YOGA PHILOSOPHY

YOGA PHILOSOPHY

In Relation to Other Systems of Indian Thought

S. N. DASGUPTA

GYAN

Published by

Gyan Publishing House
5, Ansari Road
Daryaganj, New Delhi-110002
Phone: 011-47034999, 9811692060
E-mail: books@gyanbooks.com

Distribution Network
gyanbooks.com
India, USA, Canada, UK, Australia

ISBN: 978-93-6208-209-1 (HB)
First Published, 1930

2nd Impression 2024

Printed at: Gyan Press, Delhi.

YOGA PHILOSOPHY
Author: S. N. DASGUPTA

YOGA PHILOSOPHY
In Relation to Other Systems of Indian Thought

YOGA PHILOSOPHY
In Relation to Other Systems of Indian Thought

S. N. DASGUPTA

To

Kalyānamitra Dr. F. W. THOMAS

as a humble token

of sincere and cordial friendship

and

high esteem of the author.

PREFACE

The present work on yoga was written ten years ago as a doctorate thesis of the Calcutta University and referred to in some of my later published works. As I have stated elsewhere, each system of Indian philosophy has been deeply influenced at the various stages of its growth and development by other systems of Indian thought which grew side by side with it. Yoga is often regarded as a system of practical discipline and its claims as a system of philosophical thought are often ignored. It therefore appeared profitable to me that some of the central concepts of the Yoga philosophy should be compared with or contrasted to similar concepts of other systems of Indian thought. If the work could now be re-written it could have been made more exhaustive and the historical perspectives could have been made clearer. But my hands are now so full that this hope cannot now be fulfilled. Yoga is a fruitful study and it can be approached from several other directions. Continued illness often interfered with my proper revision of the proof sheets and mistakes must have escaped my eyes, for which I crave the kind indulgence of my readers.

I beg to acknowledge my gratefulness to Mr. Haridas Bhattacharyya, M.A., P.R.S., of the University of Dacca who very kindly helped me in correcting some of the proof sheets and also to my friend and pupil Dr. Mircea Eliade Licèncié es lettres, doctorand en philosophie of the University of Bucharest, who helped me in preparing the index. It gives me also a great pleasure in acknowledging my indebtedness to Dr. E. J. Thomas, M.A., D.Lit. who during my residence in Cambridge went through my manuscript and made many corrections of transliteration and other suggestions. My general indebtedness to Dr. Thomas however extends very much further than this. I cannot say how much I must have unconsciously received from him in maturing my thoughts and ideas through his constant friendly companionship as he was my one friend in Cambridge with whom I could talk on Sanskritic matters and who was always ready with his friendly advice and criticism whenever I was in any difficulty. It gives me the greatest pleasure in acknowledging this *vidyā-ṛṇa* and the *maitrī* which was associated with it.

PRESIDENCY COLLEGE, CALCUTTA. S. N. DASGUPTA

January, 1930.

CONTENTS

INTRODUCTION

Yoga is generally understood to mean certain practices by which, it is believed, one can attain supernormal powers through concentration. It is as such often associated with hypnotism, clairvoyance, clairaudience and similar other occult phenomena. Better informed persons know that it accepts the Sāṅkhya system of philosophy, but believes in God (*īśvara*) and adopts a body of practices for the attainment of its ultimate goal—emancipation. But the difference between Yoga and the Sāṅkhya of Kapila has never been satisfactorily explained, and we often hear it asked in the purāṇas, the compendia of mythology and religion, "What is the difference between Sāṅkhya and Yoga? Who knows it is wise indeed." Yoga is counted as one of the six orthodox systems of philosophy, but if its philosophy is identical with that of the Kapila Sāṅkhya, it would be meaningless to call it a system of philosophy merely for the sake of its code of disciplinary practices. Thus we find that though the influence of Yoga on Hindu thought and life has been very great, the position of Yoga as a system of philosophy has always been misunderstood. It is probably for this reason and for the stress that it laid on its disciplinary course of practices that it sometimes wandered from its true ideal and became associated with magic, medicine and occultism.

It is true that Yoga owes much to the Sāṅkhya philosophy, but it is doubtful whether the obligation is due to the Kapila Sāṅkhya as we have it now. My supposition is that we have lost the original Sāṅkhya texts, whereas the systems that pass now by the name of Sāṅkhya and Yoga represent two schools of philosophy which evolved through the modifications of the original Sāṅkhya school; Yoga did not borrow its materials from Kapila Sāṅkhya, but, being itself a modification from the original stock, has as much right to pass by the name of Sāṅkhya as Kapila Sāṅkhya. Conformably to this we find that both the Kapila Sāṅkhyasūtra and the Pātañjala Yogasūtra call themselves, "Sāṅkhya-pravacana" (an exposition of Sāṅkhya). It will also appear, as I shall show in detail, that though the Yoga and the Kapila Sāṅkhya are fundamentally the same in their general metaphysical positions, yet they hold quite different views on many points of philosophical, ethical and practical interest.

It has been a long-felt need that the Yoga philosophy should be studied in all its metaphysical, ontological, psychological, theological, physical and practical bearings in such a manner that its different parts could be understood in their mutual relations.[1] Yoga may be admired or ridiculed for the practices it imposes, but it cannot be called a system of philosophy until it is understood as a systematic school of thought. There are the practices which are peculiar to and unique with Yoga, there is the ground which it traverses in common with Kapila Sāṅkhya, there are many divergences of views as well ; but in the interests of philosophy it is necessary that these should be properly welded together and the parts duly subordinated and inter-related with one another in such a way that Yoga might stand as a system of philosophy and not as a branch of occultism, magic, or nervous exercise.

Almost all the principal Indian systems of thought probably originated within the first few centuries of the Christian era and continued to develop side by side for hundreds of years. Adherents of different schools often discussed and disputed with one another, and these

[1] Professor Lanman says in the Harvard Theological Journal—"Yoga is accordingly one of the most ancient and striking products of the Hindu mind and character. It is therefore a little strange that, while the labours of Deussen and Garbe and others have done very much to open up the Vedānta and Sāṅkhya systems to the Occident, the history of Yoga as a body of practices and as a religio-philosophic system is yet to be written."

discussions left their permanent stamp not only on the doctrines of the different systems, but also upon the style and method of their exposition. To understand the full significance and value of the doctrines of any Indian system of thought, it is necessary that these should be taken in connection with the corresponding doctrines of other Indian systems. Most of the doctrines have a history behind them and they reflect the views of other systems on kindred points of interest and anticipate their objections. Their expositions are often in the form of debates with some imaginary opponents belonging to other schools, and without a previous acquaintance with these, it is impossible to follow these subtle discussions.

In the field of philosophy India underwent such an insular development that we can hardly trace any foreign influence. The modes of conceiving philosophical problems are therefore quite different from the current philosophical conceptions of the West. This fact causes additional difficulty for a modern student of philosophy in penetrating into the spirit of Indian philosophy, for, steeped as our minds are in modern thought, we cannot leap back into the old and unfamiliar atmosphere of Indian thought without straining our imagination. Similarities there are indeed between Indian and European thoughts, but such is the difference in the mode of expression and in the general ideal of life between ancient India and Europe, that these become altogether lost to our view. The present work is an attempt to reconstruct the system of Yóga philosophy from materials collected from Hindu philosophical works in general and especially from works on Kapila Sāṅkhya and Yoga. It has been my object here to show that Yoga is not merely a system of practices but a system of philosophy as well. It is a modification of the old Sāṅkhya doctrines parallel to that worked out by the Kapila school, and as such traverses in many respects the same grounds with it and differs from it in other respects. The disciplinary practices no doubt form the special feature of the Yoga system, but, as it will appear, it holds independent views on many other matters such as psychology, ethics and theology. I have arranged the materials as far as possible in accordance with the requirements of a modern system of thought and have avoided the peculiar dialectical style of Hindu thinking which is bound to be oppressive to western minds. Whenever I have had to deal with any important Yoga doctrine, I have not only contrasted or compared it with the kindred Kapila doctrine but also with the corresponding views of other systems, so that the Yoga ideas might stand in their true setting in relation to the views of those systems. I have always kept close to the rational parts of the system and have not laid any particular stress on the experimental portion of the practices, because though some of the phenomena, such as clairvoyance, clairaudience, etc., have been verified in some quarters in modern times, many of the other phenomena described in Yoga are of so mysterious a nature that people are rightly sceptical about them until they can be verified by the testimony of our own times.

My task here being limited to a reconstruction of the Yoga doctrines as a systematic philosophy, I have played the part of an advocate and not of a critic who sits in judgment. The Yoga system of thought remains altogether unrecognised in the modern world. I owed it therefore to this system to offer first a comprehensive and faithful exposition from a modern point of view before subjecting it to criticism.[1] If the system succeeds in attracting any notice, partial and impartial criticisms from many hands will not be lacking.

Speaking of philosophy in general, I cannot think of any system which can give entire satisfaction. Each proceeds well for some distance and then breaks down suddenly.

[1] See my *Yoga as Philosophy and Religion* published by Kegan Paul Trench and Trubner, London, 1924, and also my *A Study of Patañjali* published by the Calcutta University, 1920.

Nothing proves so much a bane to itself as philosophy. It starts off, rouses expectations and then suddenly returns to say that it has failed. But man cannot remain ever at war with himself, and though philosophy may ultimately end in proving nothing, he cannot keep his mind a blank sheet all through life. Sooner or later the psychological temperament of the enquirer makes suitable compromises, and he ends as a sceptic, a dogmatist, an atheist, or a theist. Philosophy rose to conquer faith but stooped again to allow itself to be reconquered in its turn by a newer type of faith. The Yoga system of philosophy is no exception and it has its own defects, but these are probably not greater than those of other systems. The Yoga, however, unlike other systems, does not base its claims merely on the consistency of its speculative reasonings but also on a system of practices by which the speculative results at which it arrived can be directly verified. In fact the history of Yoga philosophy shows that the speculative part of the theory was probably supplemented latterly because it supplied a rational groundwork and basis to these body of Yoga practices. The value of the metaphysical part is that of a hypothesis, which, according to Yoga, enjoys the patronage of the Upanishads and serves to explain the results of the performance of Yoga practices.

Yoga is thus formed of two inter-related parts,—firstly, the theoretical part which formulates philosophy and supports it by cogent reasoning like any other system ; and secondly, the practical part embodying a code of practices by which the truths arrived at by the theoretical part can be verified. Yoga affirms that this verification is a direct experience of the same nature as perception only much more perfect than it and as such it possesses much greater validity than reasoning or testimony. We hear of Yogins who have actually experienced this superior vision and we find that all the disputing systems of Indian philosophy are in unanimous agreement about the super-excellence of this superior vision (*Yoga-prajñā*). Under these circumstances we can neither uncritically accept their experience as true without testing it ourselves nor dismiss it unceremoniously as untrustworthy assumption.

The ancient Indian view of life as depicted in philosophy differed in a very striking manner from our own view of it. Life itself was misery; all feelings were ultimately sorrow-begetting. In our view of life pleasures and sorrows alternate with one another and on the whole we want to live because we think that pleasures so far outbalance the sorrows that they render life worth living. The Indian sage took into account our efforts and sufferings for attaining pleasures and our sufferings when we lost them and thought that pleasure was really no pleasure but only veiled pain. The wiser the person, the more sensitive did he grow and the more did the so-called pleasures grow distasteful to him.

But side by side with this pessimism there was optimism in the sense that though sorrow formed an integral part of all experience, it was not associated with the nature of our own essence, and it was possible for us to get rid of it. Sorrow is extraneous to us and if all our experiences are ultimately associated with sorrow, our experiences are also extraneous to us. But what then are we apart from our experiences? Here comes in the Hindu soul theory. Most systems think that the soul is of the nature of transcendent pure intelligence, while there are some which think that the soul is like a neutral qualityless atom in which our consciousness inheres. What the soul as pure intelligence is, philosophy cannot explain, for though it is presupposed in all experience, it cannot itself be explained by any phenomenal experience. Hindu philosophy assumes that this entity as pure intelligence remains ever in its purity and only through a transcendent beginningless illusion appears to take part in or become associated with our experience. True knowledge or emancipation consists in the apprehension of the soul or self as pure intelligence and all else as extraneous to it. When this knowledge dawns, the illusion with which the pure intelligence appeared to be associated breaks down. Such a view considers our conscious experience as the product of an illegitimate or illusory association of pure intelligence with a stuff which is the root of matter and world-experience. All the Hindu systems agree generally on these points. But few western thinkers will find it easy to acquiesce in any of these. To them the self as pure intelligence must appear inconceivable and hence the assumption of emancipation also unwarrantable.

The doctrines of *mukti* and *karma* are the two fixed postulates which Hindu philosophy could not disavow even in its highest soarings. In spite of many divergences of views, this agreement lends a uniformity to the different systems of Hindu philosophy, such as cannot be found anywhere else. These two doctrines, taken along with their necessary corollaries, sum up all the important peculiarities of the Hindu mind as it manifests itself in philosophy. These doctrines are regarded so cardinal and inviolable that there was hardly any voice (except that of the Cārvākas) in India that protested against them. But, side by side with the general agreement in favour of these doctrines, there are divergences in other matters which each system developed for itself. It is for this reason that scepticism or criticism could not be the last word of any system of Hindu philosophy. Buddhism had indeed advanced extreme sceptical and critical modes of thought but even these had been true to nirvāṇa and karma.

It was believed that the truths laid bare by philosophy were such that all earthly misery was due to ignorance of them and that as soon as this ignorance could be removed and the truths perceived, there would be a complete and perfect cessation of all pains and afflictions. Craving for worldly pleasures or for happiness in heaven is at the root of all mischief, and this proceeded from ignorance of the truth that philosophy revealed. The value of all moral conduct, self-abnegation, purity of heart, passionlessness, etc., is to be found in the help that they offer in preparing the mind for accepting the teachings of philosophy. For as long as the mind is stained with passions and worldly desires, philosophy can make but little impression upon it. When the mind is once purged of all impurities, truths arrived at by philosophical discussions carry whole-hearted conviction. Yoga holds that discussions are not enough for the purpose, for in order to be assured that our minds would not be attracted by worldly temptations, certain psychological exercises should be undertaken in order to move the mind in a direction, the reverse of ordinary experience.

When we compare, however, the solutions of many ontological and metaphysical problems proposed by Indian philosophy with those of western philosophy, we note many striking similarities which bring home to us the fact that the development of philosophy is to a great extent uniform throughout the world. The real barrier between East and West is a distrust of each other's morality, philosophy and culture. Such a distrust, ill-founded as it is, cannot remain long in existence and the clouds of ignorance are gradually passing away; the East and the West are gradually moving towards each other for understanding the respective values of their cultures and contributions to human progress and will ultimately unite and co-operate for each other's benefit. The unseen Architect of human destinies is building the massive hall of this momentous union, the greatest event of the world. I shall deem my labours thoroughly recompensed if by His grace they can render even the smallest assistance to the consummation of that end.

CHAPTER I

THE GERMS OF THE SĀṄKHYA AND YOGA PHILOSOPHY IN THE EARLIER UPANISHADS

The Upanishads reveal to us for the first time in the history of Indian thought an earnest enquiry after truth. In the later parts of the Ṛg Veda there are hymns which indicate that the sages had already begun to conceive the world as a connected whole with established laws (*ṛta*) which could not be overstepped.[1] They even wondered what there was in the beginning before creation, or whether the world was at all the result of creation or not.[2] Amidst all the diversities of cosmic change they sought to find out the ultimate and unchangeable truth. Sacrifices could no longer satisfy the minds of the thinking few. They had begun to feel that ceremonies and rituals were only intended for the mass and to substitute symbolic forms of meditation as the true worship in

[1] Macdonell's *Vedic Mythology*, p. 11.

[2] "From where did this creation spring, was it created or not? He who is its master in the sky beyond may know it or he even may not."—Ṛg Veda, X. 129.

place of the elaborate sacrifices of earlier times. But gradually, as time went on, even the symbolic forms of worship could not satisfy them, and they sought to discover the eternal and unchangeable truth. The Upanishads are replete with anecdotes and stories of the sages searching after truth. They sometimes regarded the sun as the ultimate reality, sometimes the life-breath, or space (*ākāśa*) or the like, but none of these could satisfy them or reveal the truth they wanted till they hit upon the self or ātman. Truth began to dawn amongst the thinking section of the Kshattriyas and Brahmins alike. People were possessed with the spirit of seeking it and giving it an utterance. This enquiry extended over a long period and must have been prosecuted on diverse lines by different persons. It thus did not run a course of development in one line but in divergent directions. At different stages they got different glimpses which were sometimes faint and at other times brilliant; and the Upanishads are a record of these glimpses just as they came. Not to speak of any system, there are not even any great attempts at classification. The ideas were not sufficiently definite and concrete, the problems were few and the necessity of establishing relations amongst the ideas was not often felt; and even when it was occasionally found necessary, the concepts, as they had no well-shaped corners, easily fitted in with one another. The philosopher who approaches them with a true critical spirit, expecting to find in them a well worked-out system of philosophy, cannot but be disappointed. For they are not the works of a single hand or of a single age, and the concepts of philosophy, such as we understand by them, did not evolve at the time. They were generally the untested conceptions of poets and seers ; the germs from which the later systems of philosophy developed were in them, but they themselves could hardly be identified with any of the developed products of a later age. All attempts at the identification of any of the systems of Indian philosophy with the philosophy of the Upanishads must necessarily be attended with some violence upon the Upanishad texts and it must be confessed, we have had it in abundance at the hands of commentators of a later age who always tried to identify the Upanishads with this or that system of philosophy by explaining away some texts of a refractory nature and laying undue stress on others. From a philosophic point of view the texts are of a homogeneous and undifferentiated character. They generally reveal the universal perception of the Upanishad age, of a reality which lies deep beyond the mere individual experiences of our ordinary everyday life and is supremely abiding, as the unchangeable amidst all that is changeable.

When the orthodox atmosphere of the country required that for the validity of any system of philosophy it should be necessary for it to conform to the doctrines and views taught in the Upanishads, the adherents of those systems spared no pains to show by turns that they and they alone were the true followers of the Upanishads. Personally I do not think that the Upanishad texts are a connected whole which can be identified with any of the systems formulated at a later age, although I think that we can trace in the Upanishads many of the rudimentary elements of them all. With the growth of philosophic thought the germinal differences became more and more marked, and thus gradually, with the growth of a feeling of heterogeneity among them, similar ideas began to be grouped together like *homeomeries* to form separate systems.

Proceeding with our enquiry and tracing some of the root ideas of the Sāṅkhya-Yoga philosophy in the Upanishads, we find first that the sages, having become impressed with the presence of one supreme reality, had at first set out on their quest to discover it; after testing many of the external powers, such as the sun, the wind, etc., and many of the inner functions, such as the senses, vital life (*prāṇa*), etc., they discovered the true reality in the inmost sheath of the self, the sheath of supreme happiness (*ānandamaya kośa*). Beginning with the famous hymn of the Ṛg Veda X. 129 : " There was neither Being nor Non-being," tending towards the attainment of the consciousness of unity one can trace the progress of this quest not only in the Purusha-sūkta R. V. X. 90, Viśva-karman R. V. X. 81, 82 and Brahmaṇaspati R. V. X. 72, but also in the Vāk, Aditi, Skambha and Yaksha R. V. X. 125. It is said in the Ṛg Veda I. 164 : "Of the one existence, the sages speak in diverse ways." Again in the Atharva Veda: "They call him Indra, Mitra, Varuṇa, Agni; so also is he the heaven-winged eagle ; that which is one, the seers name variously ; they call him Agni, Yama, Mātariśvan." And in the Śatapatha Brāhmaṇa, 2. 2. 1, we read : "The soul is everything." Thus we see that gradually there was growing a current of thought tending towards the consciousness of the reality of the manifold as being unity in itself. This thought found its strongest expression in the Upanishads, when not only through a general elevation of philosophic enquiry but also from the deeper experiences of the meditative process and by a negative process of elimination, through failures of lower conception of Brahman both by religious practice and by learning the sages became convinced of an all-embracing reality and identified it with the deepest self, the Brahman, as has already been pointed out.

It is indeed needless here to cite examples indicating indisputably distinct monistic tendencies in many of the passages of the Upanishads as shown by the monistic (*advaita*) school of Śaṅkara, and his followers. So far as one can understand them, it seems certain that the Upanishad texts do not formulate any well-formed system of philosophy, but represent the philosophic culture and speculations of an early age. The tendencies which are represented by these speculations can indeed be classed together to indicate the main currents of thought and their mutual connections, though taken alone by themselves they may not often be differentiated from one another in a marked manner. They do not contain only pure monistic ideas, as the followers of Śaṅkara claim, but there may also be detected a dualistic vein working in association with the uncompromising monistic ideas, which gradually developed and grew into the Yoga, Sāṅkhya, Vaishṇava and Śaiva systems. Thus in examining the Upanishads we find that sometimes the same concept of Brahman appears in association with ideas which may be regarded as characteristically distinct. There are some texts in which the idealistic bias seems to be so predominant that they are readily recognised as laying the foundation of the Vedānta system as expounded by Śaṅkara and his followers. In others the conception appears to be analogous to that of an Absolute which has yielded forth the real material order and the real mental order. It is probable that the concept of the Absolute was conceived in the earliest Upanishads on two characteristically different lines, one of which set in motion the Vedantic line of thought and the other, Sāṅkhya-Yoga and the Vaishṇava systems of thought. The stray elements of the latter type, scattered as they are in the earlier Upanishads, may briefly be classified under two groups, namely, those in which our everyday world is spoken of as real and as having emanated from the ultimately real, which was originally in an unmanifested condition, whence it desired to manifest itself and become many, and those in which the self is spoken of as being different from the creation (consisting of the world and the living beings) in the heart of which it resides. A few of these scattered ideas may thus be illustrated.

"This is true, as from a blazing fire sparks, being like unto fire, fly forth a thousandfold, thus are various beings produced from the imperishable and return therein... That which is brilliant, smaller than small, that on which the worlds and their inhabitants, are founded, that this immortal Brahman, that speech and manas,—that is this real, this immortal, that is to be achieved, O friend, know.[1] He wished, may I be many, may I produce forth. He performed penance, and having performed penance created all this, whatever there is. Having created he entered into that, and having entered became he *sat* (manifestly existing) and *tyat* (that which is unmanifest), defined and undefined, the supported and the unsupported, conscious, and unconscious (stones, etc.), real and unreal. The true (*satya*) became all this whatsoever, and therefore that is called the true.[2] Name and form are the true, and by them this prāṇa is covered.[3] There are two forms of Brahman, the material and the immaterial, the mortal and the immortal, the solid and the fluid, the manifest and the unmanifest.[4] This was originally one solitary pure being, it desired to be many and became many. That immortal Brahman is before, that Brahman is behind, that Brahman is to the right and to the left. It has gone forth below and above; Brahman is all this; it is the best."[5]

Thus the truth of the visible world is not denied but rather the reality of the changing

[1] Muṇḍaka, II. 1. 1. and II. 2 2.
[2] Tait., II. 6.
[3] Bṛh., I. 6. 3.
[4] Bṛh., II. 3.
[5] Muṇḍ., II. 2. 11.

and the mutable is reinstated by tracing its origin to an unchangeable entity.

"The sun does not shine there, nor the moon and the stars, nor lightnings, much less this fire. It is after his shining that everything else shines. By his light all this is lighted."[1] Brahman is described as "the substratum, the ground, the last resort, where the many and the differences are submerged." "Brahman is without sound, without touch, without form, without taste, without smell, without beginning and without end, beyond the Mahat, without decay, eternal and unchangeable."[2] Thus it is that a characterless substance is spoken of as the reality which upholds the visible world.

A further characterisation of this substance is found in such passages of Bṛhadāraṇyaka[3] as "In the beginning there was nothing here whatsoever. By death indeed all this was concealed; by hunger, for death is hunger. Death thought, 'Let me have a self.' Then he moved about worshipping. From him thus worshipping water was produced." Again in the Taittirīya,[4] "It was rather non-existence which was in the beginning. Out of that came the existent. That itself made its self...When

[1] Muṇḍ., II. 2. 10.

[2] Kaṭ., I. iii. 15.

[3] Bṛh., I. 2. 1.

[4] Tait., II. 7.

one finds his own nature in this invisible, in this incorporeal, undefined, unsupported, then he has obtained the fearless."

If we now try to systematise these thoughts (keeping the "self" texts outside their pale), we find that these reflect the consciousness of one reality as existing here and there beyond, in the phenomena as well as in the noumena, the upholder of the exterior as well as the interior order, not only controlling the physical forces but forming their very substratum. The mental and the material worlds are but its two forms. None of the qualities of the sensible or of the intelligible world can be found in this supreme reality, though all sensible and intelligible objects are dominated by it.

That such an undifferentiated semi-Spinozistic position was the germ from which the Kapila-Pātañjala prakṛti developed, can be inferred both from its general resemblance with the Sāṅkhya prakṛti and also from the evidence of Śaṅkara himself who says that passages of a monistic nature were often explained by the commentators of the Sāṅkhya school as referring to prakṛti.[1] Even now many of the modern students of Sāṅkhya, without an eye to these Upanishads but simply from the texts of Sāṅkhya, are inclined to find much resemblance between the uncompromising monist Spinoza and the

[1] Śaṅkara's Bhāshya, I. i. 5. ; I. ii. 19, etc.

proclaimed dualist Kapila or Patañjali. Davies has devoted a whole chapter to the finding out of this connection and Burns-Gibson does the same.[1]

In considering some of the Ātman texts we find that the self is spoken of as the controller within. Thus Yājnavalkya says, "He who dwells in the earth and within the earth, whom the earth does not know, whose body the earth is and who controls the earth from within, he is thy self, the puller within, the immortal." This is then repeated of water, fire, atmosphere, wind, sky, sun, quarters, moon, stars, space, darkness (tamas), light (tejas), and also of breath, speech, eye, ear, mind, skin and knowledge. In many other places also we find that the controller of the exterior order, the macrocosm, and the controller of the interior order, the microcosm, have been identified. Thus almost the

[1] Thus Gibson writes (1) : "Of course we must take Kapila as we find him...Yet a very little gentle manipulation might exhibit his implicit monism and bring him nearer to Spinoza. As *existents*, the many souls and one prakṛti are one co-existence, the unity of Being and Knowing, and as *pure beings* they are absolutely indistinguishable from one another and from naught. For thought, they collapse into one, and that one sinks into non-being. What then remains is Vyakta, the phenomenal world of subject and object, co-existent, co-essential and inseparable in their utter central-distinction. And this residuum of Kapila exactly corresponds with the residuum of Spinoza, when his infinite attribute of thought or consciousness has absorbed and superseded all the other infinite attributes, rendering them gratuitous and otiose hypotheses—a result that is inevitable in the dialectic of reflection."—*Mind, 1881, October.*

whole of Brāhmaṇa 7 of Adhyāya III of the Bṛhadāraṇyaka has been devoted to this purpose.

The ātman in some of the passages of the Upanishads is spoken of as having various sheaths or parts some of which are gross and even material. It is the last and the inmost kernel which is of the nature of pure bliss (*ānandamaya*) apart and distinct from all mutation and change. It is this last part on which our experiences of the dream state and the ordinary conscious states are based.[1] Again we hear of two kinds of ātman, of which one enjoys experiences and the other remains satisfied without doing any thing.[2] This superior ātman is often spoken of as "the supreme reality, the only truth of the inner and outer orders, that in which the world rests. When the phenomenal self perceives Īśvara, he is released. The self is the source from which all experiences emanate The self cannot be cognised by any ordinary perception, it is above all changes, old age, etc. It is the self which was in the beginning, and which identified itself and brought about the whole creation.[3]

Holding before us these different ātman texts, it is possible for us to see how the later Vedantic doctrine of ātman and the purusha doctrine of

[1] Tait., II. 1-5 also Sarv., 2.

[2] Muṇḍ., III. 1.

[3] Praśna, IV. 1-7. Bṛh., III. 9. Tait., II. 1-5, etc.

Sāṅkhya gradually grew out of them. With the ascendency of the monistic tendency, with the growth of the supreme importance of the Brahman as the ultimate reality, the side of the many and the concrete, both as the external world appearance, and as the sheaths of self which were spoken of as being material or belonging to the sphere of mutation or change, began to be relegated to the sphere of the non-being, māyā or illusion; only the inmost sheath of the self as the "supremely blissful" (*ānandamaya ātmā*) began to be held as the one unchanging reality.

But parallel to this Vedantic current of thought another current of a different type began to appear. The new tendency did not minimise difficulties by dropping the side of the concrete as mere non-being or illusory and having only a relative existence so long as it is not finally destroyed by the pure vision of the self as the only reality. A start was made from the supposition of self as being a combination of two distinct natures,—a materialistic nature which differed from the exterior material world only in being subtler and finer, and a non-material nature as pure intelligence, beyond the scope of any mutation or change, and the conclusion reached was that these were two distinct types of reality, one pure intelligence and the other the ultimate matter, which was the root substance of ordinary matter in its most primary state of subtle development. Thus it was the same subtle matter which developed in one chain as the mental materiality of sensations, perceptions, manas, etc., on one side, and the grosser materiality of the exterior world on the other. The intelligence, though inactive in itself, was the real upholder of the macrocosm and the microcosm, for everything was for this self. For in the Sāṅkhya, as elaborated in the Sūtras, we find that though the Sāṅkhyists agreed with the monistic doctrine that this ātman was essentially of the nature of pure intelligence, yet they held this intelligence, purusha, to be different with different persons and considered that monistic thoughts could only be tolerated in a general way, in so far as all intelligences or purushas could be spoken of as one, distinguished from prakṛtī or matter, the mutable. The Upanishads themselves had no definite systematic views on the matter, and so monistic and dualistic ideas took two different lines of development.

When we come to the Maitrī Upanishad we find that the loose ideas of the earlier Upanishads are gradually taking a definite Sāṅkhya form. It is indeed difficult to ascertain the age of the Maitrī Upanishad, but from the manner in which Sāṅkhya ideas are found to be grouped together in different parts of the work, we find ample evidence of crude as well as developed stages of Sāṅkhya thought in a process of evolution towards the formation of a coherent system. The Maitrī Upanishad, as we have it, is probably the result of a putting together of ideas of varying types, but it does not seem to us that any part of it is such as could be imagined to have been borrowed from a well-articulated system of Sāṅkhya philosophy, existing before. We have seen that in the earlier Upanishads, the traces of the elements of Sāṅkhya thought consisted mainly in the realistic attitude of some of the texts, which regarded the world as real and attributed its origin and evolution to the unfolding of the ultimate reality—the unmanifested or undifferentiated being, which desired to split itself up into many, and, when once it had finished the creation, entered into it. In the first part of the Maitrī Upanishad, we find however that though the supreme and transcendent soul retains its unique importance, yet an empirical ego (such as was alluded to in Śvet. 4.6 and Muṇḍ 3. 1. 1), is spoken of as having come forth by the shrouding over of the transcendent self by the natural qualities, (*prākṛtika guṇa*), such as passions, antipathies, etc., of man. It is here that we notice for the first time that the psychological qualities of man are spoken of as standing in opposition to the transcendent self and as generating an empirical ego of experience by shrouding the translucent one. The translucent self is still one here, though it appears as many in different persons in connection with different groups of psychological qualities (*prākṛtika guṇa*). Later on, we find that the psychological qualities are spoken of as being of three different types and as being derived from a primal being technically called pradhāna or prakṛti. From the doctrines of Maulikya Sāṅkhya (original Sāṅkhya school), as referred to by Guṇaratna in his commentary on *Shaḍdarśanasamuccaya* we find that originally it was held that each person had a separate prakṛti for himself which dissolved at the time of his emancipation. But it is difficult to ascertain when and under what influence the many prakṛtis became one, and the one transcendent self came to be regarded as many transcendent purushas behaving in their turn as so many empirical egos in association with different groups of the evolutes of the prakṛti.

It will not be out of place here to refer to some other specimens of Sāṅkhya ideas as we find them in the Maitrāyaṇa.[1]

[1] Max Müller agreeing with L. Von Schroeder holds, on the basis of pre-Pāṇinian characteristic sandhi of the Maitrāyaṇa Śākhā, which is adhered to in the MSS. of this Upanishad, that there is good reason to ascribe the Maitrāyaṇa to an early rather than to a late period (as maintained by Cowell), possibly to an ante-Pāṇinian period.

Thus we read that it is for the enjoyment of the purusha that all the senses of the body have been formed. The purusha, however, is attached to nothing; therefore, he seeming to be changing, an agent in that which is not (*i.e.*, *prakṛti*), is in reality not an agent and is unchanging. Having concealed himself in the cloak of the three qualities he appears as the enjoyer. Two kinds of selves are spoken of, the pure and the elemental (*bhūtātmā*) who is overcome by the five infra-atomic particles of matter (*tanmātra*) and the five grosser elements of matter (*mahā-bhūta*); but it is the pure self which being bewildered becomes the elemental self and suffers. Thus we find "his immortal self is (really) like a drop of water on a lotus leaf, but he was overcome by the qualities of nature. Then because he was thus overcome, he became bewildered, he saw not the creator, the holy Lord abiding within himself."[1] Again, the evolution of the prakṛti in conjunction with the purusha is described: "Even as a ball of iron pervaded by fire and hammered by smiths becomes manifold, so the elemental self pervaded by the inner man and hammered by the qualities becomes manifold."[2] The different kinds of mental qualities are classified according as they are due to sattva, tamas or rajas. The evolution of prakṛti

[1] Maitr., III. 2

[2] Maitr., III. 3.

and the reflection of the purusha in buddhi are again described thus :—"In the beginning tamas alone was this. It was in the highest, and moved by the highest it became uneven. Thus it became rajas. Then the rajas being moved became uneven. Thus it became sattva. Then the sattva being moved, the essence flowed forth. Thus is that part which is entirely intelligent, reflected in man, knowing the body."[1] Again in another place (Maitr., VI, 10) there is an attempt to speak of the relation of the pradhāna and the purusha in an argumentative manner. "The thinking purusha, when he abides within the pradhāna, is the eater who feeds on the food supplied by prakṛti. The elemental self is truly his food, his maker being pradhāna. Therefore what is composed of the three qualities is the food, but the person within is the eater. And for this the evidence is supplied by the senses. For animals spring from the seed, and as the seed is the food, therefore it is clear that what is food is pradhāna (the seed or cause of everything). Therefore, as has been said, the purusha is the eater, prakṛti the food, and abiding within it he feeds. All that begins with the mahat and ends with viśeshas, being developed from the distinction of nature with its three qualities is the sign (that there

[1] Maitr., III. 5.

must be a purusha, an intelligent subject) ...This world is indeed the food called pleasure, pain, and error; there is no laying hold of the taste of the seed (cause) so long as there is no development (in the shape of effect). And in its three stages also it has the character of food, as childhood, youth and old age; for because these are developed, therefore there is in them the character of food."

And in the following manner does the perception of pradhāna take place, after it has become manifest: "Intellect and the rest, such as determination, conception, consciousness, are for the tasting (of the effects of pradhāna). Then there are the five (perceptive organs) intended for tasting the five objects of senses; and thus also are all acts of the five active organs and the acts of the five prāṇas or vital airs (for the tasting of their corrresponding objects). Thus what is manifest is food and what is not manifest is food. The enjoyer thereof is without qualities, but because he has the quality of being an enjoyer, it follows that he possesses intelligence." (Maitr., VII, 10.)

That the Sāṅkhya doctrine had been growing in the Upanishads is further testified to by the mention of many Sāṅkhya terms and references to the modes of the evolutionary series, which Śaṅkara of course tried to explain away in his commentary on the *Vedānta-sūtra* in many cases. Thus, in Kaṭha., I. iii. 10, and II. iii. 7 the categories (*tattvas*) of Sāṅkhya, such as mahat, etc., have been mentioned and the order of evolution there from the subtler to the grosser is almost the same as the Sāṅkhya form of evolution. In the Śvetāśvatara again we find

> "The one she-goat, red and white and blackish,
> Casts many young, which are fashioned like to her ;
> The one ram leaps on her in ardour of love,
> The other ram abandons her, his companion."[1]

The manifold relations of the many purushas to the one prakṛti cannot be more effectively illustrated than by the manifold relations of the many rams to the one she-goat ; under these circumstances the reference of the description of the she-goat as "red, white, and blackish" to the three guṇas of which Prakṛti consists, is inevitable. The Śvetāśvatara also speaks of prakṛti and calls it the māyā, and speaks of a great lord eternally associated with it (*cf.* the Yoga idea). "Māyā is prakṛti and the upholder of this māyā is the great lord." The guṇas are also spoken of in various places of the Śvetāśvatara in all probability in the Sāṅkhya sense of the term. Thus we find

[1] Deussen', *Philosophy of the Upanishads* p. 251.

references to the Sāṅkhya term guṇa in many of the passages of the Śvetāśvatara Upanishad, such as "*guṇānvayo yaḥ phalakarmakartā*" (Śvet., 5. 7.), "*ārabhya karmāṇi guṇānvitāni*" (Śvet., 6. 4.), "*guṇāṃśca sarvān viniyojayed yaḥ*" (Śvet., 5. 5), "*buddherguṇenātmaguṇena caiva*" (Śevt., 5.8), and in all these places the purusha is distinguished from the guṇas as being their enjoyer, absolutely separate though mixed up with them. Living in the guṇas he produces works which bear fruits and also enjoys them."

The origin of this guṇa theory had probably an earlier form in the Chāndogya vi. 4, which states that all things of the material universe are composed of the three elements—heat, water and earth. From the list of the examples given there we find that there had already grown up a mode of thought which sought to discover the qualities of the cause in the effect in order to prove the relation of cause and effect; in accordance with such an idea the sage there tried to show that not only were different stages of a substance characterised by the predominance of any one of those qualities, but all the properties of a substance, together with its very essence or constitution, were formed by the combination of three primary forms, red (*lohita*), white (*śukla*) and black (*kṛshṇa*), and from that he concluded that all substances were composed of those things. There is however another current of thought, such as "My dear, as by one clod of clay all that is made of clay is known, the differences being only in name, arising from speech, so it is only the clay that is true."[1] If we compare these two, with a view to arriving at the idea of causation underlying them, and combine them, we come practically to the evolution (*pariṇāma*) theory of the Sāṅkhya school.

It is clear that in the examples in Chāndogya VI. 4, etc., the red (*lohita*), white (*śukla*), black (*kṛshṇa*) or heat, water, and earth, are used as principles which form the composition of different substances and generate their diverse properties. So according to it, all substances are but a product of the combination of these three, just as much as all substances, according to the Sāṅkhya theory, are regarded as the product of the combination of the guṇas. Those primary three are the only essential realities, while all the other variations are mere varieties of forms corresponding to their names.

The other passage often cited as demonstrating the causation theory of the monism of Saṅkara Vedānta, is that which asserts that the unchangeable reality is the only truth, whereas all forms are unreal and illusory. The difference between this appearance (*vivartta*) of the Vedānta theory and the evolution (*pariṇāma*)

[1] Chānd VI. 1. 4.

theory of the Sāṅkhya has been defined in the *Siddhāntaleśa*[1] as follows :—

The appearance (*vivartta*) theory of the Vedantists holds that the attributes and forms and changes have not the same reality as the substance and are mere impositions and appearances on a reality unalterable in itself, whereas the Sāṅkhya view of evolution (*pariṇāma*) holds that the appearances have a real basis in the guṇas or some ultimate entities in as much as they are in essence the same as the guṇas and are therefore real. The guṇas themselves hold together and form one composite entity, the prakṛti, and thus all forms are but the different manifestations of prakṛti. The Sāṅkhya system of thought is so far in harmony with the Vedantic position that it also holds the forms to be comparatively non-essential, since the true reality attributed to the guṇas is noumenal. The *Vyāsa-bhāshya* on the *Yoga-sūtra* quotes a passage which it believes to be the same as the Yoga doctrine of guṇas, in which it says that the ultimate nature of the guṇa entities cannot be perceived and what is perceived of them is as unreal as magic.[2] This is true of Sāṅkhya also. But it does

[1] *Vastunaḥ tatsamasattāko'nyathābhāvaḥ pariṇāmaḥ tadasamasattāko vivartaḥ* or as "*kāraṇasalakshaṇo' nyathābhāvaḥ pariṇāmaḥ tadvilakshaṇo vivartaḥ.*

[2] *Guṇānāṃ paramaṃ rūpaṃ na dṛṣṭipathamṛcchati.*
Yattu dṛṣṭipathaṃ prāptaṃ tanmāyeva sutucchakam.

not agree with the Vedānta in holding that the manifestations have not the same substratum of reality or truth as the substance, for it is the red (*lohita*), white (*śukla*), and black (*kṛshṇa*) which are the essence of all characteristics, qualities or entities. The difference therefore between the Sāṅkhya and Vedānta views of causation is to be found in this that, according to the former, the cause holds within itself the elements of difference, for the highest homogeneity as potentiality consists in the annulment of the actuality of the difference, whereas, according to the latter, difference is an extraneous element of illusion which has no place in the true cause, the pure homogeneity of abstract thought of pure self-affirmation.

It will be seen therefore that the Sāṅkhya view of causation is a reconciliation of the two lines of thought as expressed in the texts already quoted above ; whereas the Vedānta has identified itself so far with the idea of one view that it has ignored the other position altogether.

Coming to the question of god (*Īśvara*) we find that there are some texts in the Upanishads which describe a great being as the creator of the world.[1] But Sāṅkhya in constructing a

[1] The Brahman is also spoken of in the Śvetāśvatara Upanishad as the object of Yoga meditation and this corresponds with the meditation of God or resignation of everything to God (*Īśvarapraṇidhāna*).

system of duality with souls and matter had ignored this doctrine, which, to judge from the paucity of clear and distinct texts on the subject, was probably weak at the time of the early Upanishads. Yoga however took hold of this idea and gave it a distinct place in its system, as it differed from Sāṅkhya principally in the admission of God as a third principle of the system.[1] The primal matter (*prakṛti*) being a state of pure potentiality, God is introduced as the agent who, in harmony with the actions of men, will remove the barriers of *prakṛti* and help the free flow of energy in the direction thus regulated by him.

Yoga however as a system of thought or discipline, apart from the general metaphysical position which it holds in common with Sāṅkhya, cannot be traced before the Śvetāśvatara Upanishad in a marked way. In Praśna Upanishad it is said that the vital principle (*prāṇa*) derives its existence from the self and that it is from it that the other functions of upward, downward and balancing activities of the body derive their power. In other places we find that the different vital powers all owe their existence and capacity to

It is very probable that this Brahman of meditation was changed into Īśvara when Yoga doctrines were organised into a systematic philosophy.

[1] Bṛh., I. 5. 3.

the main vital principle (*prāṇa*) to which they all ultimately return. These dependent vital activities called apāna, samāna, udāna and vyāna as performing the different motor functions of the body are also spoken of in the same strain in Bṛhadāraṇyaka and Chāndogya. From this it is clear that in the Upanishads the idea of a single vital principle (*prāṇa*) which derives its existence from the self and which superintends the other functions had already gained ground.

Another passage in Kaṭha reminds us of the process of concentration in Yoga by which a man passes from a grosser stage to subtler and subtler stages until he reaches the supreme essence, the purusha.[1]

In another place in Kaṭha we find that Yoga is spoken of as restraint of the senses through which the final realisation could be achieved. Thus we find :—"When the five instruments of knowledge stand still together with the mind, and when the intellect does not move, that is called the highest stage. This, the firm holding back of the senses, is what is called Yoga."[2]

We also find from the testimony of many Upanishads, such as Aitareya, Bṛhadāraṇyaka,

[1] Kaṭh., I. 3. 13. [2] Kaṭh., VI. 10.

etc., that the differences of the diverse psychological states were already discovered, for mental states are named and differentiated from one another.

But we can notice nothing further in these Upanishads than this until we come to Svetāśvatara which is later than the other Upanishads already referred to. It is when we come to this that we reach a stage where Yoga has come to be regarded as a method of attaining salvation; here for the first time we hear of a meditative (*dhyāna*) Yoga and Sāṅkhya-yoga by which the final truth could be known, and we find, with the description of Yoga, its posture, its breath-control and the different psychical states preceding the final illumination. In the Maitrāyaṇa, however, Yoga is described as the method of fixing our thoughts on the object of meditation and most of the characteristics of this science have been mentioned there in this connection. It seems therefore that this discipline had already developed at the time as a means of meditation. It is very probable that at the time of the Upanishads this discipline had not associated itself with the Sāṅkhya doctrine of metaphysics and was resorted to by all those who wanted to attain a control over their senses and fix themselves on the object of meditation It seems therefore that these disciplinary measures were grafted on the Sāṅkhya metaphysics and thus originated the Yoga philosophy. As for the Sāṅkhya and the Vedānta, the method of obtaining true knowledge was to be found in theoretic philosophy and discussions pertaining thereto. According to them the Yoga method as such was unnecessary; philosophic enquiry and philosophic consciousness were deemed quite sufficient to dispel all darkness of ignorance, and flash upon the mind the separateness of the self from prakṛti or the unity of the self and the Brahman. Even in later times these two methods have often been described as the Sāṅkhya and the Yoga methods. Thus, Vidyāraṇya says in *Citradīpa*: "Those whose minds are engaged in diverse things cannot attain philosophic knowledge through discussion. The Yoga method is therefore important for them as destroying the pride of intellect. But for those clearer minds which are merely clouded with a thin veil of darkness, the discussion known as the Sāṅkhya brings immediate emancipation." In the Upanishads, the Yoga doctrines have no such special association with the Sāṅkhya metaphysics as we find in the Yoga philosophy as enunciated later on by Patañjali and interpreted by commentators.

This hypothesis finds further corroboration in the fact that we find a whole series of Upanishads which grew up after the Maitrāyaṇī, and dealt exclusively with the Yoga discipline with little or no reference to the Sāṅkhya metaphysics. Thus Śāṇḍilya, Yogatattva, Dhyānabindu, Haṃsa, Amṛtanāda, Varāha, Maṇḍalabrāhmaṇa, Nādabindu and Yogakuṇḍalī are all busy in describing the Yoga physiology and the practical methods of attaining concentration. In these the philosophical aspect has been largely subordinated to the elaborate physical processes of Yoga, which began to grow almost independently of Patañjali's treatment of the subject, and were accepted and assimilated later on by the sectarian schools of the Śāktas, Śaivas and also by some later schools of Buddhism.

The doctrine of transmigration, the moral qualities necessary for a philosopher and the condition of the philosopher after emancipation are all found in the Upanishads, and the fact that these are almost the same in both the systems, the Vedānta and the Sāṅkhya, goes to show that they were accepted by the Vedāntins and the Sāṅkhyists alike, before these two systems were completely developed and formulated.

Thus at the end of this brief review we find that the Upanishads contained in them the germs of thought to which are to be traced the roots of many of the important points of difference between the Sāṅkhya and the Vedānta, as regards both metaphysics and many doctrines contingent upon it.

CHAPTER II

YOGA AND PATAÑJALI.[1]

The word Yoga occurs in the Ṛgveda in various senses, such as yoking or harnessing, achieving the unachieved, connection and the like. An examination of the passages referred to in the footnote shows that the sense of yoking was not so frequent as the other senses; but it is nevertheless true that the word had been in use in this sense in such later Vedic works as the Śatapatha Brāhmaṇa and the Bṛhadāraṇyaka Upanishad.

The word *yuga* in the sense of yoke is used in many places in the Ṛgveda[2] and the Brāhmaṇas and this word with its derivative yugya (carrier of the yoke, the animal) is quite familiar to us in the later Sanskrit literature. They represent a very old word of Aryan stock which can be traced in such words as the

[1] Portions of this chapter have already appeared in a similar section of my "*A History of Indian Philosophy.*" The MSS. of the present work was ready several years before my *History of Indian Philosophy* was composed.

[2] R. V. 2. 39. 4; 3. 53. 17; 1. 115. 2; 8. 80. 7; 10. 60. 8; 10. 101. 3; Tait. Brāh., 1. 5. 1. 3; Śata. Brāh., III. 5. 1. 24. 34, etc.

German joch, Anglo-Saxon geoc, iuc, ioc, Latin iugum. The word 'yoga' however became gradually rarer and rarer in its original meaning, as it began more often to be used in the sense of yoking the senses.

With the growth of religious and philosophic ideas in the Ṛgveda we find that religious austerities were gaining a prominent place among thinking people. Thus we find in the Ṛgveda X. 129 "the one which in the beginning breathed calmly, is developed by[1] religious fervour and austerities (*tapas*)." In the older Upanishads,[2] such as the Chāndogya, Bṛhadāraṇyaka and Taittirīya, we get this word in the sense of austerity and meditative abstractions productive of mighty achievements; in the Taittirīya Brāhmaṇa[3] also we hear of such a tapas, and the commentator assures us there that tapas does not mean any such thing as asceticism, expiatory penances or the like, but devoted meditation upon the particular objects which would have to be created. Brahmacarya and tapas are also highly praised in the well-known

[1] For an elucidation of the idea of tapas see "*Hindu Mysticism*," Lecture IV by the present writer.

[2] Chāndogya, 3. 17. 4. Bṛh. 1. 2. 6: *sa tapo atapyata. tapastapyate bahūni varshasahasrāṇi.* Bṛh. 3. 8. 10 : *yajñena dānena tapasā* Bṛh. 4.4. 12, Tait. 1. 9. 1 : *tapaśca vādhyāyapravacane ca.* 3. 1. 1 : *sa tapo atapyata, sa tapastaptvā.* Tait. 3. 2. 1 : *tapasā brahma vijijñāsasva.* 3. 3. 1 : *tapobrahma.*

[3] Tait. Brāh. II. 2. 9. 1.

hymn of A.V. XI. 5. 1 and also in the Taittirīya Brāhmaṇa III. 10. 11. 3, where we are told that Bharadvāja had practised religious austerities (*brahmacarya*) during three lives, and decayed and emaciated his body, but was still willing to continue it.

In the light of the growth of these ideas of asceticism and self-control, it is easy to understand that when the force of the flying passions was felt to be as uncontrollable as that of a spirited steed, the word *yoga* which was originally applied to the control of steeds was applied to the control of the senses. That the senses were regarded as uncontrollable horses is evident from such passages of Kaṭha and Maitrāyaṇī as "the senses are called the horses and the sense objects are those which they run after" (Kaṭha III. 4), "the active senses are its horses" (Maitr. II. 6), and our expectation is satisfied when, quite in harmony with such an idea, we find yoga defined in Kaṭha II. 6. 11 as "this, the firm holding back of the senses, is what is called Yoga."

It is probable that the root "*yujir*" in the sense of connection as given in Pāṇini's list of roots is a root-form derived later from the noun-form "yoga" (yoking), or that yoga also was originally formed from "*yujir yoge*" but as yoga had taken a technical meaning in Pāṇini's time he made a confusion and invented a new fanciful root "yuja" in the sense of concentration. In Pāṇini we find that the word yoga had already attained its technical meaning, for he distinguishes between the root *yuj* in the sense of concentration (*samādhi*) and *yujir* in the sense of joining or connecting. I have not yet found any use of "yuj" the root as verb; it only occurs in the derivative forms as yoga, yogin. Pāṇini has himself used the word many times in his grammar;[1] but the sense in which it has been used in those places is that of "connecting or joining." In III. 2. 142, however he allows the formation of the word yogin to mean a man who practises religious austerities. The fact that there is no verbal use of the root "yuj" in the sense of concentration[2] goes a great way to show that the root in "*yuj samādhau*" was only an imaginary analysis of a root-form which had no use as a verb and was only found in the noun

[1] I. 2. 51; I. 2. 55; III. 4. 20; V. 1. 102; V. 4. 44; V. 4. 50; V. 4. 126; VI. 4. 74; VI. 4. 75; VIII. 1. 59.

[2] The example in the Mahābhāshya, *yujyate Brahmacārī yogam* in III. 2. 87, should not mislead us as being an use of yuj is *yujir yoge* in the passive-active voice (*karmakartṛvācya*) and not *yuj samādhau*. The same remark applies also to such passages as *sarvāṇi hāsmai bhūtāni śraishṭhyāya yujyante* (Kaushītakī, 2. 6).; *prāṇe hīmāni sarvāṇi bhūtāni yujyante, yujyante cāsmai sarvāṇi bhūtāni śraishṭhyāya* (Bṛh. 5. 13. 2); *yadyad śarīramādatte tena tena sa yujyate* (Śvet. 5. 10) *nahi sādhyasamo hetuḥ siddhau sādhyasya yujyate* (Gauḍapāda 4. 20); *tato yuddhāya yujyasva* (*Gītā* 2. 38.), etc., etc.

Śatapatha Brāhmaṇa, 14. 7. 1. 11.

Bṛh. IV. 3. 10.

and adjective forms of yuga, yugya, yoga and yogin. A consideration of the rule of Pāṇini's Grammar "*tadasya brahmacaryam*" shows that not only different kinds of asceticism and rigour which passed under the name of brahmacarya were prevalent in the country, but, associated with these, had grown up a definite system of mental discipline which passed by the name of yoga and whose adherents were called yogins. The earliest Sanskrit records where we hear of such regular adherents of yoga practice or yogins are the Maitrāyaṇī Upanishad and Pāṇini's Grammar.

In the *Bhagavadgītā* which was probably pre-Buddhistic we find that the word yogin has been used not so much in conformity with "*yuj samādhau*" but rather with "*yujir yoge*." This has often been a source of confusion. But a pretty large number of *Gītā* passages show that a yogin, in the sense of a person who lost himself in meditation, was regarded with extreme veneration.[1] In fact the importance of the *Gītā* lies in this that it has tried to chalk out a middle path between the austere discipline of a meditative abstraction on the one hand and the gross practices of a Vedic worshipper on the other, in the life of a new type of yogin who should combine in himself the best parts of the two paths, devote

[1] *Gītā*, 5. 24; 6. 15; 6. 19; 6. 27; 6. 28; 6. 31; 6. 32.

himself to his duties and yet abstract himself from any selfish motive or passion.

Again Kauṭilya in his Arthaśāstra, when enumerating the philosophic sciences of study, names Sāṅkhya, Yoga, and Lokāyata.[1] The Buddhist texts speak of character (*sīla*), concentration (*samādhi*), superior intuition (*paññā*) and meditation (*jhāna*) and if the verdict of the *Lalitavistara* be of any value in determining the state of philosophic elevation at the time of Buddha we find that *jhāna* and *samādhi* had not only been firmly established, but the forms and methods of concentration had much in common with the forms which we find in Patañjali's *Yogasūtra*. It can therefore be assumed that it is very probable that at Buddha's time and even before him, self-concentration had developed as a technical method of mystic absorption which was practised with slight variations by diverse classes of people and "yogin" was the technical term which was used to denote them.[2]

As regards the connection of Yoga with Sāṅkhya as we find it in the *Yogasūtra* of Patañjali, it is indeed difficult to come to any definite conclusion. I have already noticed in the last chapter that the science of breath

[1] "*Sāṅkhyam yogo lokāyatam cetyānvīkṣikī.*"
Arthaśāstra of Kauṭilya.

[2] Compare the texts of *Satipaṭṭhāna sutta*.

attracted notice in many of the Upanishads, though there had not developed any systematic form of prāṇāyāma. It is only when we come to Maitrāyaṇī that we find that the Yoga method attained a systematic development. The other two Upanishads in which the Yoga ideas can be traced are the Śvetāśvatara and the Kaṭha. It is indeed curious to notice that these three Upanishads of Black Yajurveda, where we find reference to Yoga methods, are the only ones[1] where we find clear references to the Sāṅkhya tenets, though the Sāṅkhya and Yoga ideas do not appear there as related to each other or associated as parts of the same system. But there is a remarkable passage in the Maitrāyaṇī in the conversation between Śākāyanya and Bṛhadratha where we find that the Sāṅkhya metaphysics was offered in some quarters to explain the validity of the Yoga processes and it seems therefore that the grafting of Sāṅkhya metaphysics on the Yoga system as its basis was the work of the followers of this school of ideas which was subsequently systematised by Patañjali. Thus Śākāyanya says, "Here some say it is the guṇa which through the differences of nature goes into bondage to the will, and that deliverance takes place when the fault of the will has been removed, because he

[1] Of the minor Upanishads the Śārīraka is a medley of Sāṅkhya and Vedānta ideas.

sees by the mind; and all that we call desire, imagination, doubt, belief, unbelief, certainty, uncertainty, shame, thought, fear, all that is but mind. Carried along by the waves of the qualities darkened in his imagination, unstable, fickle, crippled, full of desires, vacillating, he enters into belief, believing I am he, this is mine, and he binds his self by his self as a bird with a net. Therefore a man, being possessed of will, imagination, and belief is a slave, but he who is the opposite is free. For this reason let a man stand free from will, imagination, and belief. This is the sign of liberty, this is the path that leads to Brahman, this is the opening of the door, and through it he will go to the other shore of darkness. All desires are there fulfilled. To illustrate this, they quote a verse: 'When the five instruments of knowledge stand still, together with the mind, and when the intellect does not move, that is called the highest state' (Max Müller)." [1]

[1] Vātsyāyana however in his Bhāshya on *Nyāyasūtra* I. i. 29, distinguishes Sāṅkhya from the Yoga in the following way :—The Sāṅkhyas hold that " nothing cannot come into being nor can being be destroyed, there cannot be any change in the pure intelligence (*niratiśayāḥ cetanāḥ*). All changes are due to changes in the body, the senses, the means and the objects. The Yoga holds that all creation is due to the karma of the purusha and that doshas (passions) and pravṛtti (action) are the causes of karma. The intelligences or souls (*cetana*) are associated with qualities, non-being can come into being, and what is produced may be destroyed." This is indeed quite different from Patañjali's school of Yoga. It is closer to Nyāya in its doctrines.

An examination of such Yoga Upanishads as Śāṇḍilya, Yogatattva, Dhyānabindu, Haṃsa, Amṛtanāda, Varāha, Maṇḍala-Brāhmaṇa, Nādabindu, and Yogakuṇḍalī, shows that the yoga practices had undergone diverse changes in diverse schools, but none of these show any predilection for the Sāṅkhya. Thus, the Yoga practices grew in accordance with the doctrines of the Śaivas and Śāktas and assumed a peculiar form as the mantrayoga ; they grew in another direction as the Haṭhayoga which was supposed to produce wonderful bodily feats of breath-control and control of involuntary muscles and organs through constant practices of elaborate nervous, muscular and breath exercises which were also associated with the art of healing diseases, keeping the body free from all kinds of diseases and supernatural powers. The Yogatattva Upanishad says that there are four kinds of yoga, the Mantra Yoga, Laya Yoga, Haṭha Yoga and Rāja Yoga.[1] In some cases we find that there was a great attempt to associate even Vedāntism with these mystic practices. The influence of these practices on

[1] The Yoga writer Jaigīshavya wrote " Dhāraṇāśāstra " which dealt with Yoga more in the fashion of Tantra than that given by Patañjali. He mentions different places in the body (*e.g.*, heart, throat, tip of the nose, palate, forehead, centre of the brain) which are centres of memory where concentration is to be made.

See Vācaspati's *Tātparyyaṭīkā* on Vātsyāyana's Bhāshya on *Nyāya sūtra*, III. ii. 42.

the development of Tantra and other modes of worship was also very great, but these we have to neglect as they have little philosophic importance.

Patañjali was probably the most notable representative of the Sāṅkhya school of Yoga, which forms the subject of our present enquiry. Patañjali not only collected the different forms of Yoga practices, and gleaned the diverse ideas which were or could be associated with the Yoga, but grafted them all on the Sāṅkhya metaphysics, and gave them the form in which they have been handed down to us. Vācaspati and Vijñāna Bhikshu, the two great commentators on the *Vyāsa Bhāshya*, agree in holding that Patañjali was not the founder of the Yoga but rather its editor. An analytic study of the sūtras also brings conviction that they do not show any original attempt but are a masterly and systematic compilation, supplemented with certain original contributions. The character of the Yogasūtras as a compilation is evident from its division into chapters (*pāda*) according to the main topics of discussion instead of the usual divisions into books (*adhyāya*) and chapters (*pāda*) as in the works of Jaimini, Bādarāyaṇa or Pāṇini, or into books (*adhyāya*) and lessons (*āhṇika*), as in the Nyāya-Vaiśeshika schools, which were the general forms of division of original writings. The systematic manner also in which the first three chapters are written by way of definition and classification [1] shows that the materials were already in existence, and that Patañjali only systematised them in an orderly form. This explains also why we find no missionary zeal, no attempt to overthrow the doctrines of other systems, except so far as might be useful in explaining the system. Patañjali is not even anxious to establish the system, but he is occupied only with systematising the facts as he had them. Most of the few remarks that he had to make he reserved for the last chapter: the Yoga having already been described in the first three chapters, he distinguishes the existent Yoga ideas which he thus collected from his own remarks by putting an "*iti*" (the word

[1] An example of this method (which is indeed different from that of enunciation (*uddeśa*), definition (*lakshaṇa*) and examination (*parīkshā*) of Nyāya may be given by a short analysis of the first chapter. Thus Yoga is defined as *cittavṛttinirodha* (2). In (3) and (4) the nirodha and anirodha stages are distinguished. Vṛtti is then divided into kliṣṭa and akliṣṭa and these again into *pramāṇa*, *viparyaya*, *vikalpa*, *nidrā*, and *smṛti*, and these are then defined. Then Patañjali divides the means of nirodha as abhyāsa and vairāgya and classifies vṛttinirodha as asamprajñāta and samprajñāta of four kinds as savitarka, savicāra, sānanda and sāsmitā. Vṛttinirodhasamādhi is again further classified as *upāyapratyaya* and *bhavapratyaya* and the upāyas are *śraddhā*, *vīrya*, *smṛti*, *samādhi* and *prajña*. The upāyapratyaya yogins are again further divided into those who are engaged in *īśvarapraṇidhāna* and others of nine kinds according to the strength of their devotion. God is defined, and the nature of his favour is then described. The means of the removal of obstacles is then further divided according to *vīrya*, *śraddhā*, and *samādhi*. Then the chapter closes with a description of prajñā and asamprajñāta or nirbija samādhi.

to denote the conclusion of any work) at the end of the third chapter, evidently to denote the conclusion of his yoga compilation. There is of course another "*iti*" at the end of the fourth chapter to denote the conclusion of the whole work. Another legitimate hypothesis which may be formed in this connection is that the last chapter is a subsequent addition from a hand, other than that of Patañjali, anxious to supply some new links of argument felt as desirable for strengthening the Yoga position from an internal point of view, as well as for securing the Yoga from the supposed attacks of Buddhist metaphysics. There is also a marked change (due either to its supplementary character or the manipulation of a foreign hand) in the style of the last chapter as compared with the style of the other three chapters of description, enumeration and classification. The sūtras 30-34 of the last chapter seem to repeat what has already been said in the second chapter, and some of the topics introduced are such that they could well have been described in a more relevant manner in connection with similar discussions in the preceding chapters in a systematic work like this. The extent of this chapter is also disproportionately small as it contains only 34 sūtras, whereas the number of sūtras in other chapters is between 51 to 55.

We have now to meet the vexed question of the probable date of the famous Patañjali, the reputed author of the *Yogasūtra*. Weber had tried to connect him with Kāpyapātañcala of Bṛhadāraṇyaka. In Kātyāyana's *Vārttika* we get the name Patañjali, which is explained by later commentators as he for whom the hands are folded as a mark of reverence (*patantaḥ añjalayaḥ yasmai*), but it is difficult to come to any conclusion merely from the similarity of names. There is however another theory which identifies the writer of the great commentary on Pāṇini, called the *Mahābhāshya*, with the Patañjali of the *Yogasūtra*. This theory has been accepted by many Western scholars, probably on the strength of some native commentators who seem to have identified the two Patañjalis. Of these one is the writer of *Patañjalicarita* (Rāmabhadra Dīkshita) who could not have flourished earlier than the 18th century.[1] The other one is cited in Śivarāma's commentary on *Vāsavadattā* which Aufrecht assigns to the 18th century.[2] The other two are King Bhoja of Dhāra and Cakrapāṇidatta, the commentator of Caraka, who belonged to the 11th century

[1] *Pātañjalamahābhāshyacarakapratisaṃskṛtaiḥ manovākkāyadoshāṇām hantre 'hipataye namaḥ.*

[2] The śloka cited in Śivarāma's commentary occurs in some MSS. just before the opening words of the *Mahābhāshya*, but that can give us no clue to the date of the śloka as it may be a late interpolation.

A. D. Thus Cakrapāṇi says that he adores the Ahipati (mythical serpent-chief) who removed the defects of mind, speech and body by his *Pātañjala*, *Mahābhāshya* and the revision of Caraka. Bhoja says :—" Victory be to the luminous words of that illustrious sovereign Raṇaraṅgamalla who, by composing his grammar, by writing his comment on Patañjali and by producing a treatise on medicine called *Rājamṛgāṅka* has, like the lord of serpents, removed defilement from speech, mind, and body." These remarks are however based upon an old tradition that Patañjali, the grammarian, was the incarnation of Śesha (the mythical serpent) who fell upon the palms of Pāṇini (*pata*=falling and *añjali*=hands). The adoration hymn of Vyāsa, which is considered to be an interpolation even by orthodox scholars, is also based upon the same tradition. It is not impossible therefore that the later native commentators should make a confusion between the three Patañjalis, the grammarian, the Yoga editor, and the medical writer to whom is ascribed the book known as *Pātañjalatantra* and who has been quoted by Śivadāsa in his commentary on Cakradatta in connection with the heating of metals.

Professor Woods of Harvard University is therefore quite justified in his unwillingness to identify the grammarian with the Yoga editor on the slender evidence of these commentators. It is indeed curious to notice that the great commentators of the grammatical school, such as Bhartṛhari, Kaiyaṭa, Vāmana, Jayāditya, Nāgeśa, etc., should be silent on this point.[1] Though Prof. Woods does not notice it, I think this is indeed a very strong point against the identification of the two Patañjalis by a few Yoga and medical commentators of a later age.

It will not however be out of place here to notice that Prof. Woods supposes that the philosophical concept of substance (*dravya*) of the two Patañjalis differs, and that therefore they cannot be identified. He holds that substance (*dravya*) is described in *Vyāsabhāshya* in one place as being the unity of genus and specific particularities whereas *Mahābhāshya*, the work of the grammarian Patañjali, holds that a dravya denotes a genus and also specific qualities according as the emphasis or stress is laid on either side. I fail to see how these ideas can be held to be totally antagonistic. Moreover we know that these two views were held by Vyāḍi and Vājapyāyana

[1] This is particularly suspicious as Bhartṛhari gives in the second kāṇḍa of *Vākyapadīya* an account of the composition of *Mahābhāshya* and its later history till it came over to him, but does not make any suggestion as to the identity of the two Patañjalis. In the *Brahmakāṇḍa* also there was a suitable opportunity for such a reference but no reference has been made and Puṇyarāja and Helārāja are also silent on the point.

(Vyāḍi holding that words denoted qualities or dravya and Vājapyāyana holding that words denoted species). Even Pāṇini himself had these two different types of ideas, as expressed in the rules *jātyākhyāyāmekasmin bahuvacana-manyatarasyām* and *sarūpāṇāmekaśeshamekavibhaktau*, and the writer of the *Mahābhāshya* only combined these two views. This does not show that he opposes the view of *Vyāsabhāshya*, though we must remember that even if he did, that would not prove anything with regard to the author of the Sūtras. Moreover when we find in the *Mahābhāshya* dravya spoken of as the object (*e.g.*, the cow with its tail, hoofs, horns, etc. —" *yat sāsnālāṅgulakakudakshuravishāṇyartha rūpam*") we are reminded of its similarity with the definition of dravya in the *Vyāsabhāshya* as that where the parts cannot be considered apart from the whole (*ayutasiddhāvayavabhedānugataḥ samūho dravyam*). I have assured myself by an examination of the *Mahābhāshya* that there is nothing in it which can warrant us in saying that the two Patañjalis cannot be identified. There are, no doubt, many apparent divergences of view, but even in these it is only the traditional views of the old grammar scholars that are exposed and reconciled, and it would be very unwarrantable for us to infer anything as to the personal views of the grammarian from them. It may also be supposed that the writer of the *Mahābhāshya* was acquainted with none at least of the important points dealt with in the Sāṅkhya-Yoga metaphysics; as a few examples I may refer to 4. 1. 3, the guṇa theory, to 1. 2. 64, the Sāṅkhya dicta of *ex nihilo nihil fit*, to 1 to 56, the vivarta and pariṇāma ideas, the idea of time (2. 2. 5, 3. 2. 10, 3. 2. 11), the idea of the return of similars into similars (1. 1. 50), the idea of change as production of new qualities, effect and cause as manifestation (5. 1. 2, 5. 1. 3, 3. 3. 13) and the idea of the changing states of the intellect (*buddhipariṇāma*). About the obstacles of perception it seems that Īśvarakṛshṇa borrowed the idea of one of his kārikās from the *Mahābhāshya* 4. 1. 3. We may add to it that the *Mahābhāshya* agrees with the *Vyāṣabhāshya* as regards Sphoṭavāda; there is also this external similarity that unlike any other work they both begin in a similar manner (*atha yogānuśāsanam* and *atha śabdānuśāsanam*).

It may further be noticed in this connection that the arguments which Mr. Woods adduced to assign to the *Yogasūtra* a date between 300 and 500 A.D., are not at all conclusive, for, firstly, if the two Patañjalis cannot be identified, it does not follow that the editor of the Yoga should necessarily be pushed down to a lower date. Secondly, the supposed Buddhist reference is mainly found in the 4th chapter which, as I have shown above, may be a later interpolation [1]; thirdly, even if it was written by Patañjali, it cannot be inferred that because Vācaspati describes the opposite school as being of the Vijñānavāda type, we are to infer that the sūtras refer to Vasubandhu or even to Nāgārjuna, for such ideas, as have been refuted in the sūtras, have been developing even long before the time of Nāgārjuna.[2]

Thus though we cannot accept the tradition of later commentators as a sufficient ground to identify the two Patañjalis, we cannot at the same time discover anything from a comparative critical study of the *Yogasūtras* and the text of the *Mahābhāshya*, which can lead us to say that the author of the *Yogasūtras* flourished at a later date than the other Patañjali.

It is indeed curious to notice that there is another work called *Kitāb Pātanjal* of which Alberunī speaks in his *India*. Alberunī considers this work as a very famous one and he translates it along with another book called

[1] It is important to notice that the most important Buddhist reference "*nacaikacittatantram vastu tadapramāṇakam tadā kim syāt*" (IV. 16) was probably a line of the *Vyāsabhāshya*. Bhoja who had consulted many commentaries, as he says in the preface, does not count it as a sūtra.

[2] It is interesting to notice a passage in the *Mahābhāshya* which may be compared with the criticism of the concept of time by Nāgārjuna. Thus the *Mahābhāshya* says in III. ii. 123, the future, past and present—in none of these three can we locate motion : what then is meant by saying that "he goes" signifies present tense ?

Sāṅkhya ascribed to Kapila. This book *Kitāb Pātañjal* was written in the form of a dialogue between master and pupil and it is certain that this book was not the present *Yogasūtra* of Patañjali though it had the same aim as the latter, namely, the search for liberation and for the union of the soul with the object of meditation. The book was called by Alberunī *Kitāb Pātañjal* which is to be translated as the book called Pātañjal, because in another place, speaking of its author, he puts in a Persian phrase, which when translated stands as "the author of the book of Pātañjal." It had also an elaborate commentary from which Alberunī quotes many extracts though he does not tell us the name of its author. It treats of God, soul, bondage, deeds (karma), salvation, etc., as we find in the *Yogasūtra*, but the manner in which these are described (so far as we can judge from the copious extracts supplied by Alberunī) shows that these ideas had undergone some changes from what we find in the *Yogasūtra*. The idea of God in Alberunī's Kitāb Pātañjal retains its character as a timeless emancipated being; God is spoken of as handing over the Vedas, and showing the way to yoga and inspiring men in such a way that they could obtain by cogitation what he bestowed on them. The name of God proves his existence, for there cannot exist anything of which the name exists but not the thing. The soul perceives him; and thought comprehends his qualities. Meditation is identical with worshipping him exclusively, and by habituating it uninterruptedly comes in the supreme absorption in him, and beatitude is obtained.[1]

The idea of soul in this work is the same as we find in the *Yogasūtra*. The idea of metempsychosis is also the same. He speaks of the eight miraculous powers (*siddhi*) at the first stage of meditation on the unity of God. Then follow the other four stages of meditation corresponding to the four stages as we have in the *Yogasūtra*. He gives four kinds of ways towards the achievement of salvation, of which the first is the practice (*abhyāsa*) of Patañjali, though the object of this practice is union with God. The second stands for vairāgya, the third is the worship of God with a view to seeking his favour towards the attainment of salvation (cf. *Yogasūtra* I. 23 and I. 29). The fourth is a new introduction, namely, rasāyana or alchemy. As regards liberation, the view is almost the same as in the *Yogasūtra* II. 25 and IV. 34; but the liberated state is spoken of in one place as absorption in God or being one with him. The Brahman is conceived as a tree with its roots upwards and its branches downwards, after

[1] Cf. *Yogasūtra* I. 23-29, II. 1, and II. 45.

the Upanishad fashion; the upper root is pure Brahman, the trunk is the Vedas, the branches are the different doctrines and schools, the leaves are the different modes of interpretation. Its nourishment comes from the three forces (probably the three gunas); the object of the worshipper is to fell the tree and go back to the roots.

The differences of this system from the *Yogasūtra* are: (1) the conception of God has risen to such an importance here that he has become the only object of meditation, and absorption in him is the goal; (2) the importance of the two methods of Yoga self-control as yama and niyama has been reduced to the minimum; (3) the value of the Yoga discipline as a separate means of salvation, apart from any connection with God, as we find in the Yogasūtra has been lost sight of; (4) liberation and yoga are defined as absorption in God; (5) the introduction of Brahman; (6) the very significance of yoga as cittavṛtti-nirodha is lost sight of; and (7) rasāyana is introduced as one of the means of salvation.[1]

[1] Cf. *Yogasūtra* II. 1. Alberunī in his account of the book of Sāṅkhya gives a list of commandments, which is practically the same as yama and niyama but it is said that through them one cannot attain salvation.

Cf. the account of Pāśupatadarśana in *Sarvadarśanasamgraha* where Yoga is defined as the relation of individual soul with God

From this we can fairly assume that this was a new modification of the yoga doctrine on the basis of Patañjali's *Yogasūtra* in the direction of Vedānta and Tantra, and as such it probably stands as the transition link through which the yoga doctrine of the Sūtras passed over in a new channel in such a way that it could be easily assimilated from there by later developments of Vedānta, Tantra, and Śaiva doctrines of a later age. As the author mentions rasāyana as a means of salvation, it is very probable that he flourished after Nāgārjuna and was probably the same person who wrote *Pātañjalatantra* and who has been quoted by Śivadāsa in connection with alchemical matters and spoken of by Nāgeśa as Patañjali in Caraka (*Carake Patañjaliḥ*). It may also be supposed that Cakrapāṇi and Bhoja made the confusion of identifying this Patañjali with the writer of the *Mahābhāshya*. It is also very probable that Cakrapāṇi by his line "*pātañjala-mahābhāshyacarakapratisaṃskṛtaiḥ*" refers to this work, which was called "*Pātañjala*." The commentator of this work gives some description of the lokas, dvīpas and sāgaras which run counter to the description as given in the *Vyāsabhāshya*

through mind. The *Kulārṇavatantra* also says that Yoga is not a cross-legged posture of sitting or steadfast gazing at the tip of the nose but it is the true union of the individual with the self.

III. 26, and from this we can infer that it was probably written at a time when the *Vyāsabhāshya* had not attained any great sanctity or authority. Alberunī also described the book as being very famous at the time, and Bhoja and Cakrapāṇi also probably confused him with Patañjali, the grammarian. From this we can fairly assume that this book "Pātañjal" was probably written by some other Patañjali within the first 200 or 300 years of the Christian era; and it may not be improbable that when Vyāsabhāshya quotes in III. 44 as *iti Patañjaliḥ*, it refers to this Patañjali.

Next to this we find that Caraka devotes the whole of the first chapter of the book of Śārīra to proving the existence of the Purusha, as against the Buddhists who did not believe in the separate existence of souls. The description given here is so vivid and clear, and the amalgamation of the Sāṅkhya metaphysics with the Yoga doctrine as the way of salvation is so perfect that it may not be wrong for us to expect that Caraka had probably seen the *Yogasūtra* of Patañjali.

This may well serve as a guidance on the negative side against assigning any date to the author of the *Yogasūtra* which may be later than that of Caraka, who is held to have been the court-physician of Kanishka. The study of the *Yogasūtra*, however, furnishes us with such other internal evidence that on the basis of them it may be said that the *Yogasūtra* was written shortly after the close of the epoch of the early Upaniṣhads, under the influence of old Buddhism and Jainism, or when all the three had not sufficiently separated themselves and stood out from the original melting pot of ideas.

In dealing with this part of the evidence we see first that the conception of yoga as we meet it in the Maitrāyaṇi Upanishad consisted of six *aṅgas* or accessories, namely, breath-control (*prāṇāyāma*), restraint (*pratyāhāra*), meditation (*dhyāna*), holding fast (*dhāraṇā*), thinking (*tarka*) and concentration (*samādhi*). Comparing this list with the list in the *Yogasūtra* we find that in the latter two new elements have been added and tarka has been replaced by āsana or posture. Now, from the account of the sixty-two heresies given in the *Brahmajālasutta*, we know that there were people who either from meditation of three degrees or, fourthly, through logic and reasoning had come to believe that both the external world as a whole and individual souls were eternal. From the association of this last mentioned logical school with the concentration (*samādhi*) or meditation (*dhyāna*) school as belonging to one class of thinkers professing eternalism (*śāśvatavāda*) and from the inclusion of tarka as an accessory (*aṅga*) in concentration (*samādhi*), we can fairly assume that the list of the accessories (*aṅga*) given in the Maitrāyaṇa Upanishad represents the oldest list of the Yoga doctrine when the Sāṅkhya and the Yoga were in a process of being grafted upon each other and when the Sāṅkhya method of discussion had not stood as a method independent of the Yoga. The substitution of postures (*āsana*) for thinking (*tarka*) in the list of Patañjali shows that the Yoga method had now grown into a method separate from the Sāṅkhya. The introduction of non-injury (*ahiṃsā*), truthfulness (*satya*), non-stealing (*asteya*), sex-control (*brahmacarya*), satisfaction with the little that one has (*aparigraha*) as control (*yama*) and purity (*śauca*), and contentment (*santosha*), among others as superior control (*niyama*), into a system of morality, without which yoga is deemed impossible, for the first time in the philosophical sūtras, probably marks the period when the discussion between the Hindus and the Buddhists and Jains had not become so keen. The introduction of friendship (*maitrī*), kindness (*karuṇā*), contentment (*muditā*), non-apprehension of other's riches (*upekshā*) is also equally significant as we do not find them mentioned in such a prominent form in any other literature of the Hindus dealing with the subject of emancipation. Beginning from the *Acārāṅgasūtra* the *Uttarādhyayanasūtra*, and the *Sūtrakṛtāṅgasūtra* and passing through Umāsvati's *Tattvārthādhigamasūtra* to Hemachandra's *Yogaśāstra* we find that the Jainas had been founding their Yoga discipline merely on the basis of a system of morality indicated by the yamas, and the opinion expressed in Alberunī's Sāṅkhya that these cannot give salvation marks the divergence of the Hindus with the Jainas in later days. Another important characteristic of Patañjali's work is its thoroughly pessimistic tone. Its treatment of sorrow in connection with the statement of the scope and ideal of Yoga is the same as that of the four sacred truths of the Buddhists, namely, suffering, origin of suffering, the removal of suffering, and the path to the removal of suffering. Again the metaphysics of the *saṃsāra* cycle in connection with sorrow, origination, disease, rebirth, etc., is described with a remarkable degree of similarity with the cycle of causes as described in early Buddhism, though there is not the slightest reference to the doctrine of dependent origination (*pratītyasamutpāda*) and other Buddhistic developments of a later age. Ignorance (*avidyā*) is placed at the head of the group; yet this *avidyā* should not be confused with the Vedāntic view of the avidyā of the Upanishads, as it is an avidyā of the Buddhistic type. It is not declared to be anything in the way of a cosmic power nor anything like a mysterious original sin, but it is within the range of earthly tangible reality. The ignorance here is the same as with the Buddhists, the ignorance of the four sacred truths, *viz.*, the consideration of the momentary, impure, sorrow and the non-self as the eternal, pure, happiness and the self. Again we may take the example of the will to live (*abhiniveśa*). The ground of our existence is our will It is our besetting sin that we will to be, that we will to be ourselves, that we fondly will our being to blend with other kinds of existence. The negation of the will to be cuts off being for us at least. This is true as much of Buddhism as of the Yoga "will to live" (*abhiniveśa*) which i a term coined and used in the Yoga for the first time to suit the Buddhist idea, and which has never been accepted in any other Hindu literature in this sense. It is needless to multiply examples. But my sole aim in pointing out these things in this chapter is to show that the *Yogasūtra* proper (first three chapters) was composed at a time when the later forms of Buddhism had not developed and when the quarrels between the Hindus and the Buddhists and Jains had not reached such a stage that they could not borrow from one another in a clear and evident manner. As this can only be held of earlier Buddhism, I am disposed to think that the date of the first three chapters of the *Yogasūtra* must be placed somewhere between the 4th century B. C. and the 2nd century B. C. Whether Patañjali the grammarian can be identified with Patañjali the writer of the Sūtras is more than I can say, though I have already tried to emphasise the fact that there is nothing in the *Mahābhāshya* which could conflict with such a hypothesis.

In the above discussions I think I must have suggested more than once that the Yoga doctrines had undergone changes in different schools of thought, but my treatment of the subject in the following pages will be restricted to the traditional interpretation of the *Yogasūtra* as has been accepted from Vyāsa to Nāgeśa though I may in passing notice the other developments, whenever these may prove to be of interest in connection with the elucidation of the Yoga ideas.

CHAPTER III

The Guṇa Theory

The characteristic mark of the Sāṅkhya and Yoga schools of philosophy is their guṇa theory, which holds that all things (mental or material) except the pure self are made up of an admixture, or rather a combination in different proportions, of three classes of reals technically called guṇas. It is indeed difficult to ascertain the reason why these ultimate reals were called guṇas. The word guṇa in Sanskrit means (1) qualities, (2) subordinate or inferior and (3) string. Later commentators have tried to justify the use of the term from the point of view of all the three meanings. The ultimate reals are called guṇas (qualities) because each and every quality of things is due to the existence of a corresponding real, for, as we shall see later on in detail, the reals and qualities are identical in Sāṅkhya philosophy. Again the ultimate reals are called guṇas in the sense of inferior or subordinate as well, for these possess a lesser degree of constancy than the puruṣas; for, though indestructible, the reals are in a state of constant flux and change, whereas the puruṣas are ever constant and unchangeable. It is on this account that the puruṣas are given the first place, and the ultimate reals are looked upon as gauṇa or guṇa (possessing an inferior value). The other justification offered is that these are called guṇas as they behave like strings in binding the translucent puruṣas to transitory objects of interest.

But whatever may be the reason why the guṇas were so called, it is evident from the considerations we have set forth in the first chapter, that the theory itself was the result of a long process of growth, and not the work of a mythical Kapila as tradition would have it. It is, of course, quite probable that Kapila laid hold of the loose materials and built them up into a complete and coherent system, so that though he might not have been a discoverer of the root ideas of Sāṅkhya philosophy he might justly be regarded as the founder of the Sāṅkhya school as Patañjali of the Yoga.

To look at a system of Indian philosophy from the historical or chronological point of view has no doubt its value, but the more important thing is to take an estimate of the philosophic construction in the light of the analysis of our experience. It is true that none of the extant Sāṅkhya works reveal to us any such analysis of experience as might lay bare to us the inner reason of the guṇa theory, but yet we may supplement it from the point of view of modern thought and criticism. It does not matter in the least if we cannot guarantee the historical correctness of such an analysis, for it is through such procedure mainly that the philosophic value of the guṇa theory may be rightly estimated.

Philosophy, we know, is a science of abstraction which seeks to rise above the contingent aspects of things to a common platform from which it again descends to explain all phenomena of mind, life and nature. It is, therefore, expected of any system of philosophy that it should vindicate its right to acceptance by showing how its analysis of experience could lead it to the necessary formulation of its theory. In India, however, this necessary duty of philosophy was often felt as relatively unimportant, because its claims to acceptance amongst the masses of people depended not so much upon the reasonableness of the theory as upon the patronage of the Upanishads. But it is expected from an interpreter of Sāṅkhya of modern times that he should give his own construction of how abstraction from experience can lead to the doctrine of the guṇas as a plausible explanation of all phenomena.

To do this let us begin by abstracting from experience all those aspects which may be regarded as contingent or non-essential. We may take any experience and try to conceive how far it is possible for us to abstract, and beyond which it is not possible for us to go without sacrificing experience to logical consistency. Analytic reflection shows that being and movement are the two irreducible ultimates, beyond which further abstraction is not possible. It is true that Vedāntism regarded being (*sat*) only as true, and Buddhism regarded movement as true. But when we inspect closely the progress of Buddhism or Vedāntism we find that as they gradually moved towards a reconciliation of philosophy with experience, the former had to assume the "deep" (*gabhīra*) or the "essenceless" (*śūnya*) as the goal of all movement and the latter the māyā as the principle of movement by the influence of which the being resolved itself, or rather appeared to do so, into a manifold of experience.[1] But here a question may arise as to what "being" means. "Being"

[1] In Buddhism, as we find it in its early stages, we find that the causal nexus such as "from ignorance comes consciousness, from consciousness comes name, etc.," represent being only as a moment in the everchanging process. The world is the world's process. Beings are the points of the procession regulated by the law of causality, of continuous being at every moment, self-consuming and self-begetting. What we term a souled being is only an individual member in the line of this procession, one flame in this sea of flames. Being is only a moment in the process of becoming. When we come to later Mahāyāna Buddhism, we see that the doctrine of causal determination (*pratītya-samutpāda*) cannot satisfy the mind, and the void (*śūnya*) is put forward by Nāgārjuna as the substratum and goal of all causal determination (*pratītyasamutpāda*). Chandrakīrtti holds that what suffers all change and transformation must itself be the colourless void (*śūnya*), inasmuch as it is the ground of all change. It is the void which for a moment reaches the stage of being or knowledge through the principle

is not here an empty abstraction representing merely the common trait of all existences, but the universal or ultimate mode of intelligibility; as such Being is the fundamental fact of the self-position of thought which comprehends within it the positing of all objects of thought. It is the quality by virtue of which all objects become related to consciousness as a fact of consciousness. It is this element which forms the main constituent of consciousness. Without it thought could not have affirmed itself or anything else and everything would have been blind. This characteristic primarily belongs to thought and secondarily to all other things since they also can be related to thought and become its objects. This aspect of things

of causal determination (*pratītyasamutpāda*) and then sinks back to void again. It was void in the beginning and will be void in the end. Void is the only substratum—the "deep" (*gambhīra*). It is the expression of the series as well as the colourless depth where the series of existence has ceased (see Chandrakīrtti on *Mādhyamika-sūtra*, Chapter 18, and *Śatasāhasrikā Prajñāpāramitā*).

Looking at Vedāntism, we find that Gauḍapāda held that pure being was the only metaphysical category, whereas all multiplicity and change were absolutely false. Śaṅkara agreed with Gauḍapāda that the world was as unreal as the dream world, but he advanced the conception of māyā by emphasising the distinction of relative (*vyāvahārika*) and real (*pāramārthika*) existences. Vācaspati regarded māyā, the principle of change, as an accessory (*sahakāri*) cause working in conjunction with Brahman. Śrīharsha and Citsukha describe māyā as a beginningless, positive entity and yet destructible by true knowledge. But when we come to Dharmarāja, Rāmkrishṇa, etc., māyā has already come to be looked at as three guṇas after the Sāṅkhya fashion.

in Sāṅkhya is called sattva. The self-shining and lightness, or the power of being easily changed or shifted, are inseparable from the being of ideas. It is the being which in one aspect is regarded as shining (*prakāśaka*) and in another as plastic or light (*laghu*). In the objective world however this plasticity or fluidity of thought is almost lost and submerged in mass or materiality. But this positing of thought requires, as is easy to see, a subject which is to be posited. When I say "the table is," the fact of positing or relationing with consciousness is affirmed of the table. That the table can be related to consciousness as a fact of the latter's positing characteristic shows that it has in common with consciousness that attribute or substance by virtue of which it becomes a part of it. But what is posited in "the table is" is not a mere positing, but also the mass or materiality of the table. The Vedānta asserted that the positing is the only true substance, but whatever character or matter appears as posited is mere form and name and therefore unreal. But the Sāṅkhya, as it took its inspiration from experience, held fast to the principle of mass or materiality as an irreducible ultimate of experience side by side with intelligible being or sattva. The difference between the phenomena of the external world and those of the mental world, the phenomena of material things and ideas, is that the preponderating constituent of the former is the element of mass (*tamas*) whereas that in the latter is being (*sattva*). The ideas themselves, though we cannot attribute mass to them in their translucent character as the different determinations of being, may yet be held to have some tenuous quality of mass, because they can assume the form of material objects, where mass predominates. Mass can be identified in the thought world with that element which gives thought its static character. For with the element of being as shining or plasticity we can only expect a flux of shining and not clear-cut limited concepts. This hardness of concepts is similar to what we would call the impenetrability of matter. The difference of the function of this element in thought and that in matter lies in this that in the former it is extremely subordinated and submerged in being (*sattva*), whereas in the latter it is predominant. Thus the essential substance of all intellectual phenomena is *sattva* as that of all physical phenomena is mass or *tamas*.

Side by side with intelligence-stuff (*sattva*) and mass (*tamas*) we find another factor which is present in all intellectual as well as physical phenomena, namely energy (*rajas*).

It may not be out of place here to point out that in determining the relation between experience and reality, the Sāṅkhya was probably inwardly guided by the same sort of axiom as the Buddhists, namely, that each diversity of experience or sensation presumes the existence of a corresponding diversity of realities or reals.[1] The Sāṅkhya, we see, holds that corresponding to any and every affection of the sense or experience there is a real. But it classifies the infinite number of these reals into three different types, sattva, rajas and tamas, which according to Sāṅkhya analysis represent the ultimates of experience in three directions. These three the Sāṅkhya and the Yoga call the three guṇas, sattva (intelligence-stuff), rajas (energy) and tamas (mass or the factor of obstruction). It is by the union of these three in different degrees and according to their mutual superiority or inferiority that all things mental or material are generated. These three are the ultimate substances (*dravya*) and all the rest are but their modifications.

From what we have stated above two objections naturally arise ; (1) the analysis of consciousness, which cannot find out other ultimates than being, mass and energy, is imperfect, firstly because it is not complete, as it does not take any account of the "feeling" side of our consciousness which is quite as pervading as the plane of consciousness, if not more ; secondly, the ultimates generalised from consciousness

[1] *Cf.* "*Yo yo viruddhādhyāsavān sa sa nānā.*"

can hardly be put down as reals and substances. The other objection is that such a position seems to avoid the difficult problem of the correlation of mind and matter without proposing a solution for it, for the objections of the idealist (*vijñānavādin*) are not disponsed with by any supposition of irresistible convictions or ultimate necessities of thought.

The consideration of these objections again brings us to that old and tattered question "what must the nature of things be in order that they may be known?" The answer generally given is that they must be in some way akin to the mind which knows them, for the mind can only know that which is in some sense or other within the mind or is an idea, which comes to the same thing as to say that the mind can only know its ideas. Any assertion, therefore, about things is unwarrantable or, in other words, things may not exist. Our experience however tells us that we do not know ideas but things and to have an idea means nothing more than to know objects. To say that in order to be known a thing must be akin to the mind is no new revelation, as it practically means nothing more than to say that in order to know a thing, it must be capable of being known. The same fallacy of the mental nature of things is found in the doctrine which, starting from sensations as given, postulates the activity of thought in ordering and correlating the data of sensation in order to make the object: the world of nature is nothing other than the system of relations which the mind imposes on the crude data of sensations, still undetermined by relations as "the work of unknown things in themselves acting in unknown ways upon us." Green, in the interest of the intelligibility of the real world, discards things in themselves as meaningless, because while claiming to be completely independent of our knowledge and themselves never known, they are taken to be the cause of our knowledge; and causation being a relation is the work of the mind and cannot be predicated of the world of things-in-themselves. This no doubt disposes of Kant but the sensations cannot be arranged by the understanding capriciously at random. If it be not because of the inherent nature of the sensations themselves, why does the understanding give to one set of sensations a particular order different from those of other sets? If again objects of experience are made by the intelligence, we are incapable of accounting for the ways in which these sensations are made. So there must be something "not made by our intelligence" upon which our sensations are dependent; of this entity the idealists are precluded by their own presuppositions from giving any account. Thus we see that Green, after criticising Kant's things-in-themselves, is driven to speak of the "exciting cause of sensation." There is therefore an external matter which causes sensations. If it is still maintained that such things-in-themselves can have no relations or qualities, for they are the work of mind, then all the objections against Kant would re-appear. Doubtless we cannot know reality without the mind; but this cannot imply that it is a general characteristic of reality to be incapable of existence apart from the mind, *i.e.*, to be a psychical matter merely. It is unnecessary to follow the discussions of the Yogācāra with the Sautrāntikas, Mīmāṃsists, the Sāṅkhya and the Yoga, as the lines of argument are similar and differ only in details.[1]

Thus we have to admit that there is both an external reality and an inner one of mental states. But then again the question of correlation reappears. It may be held that there is only one unqualified being which is, on one side, the *viṣayachaitanya* and, on the other, the *pramāṇachaitanya*, but plurality and diversity remain unexplained. To say that matter is but thought externalised and that it follows the dialectic nature of thought is no explanation of the contingent aspect of nature as the mass, the

[1] See *Śāstradīpika-tarkapāda*, 5th Adhikaraṇa, the *Yoga Bhāṣya*, 4th Book, Sāṅkhya discussions of Vijñānabhikṣu, Kumārila's *Vārttika*, etc., on this point.

impenetrable, the datum of all change, for it is no better than a bold allegory or metaphor.

The difficulties of unqualified naturalism which would identify matter with thought are also as great as the unqualified monism of the idealistic nature just referred to. Naturalism admits that it cannot bridge the gulf between the physical and the psychical, that, in spite of its best efforts at explanation, something of a riddle remains, though it is inclined to hint that if only our knowledge were more perfect than it is, we should see that no gulf existed and that the continuity of all phenomena whatsoever was unbroken.

Since neither matter can be identified with mind nor mind with matter directly, it remains to be sought if any such things-in-themselves could be found from which both matter and mind could be derived. To find such a common basis it is necessary to lay hold on any thing which may be so crude in its nature as to be undistinguishable from both consciousness and mass and may yet be so constituted that it holds such elements of difference in itself as can explain the growth or development of them both.

Thus the question arises whether consciousness can be analysed to still simpler constituents than itself as it appears in its full development on the foreground of the mental plane. This is only possible if we can get at any such state when our mental states cannot properly be called conscious but which can be recognised as the beginnings from which later on these states mould themselves into consciousness. We can look for such a stage both as regards individual consciousness and also in the history of the dawn of consciousness in the light of its evolution. As a result of such an enquiry we find that in feeling we can detect such a primitive and crude stuff of consciousness. As we work downwards from higher to lower forms of life, the variety and definiteness of sense impressions both steadily diminish. We can directly observe in our own organic sensations, which seem to come nearest to the whole content of primitive or infantile experience, an almost entire absence of any assignable *quale*. In our sense experience generally we find the element of feeling at a maximum. Even the unity of apperception, or the comprehension as ego, does not exist in the instantaneous consciousness, for it is only in subsequent reflections upon it that it appears ; a feeling when it exists in an. for itself cannot be called "my feeling"; it is when on reflection there come up not merely faint repetitions of the feeling but, inextricably associated with it a whole set of connections with the general stream of consciousness, that we can associate the mental state with true notions of class-concept, substance, qualities, actions, names, etc.

Again in answer to the question whether a feeling can exist by itself without forming part of a consciousness we can hold with Clifford that in lower stages of development the complexity of the organism and the nerve action insensibly diminish and the complexity of consciousness insensibly diminishes also; if we descend to the molluscs, there is no reason to infer the existence of consciousness at all. There comes, therefore, a point at which one may have to infer facts out of his consciousness corresponding to them. The one way out of this difficulty is to say that consciousness is a complex of ejective facts of elementary feelings, or rather of those remoter elements which cannot even be felt but of which the simplest feelings are built up. Such elementary ejective facts go along with the action of every organism, however simple, but it is only when the material organism has reached a certain complexity of nervous structure that the complex of ejective facts reaches that mode of complication which is called consciousness. We have therefore to admit that " a feeling can exist by itself without forming part of a consciousness." It does not depend for its existence on the consciousness of which it may form a part, or, in other words, feelings are things in themselves.

If it is asked how, if in the beginning only feelings existed and these elementary feelings are the only things in themselves, relations between feelings come into existence, the answer to such a question will be that relations are just as fundamental as feelings. All that afterwards becomes thought is implicit not in mere feeling but in the primitive relations between feelings ; out of the combination of elementary feelings, having at first simple relations to one another, arises all the complexity of actual consciousness. Even when the feelings are manifested in their most developed form on the plane of consciousness it is their remarkable characteristic to be devoid of any objective reference such as is implied in knowing and willing, and therefore more or less like self-subsisting entities which have, as such, a real similarity with matter, such as cannot be found in knowing.

Apart from these considerations, which come to our mind in trying to comprehend the Sāṅkhya theory of the guṇas, the point which attracted the notice of the Sāṅkhya philosopher and persuaded him to think of the external world as made up of the three primary feelings, is the circumstance that the cognition of all external objects is associated with some kind of feeling or other ; this, they thought, could not be accounted for except on the theory that the external objects were also but the modifications of some primary feelings. Thus *Yoga Vārttika*, commenting on *Vyāsa- hāshya* 2. 15, says :— "All the mental states as well as all kinds of things are characterised as pleasurable (*sukha*), painful (*dūḥkha*), and blinding (*moha*) ; it is therefore that these guṇas, such as sattva, etc., being also transformed as the external objects such as the jug, etc., produce by mutual correlations the feelings of pleasure, pain and blindness. If the objects were not specially modified in that way, there should be no reason why with the merest connection with the objects there should rise painful or pleasurable states in the mind. It is for this reason that we hold that the modifications in the objects, which serve to determine the mental states in a painful or pleasurable way, are nothing but themselves the transformations of the elementary feeling entities of pleasure, pain, etc., for the cause must correspond with the effect that it produces; so the objects themselves are to be regarded as objectively pleasurable, painful, etc. It is important to see the force of the argument in connection with the Sāṅkhya theory of causation which holds that the effect is but the hidden nature of the cause and the casual movement is only the revelation of the cause in the form of the effect.

Thus, looking at the problem from all points of view, just as we find that feelings may be regarded as the crudest and grossest substances from which the consciousness may be thought to be derived, so also from the point of view of matter, feelings may be regarded as the subtle substances from which it has derived its existence. For it is conceivable on the one hand that such a subtle stage of matter should exist in which the elements of matter should be devoid of all such characteristics as form, colour, hardness, etc., but should at the same time possess the capability of directly assuming them: it will be difficult to distinguish these subtle kinds of matter from the entities of feelings in themselves. On the other hand, it is seen that gross matter, when it rises just a little in the scale of evolution to form the lowest organism, has already begun to generate feelings. Thus the subtler state of matter seems to be akin to that of feeling, its first development as organism produces feeling and its first and instantaneous grasp by a conscious mind reveals its nature as a mere feeling. The objection that the ancients could not have such a scheme in mind, as it involves the results of the achievements of the modern evolutionists, does not affect us in the least, as we are trying to comprehend the theory as a student of the present century should do; but it is important to remember in this connection that it was widely believed in ancient India that even the lowest organisms, the trees, plants, etc., were possessed of feelings of pleasure and pain[1] and that knowledge was only a late product as even the animals had only a blind something resembling knowledge.

In addition to these considerations which we may impose upon the Sāṅkhya from our point of view there seems to be another graver reason of a practical nature which led the Sāṅkhya to take the feelings as the ultimate things in themselves. The practical motive of all systematic philosophic speculation in India was deliverance from suffering. We know that the cardinal truth of the Buddhists was that every

[1] On account of bad deeds of previous births the plants are covered with diverse kinds of tamas; they have inner consciousness and have pleasures and pains—*Manusaṃhitā*. Medhātithi explains it as follows:—Though every thing is constituted of three guṇas, yet tamas preponderates with the plants and sattva and rajas are at the lowest; on account of the preponderance of tamas due to the effect of their bad deeds in past lives they suffer mostly pains, but on account of the presence of some sattva qualities they may occasionally enjoy some pleasures also.

The animals are described in the *Vishṇupurāṇa* as being of closed souls and full of tamas (*samvṛtātmā*) and (*tamaḥpracūrāḥ*). *Bhāgavatapurāṇa* describes them as being with knowledge and full of tamas and as discerning things they like by the smell. Śrīdhara quotes a scriptural passage in which it is said that the animals only know hunger and thirst. They can neither speak of things as known nor perceive them as such. They do not know the past, nor do they know that which is experienced and which is not experienced.

The author of *Śāstradīpikā* however differs from the above view that the animals can have only instinctive tendencies, and he holds that though the animals cannot express themselves, yet they acquire knowledge by experience and by a logical reasoning somewhat analogous to ours.

thing was full of suffering (*sarvaṃ duḥkhamayaṃ jagat*). This suffering was more manifest in the knowledge of the exterior world than when we ourselves from it withdrew to the depth of our inner thought through meditation, and Yoga was simply the practical method for such a withdrawal. Now, how could the external world be the source of suffering unless it was but the suffering hypostatised and objectified? On the side of consciousness we find that it is feeling which gives all the interest to our life. Were we incapable of pleasure and pain, of joy and sorrow, were nothing good in our eyes and nothing evil, we should be as stones, nothing could have any value for us, no event any interest, and life would be bereft of all significance. It is only because we are capable of feeling that we are interested in ourselves, or interested in each other, or have any questions to put about life and the universe, or any reason for desiring any one event to come to pass rather than another. In short, it is feeling alone that stirs to action the whole animated world; it is the root of all our experiences, of the inner as well as the outer world, and it is the sole object of the Yogin absolutely to detach himself from it; pleasure and pain have no meaning with him, for everything is but suffering to him. It is feeling, interest, which is the cause of desire that brings a man into the changing whirlpool of events the saṃsāra, and generates all experiences feeling therefore is the fundamental thing-in-itself and what we call consciousness is but its product at a certain stage of its development.

Judging from the analysis of the feelings which reveal themselves in our consciousness and taking into consideration the kinds of feeling which may be inferred from the observation of lower animals and organisms, the Sāṅkhya decided upon three kinds of ultimate and primary feelings, pleasurable (*sukha*), painful (*duḥkha*) and blinding (*moha*). All the logical, moral and noble emotions such as sincerity, mildness, shame, respect, forbearance, kindness, etc., or such emotions as are consequent upon knowledge, are regarded as belonging to the first class ; spite, anger and other immoral emotions to the second class ; and fear, scepticism, crookedness, etc., are said to belong to the third class. The three guṇas are therefore regarded as primary feeling-substances which hold within themselves the germs of infinite differences and diversities. The emotions specified above are to be regarded as indicating in terms of developed emotions their mutual differences from one another.

In the first part of the chapter, by an analysis of knowledge we had arrived at three irreducible notions. When we enquire into the substances of these ultimate things in themselves we call these three guṇas three ultimate feeling substances or reals, the pleasurable, the painful and the blinding; but when we look at them from the side of knowledge or epistemology we call them sattva, rajas and tamas with the characteristics we have noted before. These three act and react upon one another in different proportions which determine whether one guṇa should become dominant or inferior in strength; but howsoever that may be there is this harmony amongst them that though they are different primary ultimates yet they combine together to produce the exterior world of reality and the inner states of experiences and through the diverse kinds of feelings produce one flame of external reality and consciousness which is in substance a flame of feeling or rather of suffering. This harmony amongst them is maintained by the mutual correspondence of the three main functions, namely, illumination of sattva, movement of rajas and obstruction of tamas.

It is by the functioning of these three guṇas as illuminating, moving and obstructing that the phenomenon of consciousness is produced and it is thus that we find that they are the irreducible ultimates corresponding to the three entities. The external world is also produced by a similar mutual correspondence of functioning, only with this difference that here the tamas side of mass and obstruction has gained the ascendency, whereas on the side of consciousness, the tamas side has been extremely subordinated to sattva.

The solution of the correspondence of the inner and the outer has not been attempted here on the supposition of a doubleness of faces as understood of the mind-stuff theory of Clifford, but by a double line of development from one common basis. Thus on the conscious plane we have the cognitive and conative functions developed with a preponderance of sattva and rajas respectively, and on the side of matter we have a line of development with a gradual preponderance of tamas. The reality of the plane of consciousness is not only the same in substance with that of the plane of matter, but they both start from the same primal and fundamental *studium* of cosmic consciousness called Mahat only with a difference in the predominance of one or other of the constituent elements; it is therefore that the conscious plane is the same in "shining" terms as the matter plane in terms of mass. Thus it is that the correlation means nothing more than that in the development in which the character as being or shining gets ascendency it can assume in terms of sattva-predominance the form corresponding to that in the exterior world in terms of tamas-predominance or mass and materiality.

But are the reals (*guṇa*) only three or are they infinite in number? This enquiry decides finally that no idealistic exposition of Sāṅkhya philosophy is at all possible, for if the reals are said to be infinite in number, then they have necessarily to be taken as super-subtle substances. A reference to *Yoga-Vārttika* will show that there is an infinite number of reals which probably differ from one another, but which show amongst themselves three distinct types of similarities of characteristics by virtue of which they are classified under three names, namely, sattva, rajas and tamas. The reals which pass by the name of sattva are infinitesimals which have some common characteristics, such as lightness (*laghutva*) and shining character (*prakāśakatva*) by virtue of which they are called sattva. These sattva reals have many intrinsic characteristic differences between them, but we are not concerned with these, for so long as they agree with one another in laghutva, prakāśakatva, etc., we call them sattva. The same sort of classification holds good with rajas and tamas. The guṇas therefore are not three in number but infinite, and the names sattva, rajas and tamas are used only to denote that these reals may be divided into three distinct classes or types and that all these three kinds of guṇas must be present in each combination, though in any particular combination there may be more reals of one class or kind than in any other. An explicit corroboration of this is found in Sīmānanda's *Sāṅkhya-tattvavivecana*—" Though the sattva reals have many properties, such as happiness (*sukha*), complaisance (*prasāda*) and manifestation (*prakāśa*), yet it is on account of the prominence of happiness (*sukha*) that it is said to be of the nature of happiness. So rajas also, though possessed of many properties, such as sorrow (*duḥkha*), turbidity of mind (*kāluṣya*), movement, etc., yet on account of the prominence of sorrow is said to be of the nature of sorrow. So tamas, also, though possessed of many properties such as blinding (*moha*), covering (*āvaraṇa*), stunning (*stambhana*), etc., is yet said to be of the nature of moha. The quality of good or being is called sattva, and it serves the purusha the best since it brings piety; rajas is to be considered next since it brings attachment; tamas is the worst for it hinders piety. The reals, sattva, etc., are innumerable; they are continually suffering transformation every moment and are similar to one another by the qualities of laghutva, etc., and dissimilar otherwise. If each of the guṇas was of one kind only, then since creation takes place once with reference to many purushas, the guṇas have to be regarded as absolutely all-pervasive (*vibhu*); but in that case the infinite variety of created things and their limited character could not be explained. Again among created things some are all-pervasive like ākāśa or intellect (*buddhi*) though most other created things are limited and finite. Each of the guṇas must therefore be regarded as a class of reals which has some elements in it that are all-pervasive and others that are infinitesimals so that the former may be regarded as contributing to the all-pervasive nature of certain productions and the latter to the finitude of others. So the reals, such as sattva, etc., are infinite in number; they are called three in number only on account of the three types of their distinguishing characteristics (*vibhājakopādhi*), just as the Vaiśeshikas classify dravyas as nine in number. The sattva reals, however, may some be infinitesimals and others all-pervasive,[1] for otherwise rajas cannot be designated as moving (*cala*)." For if all guṇa entities were all-pervasive, movement by rajas would be impossible.

But does this scheme of presentation serve to clear up the position? After all the windings and ramblings does it come to this that consciousness is the subtle and spiritualised form of some substance of which the grosser form is matter? This is only a modified form

[1] For the utility of acknowledging the all-pervasive characteristic of the guṇas, the derivation of ākāśa in Yoga cosmology is to be referred to.

of materialism which speaks of thoughts as only forms of matter. For "forms of matter" is a phrase which is for all practical purposes almost as good as "forms of substance of which the other forms are the matter." We may admit that states of mind are but complexes of a substance having the same constituency as matter and are constantly smouldering away like flames;[1] but that does not explain the fundamental thing, the self-shining, the consciousness. Again, admitting that in the lowest stages of life we come to organisms to which we have to grant some kind of feeling or sensibility without according them any consciousness, can we say that this unconscious feeling is the same as feeling in the conscious stage? Of course, the gradation of these crude feelings from the unconscious to the conscious plane is continuous and the similarity between the unconscious feelings and the conscious ones is very great, so great indeed that they lose themselves in one another. But this only proves that the matter-stuff can form itself into complexes that imitate intelligence to an extraordinary degree and nothing more; but the fundamental fact of intelligence remains

[1] *Cittasya vṛttayaḥ dīpasya śikhā iva dravyarūpa bhaṅgurāḥ avasthāpariṇāmāḥ mūṣhānishiktadrutatāmravat svasaṃyuktārthākārāḥ triguṇakāryatvāt sukhaduḥkhamohāśrayatayā śantaghoramuḍhākhyā bhavanti* (*Yogavārttika*..:...1. 4.)

unexplained as it differs from all matter-stuff and mind-stuff in that it cannot be conceived as suffering any change; it is the pure effulgence or shining and as such unexplained by the states through which it is manifested. Moreover, even if it is said that consciousness is nothing more than the complex made up of the simple feelings, the guṇas, how should we account for the motive, the power and the order in which these are to be grouped together;[1] what is to become of the notion of the self which is continuous in all its experiences as a worldly perceiver, as the moral agent or the philosopher seeking salvation; for whom are the experiences, the order and flow of infinite world-complexes and ultimate salvation sought for in wisdom? Further, all the modifications of the guṇas being complexes of an organic nature (*saṅghāta*) it has to be supposed that there must be some one for whom these exist. If these alone were to exist they would indeed be purposeless. There must be souls who are to enjoy them. Of course the souls cannot have other enjoyers (*bhoktā*) as they themselves are the enjoyers pure and simple.

The Sāṅkhya and Yoga thus admit that there are numberless purushas or souls. The soul is

[1] *Cf.* Ward on Clifford, *Naturalism and Agnosticism.*

of the nature of a pure perceiving entity or pure illumination as such (*cf.* Vijñānabhikshu—*dṛśiratra na guṇaḥ kintu prakāśasvarūpaṃ dravyam*) and knowledge is not therefore a separate quality or attribute of the soul but the soul is an entity of pure knowledge. It is when the states (which are more or less of a material nature) are illuminated by the purusha that they are illuminated as conscious. It is by virtue of the image that there is a reflection of those states on the purusha and these appear as ideas or knowledge of a person. The difference between these states and the purusha is this that they, being of material stuff, are always changing, whereas the purusha is always the unchangeable light, and the fact that things are known and not known depends upon the contingency of the states being illuminated by the purusha. It cannot be held, however, that the states also might be regarded as unchangeable and of the nature of light, and that the contingency of knowledge depends upon the contingency of the external objects being reflected on them; for the changes of mental states do not depend upon the presentation of external objects, as they are undergoing changes of themselves even without any such external presentation, *e.g.*, in the dream state, the introspection state.[1] Thus we see that it is this

[1] See *Yogavārttika*, ii. 20; and also compare Russell's paper on "Knowledge by acquaintance and Knowledge by description."

purusha that is the perceiver. Though it is inactive in itself, yet it holds within itself the inner goal and teleology which move both the mental states as well as the external matter-complexes. It must however be noted in this connection that though the purusha is fundamentally different in nature from the buddhi or the conscious plane (the ground of consciousness holding the states as the various moments of its changes, together with the functions of the senses and the ego), inasmuch as it is the seer and the unchangeable, yet in the aspect of shining or illumination there is a great similarity between it and the purusha. In fact, of the three primal feeling-substances or guṇas the sattva is almost the same in point of shining with the purusha and it is on this account that in the supreme predominance of sattva in the buddhi it can be reflected into the purusha which it resembles completely in its shining character. The illumination of the states is transformed into the knowledge of an abiding person by the reflection on the purusha and it is principally for the sake of such an abiding personality that the world-order moves. Hence the Buddhist position has to be renounced and a soul has to be admitted.

These three guṇas and the purushas are the only principles which the Sāṅkhya admits. The Yoga however admits in addition to these the

Iśvara as a regulator of the world-order by his very proximity. The place of this Īśvara in the Yoga system will be described later on more elaborately and can therefore be left out for the present.

To understand the metaphysical position of the guṇa theory it may be useful to look at it from the point of view of a few kindred systems of thought of modern European philosophy, particularly from the aspect of "the thing in itself." Thus, according to Kant, the mind presents to itself in thought "neither itself nor other things but solely and alone that which is neither that what the mind is itself nor what other things are." The faculty of cognition hovers between a problematical X of the subject and an equally problematical X of the object. The sensibility has nothing behind it and the understanding nothing before it; in a two-fold enchanters' smoke, called space and time, rise the ghostly forms of phenomena and appearances in which nothing appears. If we assume things, Kant teaches that knowledge has not the least to do with them. Thought moves in a circle out of which there is no access to reality, in an endless series of the conditioned in which no unconditioned is to be found. But overlooking the spirit of this Kantian agnosticism there arose two distinct lines of development which grounded themselves on the certitude of their inner experiences but arrived at conclusions which have been designated as Idealism in one case and as Realism (though not so appropriately) in the other case as that of Herbart. The teaching of Kant that thought cannot get out of itself took this shape in the hand of the Idealists that consciousness can only be explained out of consciousness and by the fact that consciousness "looks at its own action" and creates thereby at once the real and the ideal series of experience—the objects as well their subjective knowledge. The fundamental general mode of this idealism is to be found in that triple characterisation of the mind as that which beholds itself. The reason is not only "in itself" as a simple ideal reality but also "for itself"; it appears to itself as "something other, alien"; it becomes for itself an object different from the subject and this otherness is the principle of negation. The doing away, the negation, the annulment of this negation, is the synthesis of the two. Following this scheme of the "in-itself" and "in and for itself" Hegel developed his dialectical method by making each conception turn into its opposite: from the contradiction of the two came out however a higher conception as their synthesis which again suffered a similar fate by finding an antithesis to itself, which demanded a still higher synthesis and so on. With Hegel therefore we find that all that is real or actual is the manifestation of the spirit or mind, and the business of metaphysics is to develop the creative self-movement of spirit as a dialectical necessity. The conceptions in which mind or spirit takes part and analyses its own content are the categories of reality, the forms of cosmic life. Philosophy has not to describe the manifold forms of reality but to comprehend them as moments of a single unitary development. The dialectical method serves "to determine the essential nature of particular phenomena by the significance which they have as members or links in the self-unfolding of spirit."

Taking the other point of view, namely that of so-called realism in the case of Herbart, we find that he denies the creative spontaneity of consciousness and finds it determined by and dependent in both form and content upon what is without. The supreme principle of all thought with him is that what contradicts itself cannot be truly real or actual. Applying this principle he said that our assumption of things as identical with themselves and yet made equal to the diversity of their qualities or attributes was wrong. Such a contradictory experience cannot but be a phenomenon; but this phenomenon must have at its basis something real which is free from all contradictions, or in other words seeming things must have absolute "reals," seeming occurrences and changes a real occurrence and change. Whatever seeming there is, there is just as much proof of being. The fallacy of ordinary thought is that something simple is thought as having differences. This difficulty can be removed only by assuming a plurality of simple beings through the relation of which to one other the "illusion" of the manifold is produced in any particular object. Things in themselves exist, not one but many. There is a simple and unchangeable real as the basis of each of the simplest characters or attributes that we ascribe to the substance. Every real strives to preserve its identity against disturbances on the part of other reals. One and the same real will therefore behave differently in maintaining itself against others. There is no real change in the real; it asserts its quality or preserves its essence against all disturbances threatening it. "Even if there were no opposition, if it existed alone, it would preserve its quality. The real is constant and unchanging in the face it presents, but various degrees of efforts are necessary for it to preserve its own calm against the different degrees of opposition of other reals. The presence and opposition of other reals do not change the nature and state of any real, but they arouse different degrees of self-preserving activities. Space, time, motion, matter, all that appear, are not reals but objective appearances of reals due to their different kinds and degrees of self-preservative activities. The being (the reals or absolute qualities) is "absolute position." Each of these has its own unchangeable determinations but the relation which arises between two reals is not essential to either and has not its basis in either. The Eleatic rigidity of these reals in no wise permits us to form an idea of the kind of actual relation which is held to obtain between them. The soul as a simple substance is naturally unknowable, but the ideas are the self-preservations of the soul against the disturbances by other reals. These ideas exist within the soul which simply furnishes the indifferent stage for their co-existence; they disturb each other, and the whole course of psychical life is to be explained from the reciprocal tension of ideas.

The Sāṅkhya is idealistic as far as it accepts the Vedāntic Brahman as pure "*jñānamaya*" as its purusha and insists on its permanent and unchangeable character as uncompromisingly as any Vedāntist or Eleatic would do. But it differs materially from the school of idealists we have referred to in that it would deny all change or process as being any part of the shining purusha. All processes and transformations as such belong to matter, and movement involved in thought must be regarded as alien to the purusha. Their connection with the purusha only takes place by their mystic reflection on the purusha by virtue of which they appear as illuminated by it and as the experiences of a person. The truth of the dialectic method appears here only so far as all objects mental or material are regarded as the development of one mind-stuff, the three guṇas in eternal conjunction. The causal movement by diverse kinds of re-groupings of the guṇas serves only to actualise the manifold potentialities of the guṇas (*cf.* Aristotle). But there is nothing here of the self-criticism of thought in the sense in which it is used by the modern idealists, and this causal movement is also almost a mechanical necessity of the guṇas in accordance with a moral or ethical teleology. The main point of view which has been emphasised in Sāṅkhya and Yoga is that the ideal content of thought must be distinguished as being essentially different from the knowing principle or the subject. The element of unity must be absolutely distinguished from the element of variety, and it is the confusion of these two parts as together representing the nature of thought as unity in diversity, that is the cause of all mischief. Diversity and change as such belong to matter, whereas thought as pure illumination is the unchangeable subject. It is the object of philosophy to convince its students that those are essentially different from the purusha, as they are made up of the same stuff of which matter is made.

The realism of Sāṅkhya consists in the fact that it does not agree with the idealist in holding either that it is only thought which exists or that the world is but the determination of thought objectified, though it holds that the world of matter is bound up with pure thought or purusha, inasmuch as all its changes are guided by an inner purpose, namely, that of bringing about the experiences of the purushas and their final liberation. All else except purusha are made up of the three guṇas or reals which are in a state of eternal movement. *Yoga-vārttika* holds that these are called guṇas (*cf.* Sanskrit, gauṇa) because they are subordinate to the purusha and because their identity is less real than that of the purusha, they being always in a state of movement.[1] But so far as the guṇas themselves are concerned, they exist as eternally as the purushas. But, in spite of this realism, the idealistic element becomes noticeable when we consider that the guṇas in their noumenal character cannot be known. It is true that the modifications of the manifold

[1] The word guṇa is not used in Sāṅkhya and Yoga in the sense of attributes as it is used in the Nyāya and Vaiśeṣika, but is used in the sense of ultimate substances (*dravya*).

outside are but the modifications of these reals, and that all the affections of the exterior world upon us through the senses are also the modifications of these reals and are therefore also real; but these our affections or impressions of the exterior world are in themselves but phenomena, which do not represent correctly the real modifications of the exterior world. The exterior world is no doubt the common source of all impressions, but the sense-data that each individual receives from it depend to a great extent upon the modifications which are imposed upon the original stimuli by his senses. Thus it is that what we call the exterior world of colour, sound, etc., is but the phenomenal world created by the co-operation or conjunction of the changes in the reals of the external world and those in the senses of the individual perceiver. Phenomenal experiences cannot therefore be said to represent correctly the true state of things in the exterior world, for they have largely been modified by the elements imparted to it by our senses. From this point of view this realism of Sāṅkhya may favourably be compared with that of Herbart or Lotze.

The reals of Sāṅkhya however have not much more in common with the reals of Herbart than that they are both real existents. Instead of the infinite number of Herbart's reals corresponding to each and every quality of substance, we have here in Sāṅkhya only three kinds of reals. Each one of these can show an infinite series of qualities or manifestations of a particular type according to the manner or degree in which it dominates the other two reals or is dominated by them. Each one of the guṇas is taken as if it were the potential unity of an infinite series of manifestations of a particular type. The appearance of these manifestations is helped or regulated by the various degrees of domination, determined by the other two reals, so that the three guṇas being each determined in the presence of the other two show their joint peculiar characters in each and every modification. The phenomena or appearances in Sāṅkhya however are not as phenomenal as in Herbart, for all determinations have a true reality, inasmuch as they are the modifications of the three guṇas; space therefore has its external reality, and time also has its basis in the unity of movement of an atom through its own unit of space. Our impressions of external reality are therefore phenomenal only because some new elements have been added to the external impressions from the senses. But these additions are also real additions, and in that sense the world of ideas is not mere phenomenon or illusion in any way. In Herbart the relation is non-essential to the reals, and hence it is difficult to understand how the reals can come into relation with one another. With the guṇas however such a difficulty does not arise, for they are always in eternal relation with one another, or rather they are so intimate with one another that they are three in one, and relation is not therefore a different category but is involved and merged in their reality. What we call relation is but a mode of looking at these guṇas.

Herbart's fictitious psychological calculus of explaining all ideas as being due to the reciprocal tension of the simple essence like other simple essences is fundamentally different from the psychology of Sāṅkhya; for the soul is here essentially different from the guṇas and beyond any stress, strain, or change. Here in Sāṅkhya we know that the difference between the mental and the material modifications of the guṇas lies in this that in the former case we have a predominance of the sattva and the rajas elements, whereas in the latter it is the tamas which predominates.

The guṇa theory approaches the Buddhist doctrine of impermanence and change so far as the guṇas, and with them all substances and qualities and appearances, are in a state of eternal change; but here there is the substratum of change, the guṇas, whereas in the earlier Buddhism there is apparently at least no substratum of change or permanent entity. If we however take the doctrine of Śūnya in the light that the śūnya is the substratum which undergoes all forms of change but is in itself pure void, we see that it approaches the guṇa theory only so far that, in the noumenal equipoise of the guṇas in the prakṛti, the guṇas are absolutely colourless and absolutely as devoid of any determinations as void itself. Even then however there is the most important difference that there is no permanent soul in Buddhism, whereas it is the soul which is regarded here as the most fundamental reality.

The guṇa theory mainly differs from the Vaiśeshika view in according no separate existence to the attributes, the relation, the universal, or the particular and speaking of the grosser elements as being only the modifications of the primary guṇas, but it agrees with it in the recognition of the plurality of souls. But even here the essential distinction must be noted that the Vaiśeshika soul is not pure knowledge or intelligence as is the Sāṅkhya purusha, for knowledge in the Vaiśeshika system is only a quality which inheres in the substance of the soul or ātman. Time, space, and mind (*manas*) are regarded as separate substances in Vaiśeshika, whereas in Sāṅkhya they are regarded as evolutes or products of the combination of the guṇas. These differences necessarily presuppose a difference in the theory of causation which appears here as mere actualisation of the potential whereas according to the Vaiśeshika it is the formation of a new existence.

Such is its similarity with Vedānta that we find the guṇa theory accepted in later days by most Vedāntists. The main point in which it differs from the Vedānta is its doctrine of the multiplicity of purushas.[1] With a liberated person the effect is almost the same in both systems, though Chitsukha finds fault with the Sāṅkhya for the absence of ānanda in the purusha. The subtle point of difference with regard to the manifold lies in this that with Sāṅkhya the manifold continues to exist independent of the purusha quite as eternally as the purusha, whereas in the Vedānta it has only a relative existence till salvation is attained. In the noumenal state however prakṛti is hardly distinguishable from māyā as it holds within it the principle of the many and is in itself devoid of any character, and we know that the Śvetāśvatara actually identified the māyā and the prakṛti.

Thus we find that, according to Sāṅkhya, there are two noumenal realities, the purusha and the prakṛti or the unity of the guṇas in equipoise. All the manifold is produced out of

[1] It may be noted in this connection that the Sāṅkhya has no objection to speaking of one universal Brahman in the Vedānta fashion in the sense of a class notion. (See *Sāṅkhya-Sūtra.*)

this prakṛti in conjunction with the purusha or pure intelligence. Sāṅkhya may thus be characterised as the union of transcendentalism in realism and realism in transcendentalism.

CHAPTER IV

Some Important Ontological Problems in the Light of the Guṇa Theory

The problem before the Sāṅkhya was that of explaining the diverse transformations and changes of this world of many, as originating from some such ultimate ground as could be demonstrated as the ultimate cause. The realistic tone, which must have been very remarkable even in the case of the earliest Sāṅkhya thinkers, made it difficult for them to agree with monistic ideas which ignored the importance of the ordinary experiences of our everyday life. The Vedānta, so long as it remained in this attitude, either in the later Vedāntic Upanishads or even in the *Brahmasūtra* (which is more a summary of the main contents of the Upanishads than a systematic philosophical treatise), was more a theological or philosophical mysticism than philosophy proper ; for philosophy demands a consistent system of thought which can put diversified experiences on a more stable basis whence it may illuminate the problem of existence from a new angle. The more the speculator strives to lay stress on any particular part of the truth to the negligence of the importance of other necessary parts, the more defective does this system become from the point of view of systematic philosophy. The Sāṅkhya in its deep insight grasped the problem of philosophy, and accepted the world of change as real, and, following the Vedāntic lines of thinking in its own way, argued that since these everyday realities of change and limitation are but modifications of a limited nature they necessarily presuppose an unlimited, infinite, and unqualified principle as their ground and cause. The Upanishads held that in all modifications the substratum alone was true, whereas the Sāṅkhya declared that in all modifications the substratum underwent change; the modifications therefore were as much real as the substance itself and they demonstrated only how the substance revealed itself under a variety of forms. The modifications were finite and limited in quantity, character and attributes, and this only showed that they were but finite forms and determinations of a principle infinite in its nature, the prakrti.

The Sāṅkhya holds that the effects are not non-existent only because the ground or cause is the only thing perceivable in all changes, for it is the nature of reality to change the states of its existence and reveal itself in diverse forms. The diverse forms or effects are already in existence in the cause and the work of the conditioning factors consists only in revealing them as different aspects of the cause gradually brought before our view in an unending series. In our ordinary experience also we find that we have a natural expectancy that some effects exist in some causes, which are not looked for in other causes. He who wants oil takes mustard as that in which it exists and not sand for he knows that there is no oil therein. If the oil did not exist in the mustard, no amount of effect would be able to get it out, for *ex nihilo nihil fit*, out of nothing nothing comes (*nāsato vidyate bhāvo nābhāvo vidyate sataḥ*). The relation that exists between the cause and the effect is only that the latter exists in the former ; for had this not been the case, we could not have expected to get it from that. The effect, if it is non-existent, is non-existent everywhere, for negation is perfect homogeneity, and there is no reason why we should get curd from milk and not from sand ; for if the curd had been as much non-existent in the milk as in the sand it would not follow that milk should produce it rather than sand ; negation possesses no speciality or characteristic in one case which is absent in the other. If there were indeed differences in the nature of the non-existence in the milk and in the sand this would be tantamount to existence. Thus the reason why some things are produced from some things and not from others proves that some effects are present in some causes and absent in others. Moreover if the effect had been extraneous to the cause, how could it relate itself with the cause? The causal movement is only the effectuation or bringing into appearance of such a state or modification of it as had hitherto been concealed, either lost or hidden in the causal form or appearance.

To explain the phenomena of change we find that the appearance of bodies or things changes with the change of the relative position of the atoms amongst themselves. The change of the appearance of things and bodies only shows the change of collocation of the atoms, there being always a change of appearance in the bodies consequent on every change of the position of the atoms. The former therefore is only a manifestation of the change that takes place in the substance itself; for the appearance of a thing is only an explicit aspect of the very selfsame thing, the atoms; thus the Bhāshya says that qualities are nothing but the substance itself,—it is only the changes of the state of the substance that are noted by the manifestation of the qualities. All bodies are continually changing their constituent collocating atoms and their appearance. Therefore in the smallest particle of time or kṣaṇa, the whole universe undergoes change. Each moment or smallest particle of time is only the manifestation of that particular change. The appearance is called the quality (*dharma*) and the particular arrangement of atoms or guṇas which is the basis of the particular appearance is called the dharmin. The change of appearance is therefore called the *dharmapariṇāma*.

Two other aspects, which, though not intrinsically different from the change of appearance, have their own special points of view that make them remarkable. These are *lakṣaṇapariṇāma* and *avasthāpariṇāma*. Taking the particular collocation of atoms in a body for review, we see that all the subsequent changes that take place in it exist only in a latent way and will be manifested in the future. All the previous changes of the collocating atoms are not lost, but exist only in a sub-latent way in the particular collocation of atoms present before us. For the past changes are not by any means destroyed, but preserved in the peculiar and particular collocation of atoms of the present moment. For had not the past changes taken place, the present could not have been. The present was hidden in the past, just as the future is hidden within the present. It therefore only comes into being with the unfolding of the past, which therefore exists only in a sublatent form in it. It is on account of this that we see a body come into being and die away. This birth or death, though it is really subsumed under the change of appearance, has its own special aspect on account of which it has been given a separate name *lakṣaṇapariṇāma.* It considers the three stages of an appearance—the unmanifested which is to exist in the future, the manifested moment of the present, and the past when it has been manifested and now lost to view but conserved in all further stages of evolution. Thus when we say that a thing has not yet come into being, that it has just come into being, and that it is no longer in being, we refer to this lakṣaṇapariṇāma, which records the history of the thing in the future, the present and the past, which are only the three moments of the same thing according to its different characters as unmanifested, manifested, and manifested in the past but conserved. When the changes that a thing undergoes are of so remarkable a nature as to affect the constitution of the body materially we call it new or old, or say that it has suffered growth or decay, and this aspect of the change is called *āvasthāpariṇāma.*

Thus we see that the dharmin or substance is that which remains common to the latent (as having passed over), the rising (the present) and the unpredicable (future) characteristic qualities of the substance.

A substance, (for example) earth, has the power of existing in the form of particles of dust, a lump, or a jug by which water may be carried. Now taking the stage of lump for review we may think of its previous stage, namely that of particles of dust, as latent, and its future stage as jug, as unpredicable. The earth, we see here, is common to all these three stages which have come into being by its own activity and consequent changes. Earth is here the common entity which remains unchanged in all these stages and so relatively constant among its changes as particles, lump and jug. This earth is therefore regarded as the dharmin, the characterised one, the jug and its stages as its dharma or qualities. The transformation of the substance looked at from the point of view of change of qualities is called dharmapariṇāma; from the point of view of temporal change as determining present, past and future it is called lakshaṇapariṇāma; and from the point of view of the effect on the constitution of the thing (as growth or decay, etc.) as determined by the temporal change of lakshaṇapariṇāma it is called avasthāpariṇāma.

We now see that the substance has neither past nor future. The appearances or the qualities only are manifested in time by virtue of which the substance also is spoken of as varying and changing temporally, just as a line though unchanged in itself acquires different significances according to the number of zeros that are placed on its right. The substance by various changes of quality appears as the manifold varieties of cosmic existence. There is no intrinsic difference between one thing and another, but only changes of character of one and the same thing, just as water and earth particles acquire various qualities and appear as the various juices of all fruits and herbs.

The guṇas are the final or ultimate substratum of all things. They are always in a state of commotion, forming the diverse relative substances, appearances and characteristics. There cannot however result any new kind or existence, but only new attributes and with them relatively new substances.

The Śakti (power, force,) and the Śaktimān (the possessor of power or force) are again as undifferentiated and identical as the quality (dharma) and the substance (dharmin) which we have just now discussed. So the prakṛti and all its emanations or modifications are of the nature of substantive entities as well as of power or force. Their appearance as substantive entities and their appearance as power or force are but two aspects, and so it will be erroneous to make any real distinction between the substantive entity and its power or force. That which is the substantive entity is the force and that which is the force is the substantive entity. Of course, for all ordinary purposes we can make some distinction but that distinction is only relatively true. Thus when we say that earth is the substantive entity and its power of transforming itself into the jug or lump as its attribute, we see that no distinction is really made between the appearance of the earth and its power of transforming itself into the jug, as this power of transforming itself into its diverse modifications always abides in the earth ; when the power is in the potential state we say that the jug is in the potential state and when it is actualised we say that the jug has been actualised. The potentiality or actuality of any state is the mere potentiality or actuality of the power which its antecedent cause has of transforming itself into it.

Coming to the other kindred questions of genus and species or of whole and part, we find that substance is here regarded as the unity of the genus and the species, of the whole and of the parts. There is one universal genus, namely that of the three guṇas, and it is these that in collocations show themselves as the different sub-genera or sub-species in their diverse characteristic qualities. The Sāṅkhya-Yoga holds that in our experience we notice the genus and the species as being quite undistinguished and undifferentiated from one another in experience. The individual and the parts cannot be ignored for the genus or whole appears to be existing in them, though it must be admitted that we cannot notice any other separate whole or genus which is different from the parts or the individuals. Thus it is that the universal in the jug is its character as the atoms (*paramāṇus*) which are the colour, form and other characteristics appearing as the jug; for the colour, movement, etc., are themselves in spite of their individuality also universal substances. It is these individuals that continue to exist in spite of some modifications or changes amongst themselves, which we call the universal. It is not denied that the universal is observed in experience, but it may be asserted that all we can deduce from such an experience is that the universal or genus is the substance, and not that the universality is a quality or attribute of the substance. There is no other substance given in our experience which may be thought of as the residence or vehicle of universality and individuality. There are no hills apart from stones grouped together. Thus substance is to be taken as being of the nature of the universal and the individual together, as there is no contradiction between them. The universal is but a mode of the individual itself.

It is well to note in this connection that conglomerations are viewed from two different points of view, (1) linguistic and (2) constitutional. Thus we speak of a body, a tree, a herd, or a forest, and we speak also of "gods and men." In the latter case language distinguishes the two parts as being separate though they together no doubt form a conglomeration. In the former case, however, though the trees stand apart from one another, yet the word "forest" carries the idea of a whole or conglomeration, as the idea of the parts does not arise in the mind. The forest again may be spoken of with a distinct idea of the separateness of the trees or of the parts as a forest. Thus it is that the unity as a whole, or diversity as parts, depends upon the aspect from which these are looked upon; the same thing which appears as a whole, when it is looked at from one point of view, appears as the many of the parts from another point of view. When appreciable space-distances exist between things, such a relativity of the notions of "whole" and "parts" becomes quite intelligible but when there are no visible space-distances (*e. g.*, in the case of *ayutasidhāvayava*) between things, the group appears as one whole or undivided thing, and not as mere collection of parts.[1] Thus the "body," the "tree," or the

[1] See Nāgeśa's commentary, iii. 43.
See also *Vyāsa Bhāshya* and *Tattvavaiśāradī* on *Yoga-Sūtra*, iii. 44.

"atom" (*paramāṇu*) are all composed of parts. But their distinct appearances not being perceptible for want of visible space-distances, they appear as indivisible wholes or units.

Thus in *Yoga-sūtra,* iii, 44 we find that the objects of the material world have five forms: (1) as they appear with their diverse physical characteristic qualities or attributes, (2) as things or substances forming the unity of genus and species, or as wholes or unity of parts, (3) as subtle causes, the tanmātras, (4) as the ultimates or universals of the three guṇas, (5) in the teleological aspect as conducive to the experience and salvation of souls. But in all these diverse aspects it is the three guṇas which manifest themselves.

The views of Kapila and Pātañjala-Sāṅkhya are probably the same regarding the ontological problems discussed above; the views of other Indian systems on some of these problems deserve special notice in this connection, as they will aid us in comprehending the true Sāṅkhya position with reference to other Indian systems and in forming a right estimate of the value of Sāṅkhya speculations. Let us take the grammatical school first.

Taking for example the question of genus and species or substance and attribute, the earliest pragmatic answer is to be found in the reconciliation offered by Patañjali (the grammarian) in accordance with the common sense metaphysics of grammar, of the two extreme views of Vyāḍi and Vājapyāyana. Thus Patañjali described substance (*dravya*) in one place as the visible object (cow) with all its individual peculiarities and yet finds in it a permanent universal aspect, which exists in spite of the changes that the individual may suffer. He says that one and the same word, is used to signify both the universal and the individual. A substance is in one aspect an individual and in another a universal; the two remain together, and the one cannot be had without the other. But the two have not one identical reality, for the universal rests upon the individual, so that even if the latter be destroyed, the former remains intact (*tadyathā vṛkṣasya avatāno vṛkṣe chinne api na vinaśyati*). This is to be distinguished from the Nyāya view of sāmānya or genus as a special kind of substance; Patañjali would admit grammatically a universal even of the universal, which is impossible with Nyāya, for the maxim of the grammatical school is that whatever seems to have existence in our ordinary common sense experience and corresponding literary usage, must be admitted. Thus Kaiyata says—

The class-concepts "horse" and "cow" are different, but yet they are similar, since they are both class-concepts; so even class-concepts may have further class-concepts. The Nyāya view that class-concepts cannot have further class-concepts is not admitted by the grammar school which holds that categories have to be admitted whenever they have a legitimate purpose or function to fulfil. Thus in spite of such an extremist view of sāmānya we find elsewhere that the universal and the individual lie undistinguished from each other.[1] Coming to the subject of substance and attribute he takes the view that in common experience the attributes alone can be noticed ; no other thing than these can be got in experience; but in the light of inference we can get at the notion of the thing. It is that which makes the difference between cotton and iron, fragility and hardness, or rather the mass or the materiality that is to be called the things, or that which remains constant amidst the diverse modifications or changes of qualities, the substratum of change and qualities that is to be called a thing or dravya.[2] (*Cf.* *Yoga-sūtra*, III. 14 *śāntoditāvyapadeśyadharmānupātī dharmī.*) There are other passages in which the cause and effect are regarded as being identical, *Mahābhāshya* (3, 3,

[1] See *Mahābhāshya*, 1. 1. 56. ; 1. 2. 45. ; 1. 2. 64. ; 1. 2. 58,; 2. 1. 51.; 1. 44. ; 4. 1. 63. &c. See also for further elaboration of the grammar school of ideas in this connection the chapter *Jātisamuddeśa* of *Vākyapadīya* and *Prakīrṇaprakāśa* of Helāraja.

[2] See *Mahābhāshya*, 5. I. 129.

163). These examples go to show that the solutions that the grammatical school of thought proposed, did not enter into subtle metaphysical niceties ; it accepted the points of view which appealed to common sense without trying to reconcile these with a consistent metaphysical theory of a comprehensive nature.

Turning to Buddhism we find that Paṇḍita Aśoka refutes the idea of Nyāya of the existence of a "whole" as separate and distinct from the parts but residing in them in the relation of inherence, and says that there is no separate "whole" apart from the individual appearances called the parts. It is the atoms which appear as spreading in space and the notion of grossness (*sthūlatva*) is nothing but extension in space. So it is that when the many partless ones shine in one knowledge, there comes the appearance of grossness which rises at the time of the appearance but is really non-existent, as it does not exist in any one of them. Nothing can be argued from the fact that the intervening spaces cannot be perceived, for pure space cannot be perceived. In movement also it is always the movement of atoms that is designated as the movement of the whole.

Regarding the nature of the universal and the individual also, contrary to the Nyāya-Vaiśeshika view, Paṇḍita Aśoka says in his *Sāmānyadūshaṇadikprasāritā* that we always perceive the individuals; we have no doubt class notions but these cannot be perceived from outside, but are always generated in the inner consciousness through positive and negative experiences and then superimposed upon external objects. (*antarmātrābhiniveśine bhāvābhāvobhayānubhavāhita vāsanāparipākaprabhāvasyādhyastabahirvastuno jñānākārasya dharmitayopayogāt.*) The supposition that the genus and the individual are given in one act of experience also does not meet with his approval, for in that case both being mixed, none of them would be visible He sums up the debate by saying that among the five fingers that appear before us he who sees the "fingerness" universal, as the sixth, will also probably see a horn upon his own head.[1]

[1] It is interesting to notice in this connection the main points of the Buddhist objections as they were taken note of by the Hindu writers. As an example reference may be made to some of the most important points from Jayanta's *Nyāyamañjarī* :—

(1) We cannot experience class-concepts or guṇa universals by perception, for the essence of the notion of class-concepts consists in the assimilation of the common characteristics experienced in the past and in the present, and so it is altogether a mental affair.

(2) There is no mode of any such existence (*vṛtti*) in which the guṇa universals may be said to reside in the individual, for it could not do so either wholly or in part; for if the class-concept consisted in one individual wholly how could it apply to other individuals? If it consisted in part in all individuals having the same class-concept, then the class-concept being only in part in each individual could not apply wholly to any one of them.

(3) The relation of form and substance does not hold, as also of character and the characterised.

To multiply examples from other systems is needless, as this will be enough for our purposes to show the different points of view from which these problems were looked at by different Indian systems in accordance with the peculiarities of each system.

Returning to the problem of the doctrine of the existence of the effect before the operation of cause (*satkāryavāda*) we find that the Vedāntist could not take change as reality and naturally thought that "being cannot become, for then it were only illusion. Who so lets anything come to be, lets that come to be that was already there."[1] This position is to be distinguished from the Sāṅkhya position of *satkāryavāda* for its special import is that all effect as such is mere illusion and imposition on the cause which alone is the unalterable reality; it is the cause (*kāraṇa*) or cause which is existent, (*sat*) whereas all effect (*kārya*) as such must be taken as non-existent (*asat*). Plurality or change as such cannot in any way be brought into relation with the unity

(4) Nor can it be noted that both the notions are generated without suffering any contradiction, as no such relation is intelligible.

(5) The notion of jāti has merely conditional subsistence (*aupādhika*) without any reality behind it; it exists merely from the point of view of a positivity, derived from negative processes of the exclusion of the opposites. There are no positive entities at the back of any class-concept, *e. g.*, horse, but the class-concept horse only subsists by the exclusion of other concepts which it implies.

[1] *Māṇḍukyakārikā.*

which is the one reality full and completely relationless within itself.

The other form which some monists hold and which seems to be an attempt at a compromise with the Sāṅkhya view is to define the material cause as the producer of effects which are not different from itself the cause (*svābhinna-kāryajanakatvam*). This, as the meaning signifies, meant that the cause produces the effect, but that the effect is identical, all the while, with the cause. Such a position may in some senses be compared with that of Green in his idea of ground and consequence. This position must however be distinguished from the Sāṅkhya-Yoga position where all the modifications have the same identical reality in their nature as the guṇas, yet all the modifications forming the ground of different substances are in themselves real, as much real as the guṇas of which they are the modifications. It is for this reason that there is no emphasis here on the identity (*abhinnatva*) of the primal cause in the causal demonstrations. The effects are as true and real as the cause, and their substantial identity with the primal substratum is not the only remarkable point about them. It is thus that we say here that the effects are existent in the cause and that the causal movement only reveals or actualises the diverse combinations of the guṇas to be designated as effects. So the

17

main point here as distinguished from the Vedānta is to be found in the fact that the effects are to be regarded here as a mere unrolling or manifesting of states already in existence, but only in a potential manner. The incongruity and inexplicable character of the relation between cause and effect are solved in the conception of the movement of the substance in which the cause and effect are posited only as preceding and later stages. Here is indeed a philosophical standpoint in which the movement, the moved and the unmoved are not set against one another in opposition but are conceived in their actual and necessary form. The Naiyāyika, however, thinks of the movement as a separate entity from the unmoved but subsisting in it in an inexplicable relation of inherence. He separates the two and tries in vain to get at the Sāṅkhya conception of abhivyakti, and finds fault with it. Thus Jayanta asks what can be the meaning of the Sāṅkhya evolution (*abhivyakti*)? If it means effect (*kārya*), then as it did not exist before, the theory of the previous existence of effects (*satkāryavāda*) fails. If it really existed before, then, the actions of the instrumentals or agents to bring it about become unnecessary. If it means the particular arrangement of the atoms, then so far as the existence of the atoms is concerned, there cannot be any dispute, for we also are agreed on that point. If however evolution (*abhivyakti*) means appearance as knowledge, then that depends on one hand upon the subjective activities of the senses, and on the other hand (in the case of the jug) upon the lump of earth, the potter's wheel, the stick and the agency of the potter, and it cannot be said that a thing which depends upon the collocation of so many things could exist already in the lump of earth. Moreover the effect could not exist as a mere potency, for the question whether this potency is the same as the effect or not leads to an unanswerable dilemma. The objection that if any effect comes out of non-being, we might expect the production of a non-existing effect as well like the hare's horn, is illogical as the converse does not follow (*yadasat tatkriyate iti neyam vacanavyaktirapi tu yatkriyate tadasat*).

Again it is absolutely meaningless to speak of the existence of the effect as the being of the potency (the substance as the datum and the instrumentals as extraneous), for that would mean that an effect would come out of an effect; and if the effect is already in existence there is neither production nor material cause. Experience also shows that the cause and the effect are different, it is therefore mere confusion of thought to speak of the effect as being existent in the cause.

Vijñānabhikshu brushes away these objections by saying that if at any change that a substance undergoes it is to be urged that a new thing has been created, then such changes are always occurring, and consequently we are always having a succession of new things, the preceding ones being gradually destroyed one after another; and this will bring in the Buddhist doctrine of the momentariness of things.

It is indeed interesting to notice that while the Sāṅkhya had united the cause and the effect or the part and the whole in one process of movement, the Buddhists had merely laid stress on the side of the series of succession of existence without observing anything permanent in them. Thus a Buddhist will say that he perceives only modification (a being destroyed and replaced by another) and no permanent substance which continues to subsist throughout the changes as their substratum; he perceives only individuals and the idea of the genus, as the one universal subsisting amongst them all, is only an illusion of the mind; he perceives only the parts and not the whole, which is merely a convenient fiction of the mind. Sāṅkhya also agrees with the Buddhist that the modifications are coming into being and passing away every moment, but it asserts at the same time that these are only the appearances (*dharma*) and behind them is the substance (*dharmī*), whereas with the Buddhists it is only the appearances, the impermanent, the momentary revelations which exist which have no other reality behind them.

Again with reference to the relation of the individual and the universal, the Sāṅkhya does not say like the Buddhist that there is no universal, but asserts that in one sense the universal is identical with the individual, and in another sense the two may seem to be different ; they cannot be separated from one another like milk and water, for even when we look at the aspect of the individual, the aspect of the universal persists.

On the point of the relation of the part to the whole also Sāṅkhya agrees with the Buddhists that the parts are the only reals but it does not agree with them in holding that the whole is merely an illusion, for if this were so, then the minute parts themselves being invisible, all knowledge would become false and illusory ; it must therefore be admitted that the whole is an attribute of the parts and fulfils its existence in each one of them ; it does not depend upon them all for its existence or manifestation, *i.e.*, it is not *vyāsajyavṛtti*, or relative mutually to all the parts like the conceptions of number such as two, three, etc. ; for had it been so, then from the obstruction of any part the whole would become invisible.

The view which comes nearest to the Sāṅkhya-Yoga doctrine on these points (namely, the relation of the universal and particular or of the whole and the part) is that of Kumārila Bhaṭṭa as we find in *Śāstradīpikā*, though attempts have been made there to refute the Sāṅkhya doctrine which holds the world to be a product of evolution; for Kumārila's agreement is mainly based on experiential grounds which cannot be extended beyond a certain limit as neither Kumārila nor Prabhākara would believe in the creation and dissolution of the Universe as a whole. The author of *Śāstradīpikā* points out that since we can say "this is a cow" the class-concept can be considered as identical with the individual. But since the class-concept is applicable to different individuals at the same time, the class-concept cannot be identified with individuals. So the class-concept is at once one with the individual and different.

The main Sāṅkhya conclusions may thus be summarised. First, it agrees with Buddhism that the facts of experience come into being or are revealed, change and pass away; but it differs from it in that it holds such changes to be no mere fleeting states, no mere present, past and future, no mere impermanence, but it believes that there is a permanent background, the workings or self-modifications of which are noticed as "not yet," "now" and "no longer" characters, and qualities.

Secondly, it differs from the Nyāyavaiśeshika

view in that it does not regard the characters or qualities as different in nature from the substances, but as the manifestations of their modifications as appearing to our consciousness through the senses; so also other changes which lead to the distinction of cause and effect, universal and particular, or whole and part, are only relative distinctions and do not justify the Vaiśeshika idea that these indicate permanent and unalterable difference in existence; for these are only relative distinctions based upon the reality of a substance which reveals them by their own constitutional or collocational modifications.

Thirdly, it agrees with Vedānta that only the substance is true reality, but it does not agree with it in holding that all movement and change are mere extraneous and illusory impositions. Change, character, diversity, and plurality are as much a reality as the substance itself, though these are involved in the nature of the substance itself and are not mere extraneous impositions of an illusory nature. The facts of experience are therefore not unreal but are modifications of the real.

CHAPTER V

THE THEORY OF SOUL

The Cārvākas and Buddhists do not believe in the existence of any permanent soul or self. All the other systems of Indian Philosophy however believe in its existence, but differ as to its nature and relations with conscious experience. To understand properly the peculiarities of the Sāṅkhya-Yoga theory of soul, it will be to our advantage to bear in mind the criticism that all the Hindu systems make in common, of the Cārvākas and the Buddhists, and then pass in review the peculiarities of the soul-doctrine in important systems. To do this I shall first examine how the Cārvākas and the Buddhists try to do away with the theory of a permanent soul in the light of the criticisms offered against them by Nyāya. The peculiarities of the soul-doctrine of Nyāya, the two schools of Mīmāṃsā and Vedānta will then be compared and contrasted, so that we may attain a position from which it will be possible to form a correct estimate of the Sāṅkhya-Yoga theory of soul, as it is in itself and in relation to other Indian doctrines.

The Lokāyata school of Cārvākas asserts that the body is endowed with intelligence and there is no separate soul; life and intelligence are only by-products of the transformations of matter at a certain stage as they appear in the body of an organic being just as molasses can in certain forms cause intoxication. It cannot be argued, they say, from the feeling of "I know," "I desire," "I am happy," or "I am sorry," that we really directly perceive such a self or soul within us, for these are mere linguistic usages, and such notions do not really signify any perceiver but merely perceptions as knowldge, desire, etc. It is easy to see that such an introspection will naturally mean that the self can at the same time be both subject and object of its cognitions. It cannot be said that in such an expression as "I know the things," the "self" is revealed in knowledge. as there is no distinction between this and the perception "Here is the thing," except that in the former case the *knowledge* of the thing is directly made the object whereas in the latter case it is the *thing* which is made the object of knowledge. To say that in such cases of introspection as in the self-knowledge involved in "I know myself," the self is revealed as the seer, is all the more absurd, for the single self cannot cut itself into two, so that one part may see the other. We are therefore forced to the conclusion that in all cases of self-knowledge it is the body that is known and not a separate self. Linguistic usages do not count for much, as we are just as accustomed to say "my body" as "my soul" Objections similar to those found against the direct perception of the self in our experiences are also to be urged against any inference of the self as the seat of knowledge, feeling and willing, and the body may equally well be designated as their seat.

The other school designated by Jayanta as the learned (*suśikshita*) Cārvāka though ready to admit that there is a separate subject who is the perceiver in man, does not admit as to the immortality of such a self, as we have no memory of any of our past lives.

Buddhism also rejects any permanent soul, but not in the manner of the materialists of whom I have just spoken. The body as well as the soul exists only as a complex of manifold interconnected origination and decease, but neither has any existence as a self-contained substance, existing *per se*. Sensations, perceptions, and all those processes which make up the inner life, crowd upon one another in motley variety. In the midst of this psychical flux stands consciousness. But consciousness is not different from the perceptions, sensations, ideas, etc., which come and go, though it may in a way be said to superintend them. "We are accustomed to realise our inner life as a comprehensible factor, only when we are allowed to refer to its changing ingredients,—every individual feeling, every distinct act of will,—to one and ever identical ego; but this mode of thinking is fundamentally opposed to Buddhism. Here as everywhere it condemns that fixity which we are prone to give to the flowing current of incidents which is falsely interpreted as abiding substances. A seeing, a hearing, a conceiving, above all, a suffering takes place; but an existence which may be regarded as the seer, the hearer, the sufferer is not recognised." The stream of saṅkhāras appearing and again vanishing admits of no "I" and no "thou," but only a phenomenon of the "I" and "thou" which many in their illusion think to be a manifestation of personality. It is like the flame which appears to be at rest but is yet enduring continuous self-production and self-consumption. The arguments against the existence of a permanent self are the same as against the permanence of all other things; for applying their maxim of causal efficiency *arthakriyā-kāritva*, the Buddhists declare all things to be momentary and revealed as a moment in the process of origination and decease. [1]

[1] For Buddhistic arguments in favour of the doctrine of momentariness (*kshaṇabhaṅgavāda*) see *Nyāyamañjarī* of Jayanta and *Nyāyavārttikatātparyyatīkā* of Vācaspati. Ratnakīrtti's contributions in this direction through *anvayavyāpti* and *vyatirekavyāpti* are invaluable. For the Mādhyamika view see Nāgārjuna's Kārikā, 18th Chapter, and Candrakīrti's commentary.

As against the Cārvākas, Nyāya argues that it does not matter whether the molecular transformation of changes (*piṭharapāka*) or the atomic transformation of changes (*pilupaka*) be accepted, for in either of those views, the body, since it must suffer changes in the different stages of growth and decay, cannot be held to be the seat of knowledge, desire, etc., or the subject of an unchangeable notion of self. Intoxication cannot be compared with knowledge and the fact that food enhances the power or strength of consciousness, means nothing more than this, that food improves the physical body and with it the power of the senses, and thus the powers of cognition are also enhanced. The senses too cannot be the self, for they are not only as material as the body but require an organiser and common perceiver and are also often contradicted by one another Neither can the mind (*manas*) be regarded as the seat, for it is but the organ of knowledge, desire, etc. So Nyāya holds that a separate self is to be admitted as the seat of knowledge, desire, happiness, etc.

As against the Buddhists, Nyaya contends that causal efficiency (*arthakriyākāritva*) is not the criterion of existence but whatever appears as existent without any contradiction to experience (*abādhitasadbuddhi*) is to be regarded as existent. Moreover even if the maxim of causal efficiency (*arthakriyākāritva*) be accepted,

Nyāya holds that the momentariness of things cannot be proved. A thing suffers destruction only when it is destroyed by the operation of an extraneous agency (*kārakavyāpāra*).[1] Again, the phenomena of memory and recognition, those of continuous perception and rebirth, also prove the doctrine of momentariness to be invalid. Thus the doctrine of momentariness of the Buddhists being dislodged, their theory that there is no permanent soul also falls to the ground.

As to the nature of this soul, Nyāya holds that it can neither be of the nature of pure consciousness (*cit*) nor an object of pratyaksha, for then it would have revealed itself even without the action of the mental organs; again even if it could reveal itself how could it be itself its subject as well as the object. So the soul is without any natural consciousness of itself (*jaḍa*); and it is with the acquirement of the attribute of consciousness that it becomes conscious It can be inferred as the constant seat of its own attributes such as consciousness, etc. It is only its nature that these attributes rest on it alone and not on any other thing, just as smell is the property of earth and not of fire. This soul is eternal, for as it has no parts it cannot

[1] For Nyāya arguments against momentariness (*Kshaṇabhaṅgavāda*) see *Nyāyamañjarī*.

be destroyed by the dissolution of parts; as it is not an attribute it cannot be destroyed by the dissolution of any substance, and there is no conceivable cause by which it could be destroyed. This soul is also omnipresent, for being without any physical body it cannot be carried with the body from place to place, and yet wherever the body may be carried there is knowledge, etc., associated with it. Moreover it cannot be atomic, for then we should not have feelings all over the body. It cannot be occupying the extent of the body, for then it would have different dimensions with different bodies; and if it could suffer such changes it would not be eternal. So it has to be admitted that the soul is omnipresent. Souls are many, for without this assumption the different experiences of different men as pleasure, pain, bondage, etc., could not be explained. The soul is not actually connected with any action as real mover, but its agency consists in possessing knowledge, desire, etc.; the actual action is performed therefore by the accessories such as the body and the senses. From all these considerations we find that there cannot be any objection against the eternality of the self, and this is further strengthened by the presence of instinctive fear, desire, etc., in children, which proves that they must have felt them in another birth. Prabhākara's view agrees in general with the

Nyāya theory of soul except as to the self-luminosity of knowledge and its necessary consequences. The Nyāya holds that the soul is to be inferred from knowledge, desire, etc., as one constant entity capable of possessing them, but Prabhākara holds that both the self as the notion of "I" and the object are revealed in self-luminous knowledge and so there is no necessity for any inference or for accepting the view that it is through the mind that the self is known, for then the self would become the perceiver as well as the perceived, the object and the subject are revealed in one self-revealing knowledge. The soul is the notion of "I" and as such directly given in knowledge. Kumārila differs from Prabhākara in holding that the soul must be the substratum or object of the notion of "I."[1] The soul therefore according to him is known by mental perception. The nature of soul is pure consciousness (*cetanā*) and therefore consciousness here, is not a quality of the soul as in Prabhākara and the

[1] Even if it is accepted that the soul is perceivable directly, yet for inferring the soul in general of other people, the inference is necessary.

It must be noted in this connection that the inference of soul is not from changing acts of knowledge to a permanent entity or from effect to cause, but according to Nyāya the relation of substance with attributes and actions is that attributes and actions must inhere in substances. So cognition (*jñāna*), desire (*icchā*), etc., being attributes (*guṇa*) must have a permanent substratum in which they may inhere. This substratum is the self.

Nyāyavaiśeshika. The souls are, however, many as in the systems of Prabhākara and Nyāya, eternal and omnipresent. The objection of Prabhākara to mental perception (*mānasa-pratyaksha*) applies therefore directly against Kumārila and he rightly turns the table upon Prabhākara, saying that the objection of the same thing appearing both object and subject applies to the self-luminous knowledge of Prabhākara also. The self is thus according to Kumārila "pure intellectual energy" (*citiśakti*) and in the emancipated state there is no knowledge and no bliss (*ānanda*) such as a Vedāntin would hold, for the soul exists in this state in its own true nature as pure power of knowledge (*jñānaśakti*).

Rāmānuja holds that the self is a non-material principle, which means that it shines by itself nd does not require the aid of knowledge for its illumination. It is of the nature of bliss (*ānandarupa*) and exists for all time, *i.e.*, is eternal. It is atomic in size, and yet can feel the affections in distant parts of the body, for just as the rays of the sun radiate to a great distance, so likewise its knowledge spreads all over the body.[1] It is beyond the knowledge of the senses, changeless,

[1] The simile used by the Jains in explaining the pervasion of the body by the soul is just the same though on the basis of their expression "*aṇugurudehapramāṇa*" they are charged with thinking the soul to be of the size of the body it occupies.

partless and a receptacle of knowledge (as contrasted with the Vedānta of the Śaṅkara School). It is itself agent and enjoyer, though worldly actions are said to be due to the connection of the guṇas. The power of this agency however is ultimately derived from God (Īśvara) and the agency of the soul is realised in action only through Īśvara's will. But the soul is responsible for its actions, because Īśvara fulfils its agency in the way in which the soul desires to act (*cetanakṛtaprathamaprayatnam apekshya Īśvarah pravarttayati*). It exists in absolute subordination to Īśvara, of whose body it forms a part. Souls are infinite in number. They are associated with avidyā and desires, etc., by being associated with acit or matter. Knowledge of the self is also like it an eternal non-material substance of the nature of ānanda, but the difference between them lies only in the fact that though itself a substance (being non-material as well as endowed with movement and qualities) it is an attribute of the soul and unlike it, capable of contraction and dilatation, and of illuminating all other things though it remains dark with regard to its own nature.

The Vedānta of Śaṅkara however holds that it is one Brahman which appears as many souls. For the sake of convenience it will be well to note here only three typical explanations offered by the different exponents of the appearance of the one as many souls :—

(1) Reflection theory (*prativimbavāda*). The Brahman as pure consciousness and bliss being reflected in the ajñāna (nescience) of mind (*antaḥkaraṇa*) and its states, appear as individual souls. It is called reflection for like it, the thing reflected (Brahman) is outside, and yet is not different from the image it has projected which appears in the ajñāna (of the reflection in a mirror). As the antaḥkaraṇas are many, souls appear as many, though none have any real existence. Its characteristic as image is due to the fact that though like an image it appears in the mirror of antaḥkaraṇas it is not affected by the limitat ions of the reflector.

(2) Limitation theory (*avacchedavāda*). The Brahman as associated with ajñāna appears as many souls on account of the plurality of the ajñāna. Each soul has its own creation and it is only on the basis of similarity that there is agreement regarding the objective perceptions of the souls (*pratijīvam viyadādi prapañca-bhedasca*).

(3) The idealistic theory of self-creation of all perceptions (*dṛshṭisṛshṭivāda*). In this view the Brahman appears though itself unchanged through beginningless māyā, as jīva, but this illusory appearance is due to ignorance

(*kaunteyasya eva rādheyatvavat avikṛtasya ātmanaḥ avidyāvaśat jīvabhāvaḥ*). There is thus only one soul and both the many souls and the world are merely its imaginary creations.

The reasons which all Hindu systems adduce against the Cārvāka and Buddhist schools are (1) that the notion of a self or personality as a permanent entity in all experiences cannot be adequately justified in the case of either the ever-changing body or the ever-changing flux of ideas. (2) On ethical and eschatalogical grounds, also there should be one unchanging soul responsible for all actions, experiences, sufferings and emancipation. The quarrel therefore which the Hindu systems have amongst themselves is only with regard to the nature of this soul or to the substance of its being, its knowledge, experience, etc., and connection with external nature.

The Sāṅkhya-Yoga agrees with the Buddhists in holding that the citta or plane of consciousness is always in a state of change undergoing constant modifications not only when it has to relate itself to the external world but also when it is without any such relation, as in the dream state. There is of course a fundamental unity of relations amongst the mental modifications themselves, and also between them and external nature, as they are all grounded in the three guṇas, but this unity of relations and actions in the production of a unity in the diversity of effects presupposes an intelligent being for whom they are intended (*cf.* their dictum of *saṃghātaparārthatvāt* which hold that all complex groupings imply a teleology or purpose). This teleological attitude is the most important philosophical consideration which led them to postulate a permanent soul as against the Buddhists. With the Nyāya, knowledge, etc., were qualities and thus presupposed a substance in which they could inhere and their interest in refuting the Buddhists was mainly centred in establishing the existence of permanent substances. Knowledge, pleasure, pain, etc., were not qualities according to Sāṅkhya but states or modifications of citta, or the plane of consciousness and this succession of states could not be said to know itself. It was therefore necessary that there should be a permanent intelligence to whom these might appear and thus be co-ordinated and expressed as the experience of a person for the states must be the states of a perceiver. Sāṅkhya-Yoga holds that there is an essential difference between this element of permanent perceiver and the general content of mental states as appears in experience. For the content of states not only assumes the forms of the external world but also suffers change at every moment. The element of the personality is however always abiding. So far as the content of experience has the form of external objects generally or any other kind of form, it is not different in essence from the objects which it copies. The perceptions therefore when looked at apart from the experience of a person are no more than mere reflections, copies, or photographs, as it were, of the gross world of matter. This gross state is at once transformed into a state of effulgence as intelligent experience as soon as it is related to the self of the personality. So far as the notion of personality is concerned it is again a mental state and as such non-intelligent and gross, and as such must be distinguished from the pure intelligence involved in it which like a light enlivens the states into intelligent experience. The essential distinction of this pure noumenal intelligence which intelligises all experience, from the mental states is, that it always remains constant and permanent in its true nature as pure intelligence (*citśakti*).

The Nyāya holds that our knowledge of self does not rise above the descriptive stage as being aware of something, *e.g.*, a book, of desiring something, of feeling pleasure or pain. The self is therefore nothing more than that entity with which the awareness of the different sense data, the feelings of pleasure, pain, etc., can be associated by inference. But is this true ? Let us take the proposition "I am aware of this awareness," it is not merely a judgment that some person has an awareness of an awareness but it also asserts that the person who is aware of the awareness is the person who is making the judgment. How can I assert this identity if 'I' can be known only by description? In that case I am aware of this awareness and of making a judgment and I may be entitled to conclude that there is some one who is aware of the awareness and that some one is making the judgment since both awareness and judgment require persons to make them. It may be that "the person who is aware of this awareness" is an exclusive description of the person to whom it applies. But how do I know that the person thus described is the person who makes the judgment? If I am not aware of myself, the only thing that I know about the person who makes the judgment is just the description "the person who makes this judgment." Granting that this is an exclusive description, I am still not entitled to say "I am aware of this awareness" unless I know that the two exclusive descriptions apply to the same person. If the person is known only by these descriptions or by other descriptions it is not possible to know anything of the sort. If 'I' can be known only by description it seems impossible that I can know that I am aware of this awareness or of anything else, since the judgment "I am aware of this" always means that the person who knows this is also the person who makes the judgment.

If, however, I perceive my self, there is no difficulty in justifying either the proposition "I am aware of this awareness" or "I am aware of this thing." If it is said that this means that I know the self with the two characteristics of having the awareness and of making the judgment, the answer will be that to know the "self" to be the possessor of those two qualities, the self must be known not merely in an indifferent manner as their vehicles but as the "I," the experiencer. The person who has the awareness is the same that passes the judgment; the volitional aspect (*kartṛtva*) and the aspect as enjoyer of experiences (*bhoktṛtva*) go together and reveal themselves in the notion of the self and this manifestation of the self in experience at once raises it to the plane of intelligibility; without it the awareness as such (though it might be mine) would be as intelligenceless as the direct awareness of other persons is to me. Purusha has thus to be admitted as the principle of intelligence. The Nyāya and Jaina objections that if purusha were the principle of intelligence, then all things should be directly illuminated by it, and there would be no need of the help of any organ such as the Buddhi, is groundless, for knowledge in our ordinary sense means, that a limited content should appear revealed as the experience of a person; it cannot therefore be supposed that pure knowledge which is without any content can be known. The knowledge that we speak of can only be of a certain content in the domain of relativity, change and limitation. So the pure intelligence though it is self-revealed and though it illumines and reveals the ordinary contents of our knowledge and feelings, is yet an entity which cannot be interpreted in terms of ordinary consciousness.

Self-consciousness can therefore be affirmed of such an entity in the sense that it is pure intelligence and yet denied in the sense that it has no self-consciousness in the ordinary sense of the term, for what we call self-consciousness is but the illumination of a content, and thus limited in its nature, and hence the result of the union of the self with the states of the plane of consciousness.

Hume went side by side with Buddhism when he supposed that our selves were nothing but bundles or collections of different perceptions which succeed one other with an inconceivable rapidity and are in a perpetual flux and movement. The fallacy of such a position lies in this that though all the contents of self, pains, pleasures, griefs, joys, sensations, etc., fall within various mental states, yet while these change, the self remains the same. The self again which was not intelligence by its own nature and which only acquired consciousness by the ordinary processes (as in the case of Nyāya) would be in its pure and emancipated state in no way better than pure vacuity and in the ordinary state also there is no reason why knowledge should be its peculiar gift or property.

It may now be objected from the Rāmānuja and other similar points of view that since personality involves the notions of a determiner and experiencer, it is better rather to say that the soul actually experiences and determines, the answer is that if it really experiences and determines diverse contents, it must change itself with them for if it be absolutely the same it can never determine or experience different things at different times; for that which is absolutely the same cannot itself change its relations with other things. It is for this reason that it is held that it is the things, the contents, which are modified and changed in such a way that they are all illuminated by the purusha and thus project the appearance that it is the purusha which is determining or experiencing. The purusha remains however the pure and unchangeable entity of pure intelligence which never really determines nor experiences.

Both the Prabhākara and the Bhaṭṭa schools are guilty of the charge of self-objectification of knowledge and of self respectively, as each has pointed out of the other. Prabhākara moreover inverts the true relation in holding that it is the knowledge which reveals the self and not that the self that reveals knowledge.

As regards the Śaṅkara school, it holds that (1) bliss or ānanda does not mean anything more than happiness and this is always an object of knowledge; so if at the state of emancipation there is this happiness then it presupposes that there also must then be a subject who feels it and thus monism fails. It cannot be said again that it is of the nature of happiness to be identical with intelligence (*cit*) for these are related as object and subject and hence cannot be identified. (2) The Vedānta explains all the appearance of the world with the help of avidyā, but when asked to describe its nature gives evasive answers and when further pressed says that it is illusory and has no real existence. If it is at the root of all worldly appearances, it has necessarily to be admitted that it has real existence, for, if inspite of its hand in bringing about this manifold world and diverse experiences of the world appearance, its existence could be denied, then verily the existence of anything and everything could be denied. (3) Its doctrine of the Brahman appearing as numberless souls stand refuted in all other systems of Hindu thought as it cannot explain any of the questions relating to individual birth, death, experiences or salvation.

Thus the Sāṅkhya-Yoga holds that the soul is pure intelligence and that all the cognitive states of ideas, feeling, etc., are illuminated by it. (2) As against the Jains and the school of Rāmānuja, it agrees with the Naiyāyikas in holding that the souls are omnipresent. (3) They are numberless, absolutely actionless, and passionless, remaining ever the same with absolutely no change.

The most important problem in Sāṅkhya-Yoga philosophy is therefore the establishment of the relation of the purusha with the prakṛti or the three guṇas which form the substratum of the conscious plane on one side and of the objective world on the other. The difficulty lies in this that purusha in its nature as pure intelligence is absolutely unrelationable with any change, but the states in which we find it reflected are all made of the stuff of the guṇas which are constantly changing. Change is as much the character of the prakṛti as changelessness of the purusha; intelligence is the essence of the purusha, whereas non-intelligence is the characteristic of the prakṛti. Yet it is said that all the movements of the prakṛti are for the experiences and liberation of the purusha and it is held at the same time that the purusha stands always as emancipated, and cannot be the determiner of the prakṛti. How are the two to be brought together and yet held in such a state of aloofness that the purity of the purusha may remain intact ?

We know that according to Sāṅkhya-Yoga the prakṛti takes two developments, one on the mental side, another, on the side of the exterior world. The mental plane takes the copy or the reflection of the external objects and the result is the perceptions which are but the reproductions (though distorted through the senses) in the stuff of the mental material. These mental images are enlivened by the influence of the pure intelligence, the purusha. The material of both the mental plane and of the exterior world is the three guṇas. Of these, sattva, which we have already described, resembles most the nature of the Purusha ; in fact it is called in the *Bhoja-vṛtti* the second citśakti with this difference only that its cit requires for its manifestations association with the purusha. It is through this sattva that the Sāṅkhya-Yoga has striven to solve the vital difficulty of the system, namely that of connecting the purusha with the prakṛti. The commentators have tried to understand this connection in diverse ways. Some have taken the sattva to be a second kind of intelligence, which is kindled by the influence of the purusha ; others have taken the sattva to be so translucent that intelligence is reflected in it, though there is no real contact, while others have held that there is a real contact between the two. Let us take these views one by one. Bhoja says that just as the proximity of a magnet manifests the power of movement in a piece of iron, so by the mere proximity of the purusha, the cit which exists in a potential manner as it were in the sattva, becomes manifest and this manifestation of cit which illumines the whole vṛtti or state becomes the object of purusha's experience partly because of the closest proximity of the purusha and partly because the whole process of prakṛti's transformations is for the experiences and the liberation of the purusha. Prakṛti is not conscious that it will serve the purpose of the purusha but its forward and backward transformations are called its tendencies for the services of the purushas. The prakṛti naturally possesses these two tendencies though it is unconscious. When it exhausts its powers in this way with reference to a purusha it cannot again repeat the process. As both the prakṛti and the purusha are omnipresent, there cannot be any actual contact or saṃyoga. It is the proximity and the teleology of the purusha that effects the illumination in the citta the object of the purusha's experience so far only as it is kindled by its presence. So there is no actual reflection also; but when reflection or prativimba is spoken of in this connection, what is meant is that as in a reflection there is the projection of a similar image so here also by the proximity of the purusha an intelligence is manifested in the sattva which is quite similar to the intelligence of the purusha.[1]

Vācaspati Miśra however seems to hold that there is no saṃyoga or contact of the buddhi with the purusha but a reflection of the purusha is caught in the states of the buddhi, by virtue of which these become intelligised and transformed into consciousness. But this view is said to be open to the objection that it does not explain how the purusha can be said to be the experiencer of the conscious states of the buddhi, for its reflection in the buddhi is merely the image, and there cannot be any experience (*bhoga*) on the basis of that image merely, as actually there is no connection of the purusha with the buddhi. The answer of Miśra is that there is no contact (*saṃyoga*) between them in space or time but the "*sannidhi*" or proximity here means "*yogyatā*" or passive capacity of being treated and by virtue of it the purusha, though it remains aloof, is yet felt to be united and identified with the buddhi, and as a result of that the states of the buddhi appear ascribed to a person. The modifications of the buddhi as states, on account of their extreme translucent character,

[1] *Bhojavṛtti* IV, 22 and II, 23.

catch the reflection of the purusha and are not only intelligised but become expressed as the experiences of a person or purusha, and it is in this way that it may be said to have been useful to the purusha. Thus it is that though the purusha remains absolutely pure and unperturbed yet it experiences the states of the prakṛti.[1]

Vijñāna Bhikshu differs from Vācaspati as to this being the Sāṅkhya doctrine. His objection is first, that such a yogyatā or capacity on the part of the purusha by virtue of which even though it may not be in touch with the buddhi yet the states of buddhi can continue to be expressed in terms of an experiencer, will continue even in the state of emancipation; for it is the nature of the purusha, and so the experience will continue even in the emancipated state Second, if the beginningless experience of states be said to be serving the purpose of saṃyoga or contact, then the assertion of the Bhāshya that this seeming union is due to avidyā potency breaks down. Thirdly the objection of Vācaspati that a saṃyoga of the buddhi and the purusha will necessarily mean that the purusha is exposed to change is groundless, for saṃyoga and change are not synonymous. The ākāśa has also saṃyoga, but it is

Tattvarvaiśāradī II. 17 and I. 4

not by virtue of that called pariṇāmin or changing. Change means the rise of new qualities. It is the buddhi which knows or forms its states (either through the inner action of its own potencies or by copying the objective world directly) and when this is reflected in the purusha, there is the notion of the person or the experiencer in the purusha and when the cit is reflected in the buddhi there is the knowledge as conscious state in the buddhi. The notion of the knower as "I" the experiencer cannot be generated in the buddhi by the reflection of the cit, for the mere reflection cannot be said to be of any purpose. It is when by the reflection of the cit, the states of buddhi become intelligised, that the purusha shines forth through their reflections as the cogniser of those states.

If the notion of cogniser had also been in the buddhi, then there would be no necessity of a separate purusha. Thus the bondage continues so long as this mutual reflection continues through the action of the prakṛti The cit does not become actually a part of the states of buddhi but just as by the mere presence of fire the iron becomes redhot, so by the mere proximity of purusha the mind becomes illuminated ; and it has to be assumed that this contact (*saṃyoga*) is due to the manifestation of that translucent character in the citta, the sattva, for purusha is unchanging and could not therefore be made responsible for the connection. Thus we see that to account for the knower in knowledge the purusha has to be admitted as the pure entity which intelligises all states by reflection. The Naiyāyikas are wrong in saying that the self is the vehicle of jñāna but Bhikshu agrees with them so far that the jñāna is no real part of the person the knower or the self, and that their unity "I know this" as a mental state is false so far as the "I" is concerned. Yet this union is necessary for revelation even of the "I" as its notion in a conscious state.

When we look to the *Yogasūtra*, we find that questions regarding prakṛti and purusha have been discussed in *ii.* 6, *ii.* 20, 21, 22, 23, 25, *iii.* 35, *iv.* 22, etc. In *ii.* 6 dṛk or purusha, the seer is spoken of as power (*śakti*) as much as prakṛti itself, and we see that their identity is a seeming one. Vyāsa in his *Bhāshya* explains "*ekātmatā*" or identity as *avibhāga-prāptau iva*, *i.e.*, as if they were so mixed up that no distinction could be made between them; and Pañcaśikha writes, "not knowing the purusha beyond the buddhi to be different from it in nature, character, and knowledge, etc., a man has by forgetfulness the notion of self therein." Thus we see that when they are known to be separate the real nature of the purusha is realised. This seeming identity is again described as "*pratyayānupaśya*"—it illuminates the conceptual forms of thought and though different, appears as if it were identically the same as the concepts of thought.

The purusha cognises the phenomena of consciousness after they have been formed and though its nature is different from them, yet it does not appear to be in any way different from them. Vyāsa in explaining this sūtra says that the purusha is neither quite similar to the buddhi nor altogether different from it. For the buddhi must be said to be changeful according to the change of objects that are offered to it, and according as it knows objects or does not know them. But the purusha is not such, for it always appears as the self, howsoever the other contents or objects of knowledge may change. As the contents of knowledge belong to the buddhi and as its connection with the "I" only intelligises these into the conscious states of a person, the purusha may be said in a way to see again that which was perceived by the buddhi and thus impart consciousness by transforming its illumination into the buddhi. The buddhi suffers modifications according to the forms of the objects of cognition and thus a state of conscious cognition in the shape of "I know it" results when it becomes connected with the constant factor of the transcendent reflection or identification of the purusha with the buddhi. Whether the process can be called a reflection is open to objection and criticism. But the Sāṃkhya-Yoga rests here on its analysis of consciousness, as also on the traditional teachings of the Upanishads, that the self, as the permanent experiencer which reveals itself as the notion of "I" in consciousness, has an essentially different nature in its character as permanent and unchangeable, though in point of mere intelligence it highly resembles the sattva. What gives the conscious states their true character as conscious is not merely their intelligent character, but their expression in connection with a person or rather as the experiences of a person. The notion of "I" however is not the principle as a Prabhākara would say but merely the product of the unity of the self with the buddhi. The substratum which I perceive of the notion of the "I" through mental perception is not also the self as a follower of Kumārila the great Mīmāṃsā philosopher might think, but the self is that element by coming in touch with which the states of buddhi become expressed as my experiences or the experiences of an "I" as the experiencer. The "I" so far as it is a vṛtti or state is a modification of the buddhi, but it does not change like other contents and is an indication of the permanent self as intelligising the states.

The knowledge belongs to the self, but the states belong to the buddhi. The self is no part of buddhi, but yet as the *Bhāshya* says it appears as a state of buddhi as the notion of self experiencing the cognitions and as such within them. The sattva element which predominates in buddhi is so pure and of so intelligent a character (as we have noticed many times before), that it can become as absolutely contentless as the purusha.[1] So when the buddhi has been modified into its states, it may be said in some sense to have been intelligised, for buddhi is itself of a translucent nature, but even this state is called jaḍa as there is no self, no knower, and the only distinction between intelligent states and material states is this element of self or "I." This modification of the translucent buddhi therefore cannot ultimately be distinguished from other material states, as the difference between the two is one of degree of manifestation of ṣattva and not of kind. It is when the self comes in that the distinction

[1] The sūtra "*sattvapurushayoḥ śuddhisāmye kaivalyam*" supposes that the buddhi can be as pure as the purusha and this state in which it reflects the purusha in its absolute purity without any other content does not materially differ from the state of oneness (*kaivalya*), for the next stage is only the return of the buddhi to prakṛti and the ultimate escape from sufferings and experiences came about when the buddhi could no longer bind the purusha again. The only distinction is that when the buddhi is as pure as purusha, it is still a phenomenal state, whereas when it returns to the Prakṛti the state is metaphysically reduced to a noumenal one.

becomes one of kind as apart from that of degree. These states of buddhi have therefore to be intelligised over again by coming in touch with the self. So our process of knowing an external object may be said to be one of double-intelligising, first by being imaged by buddhi and then again by the perception of the light of the purusha and of being transferred over to it for interpretation as its experiencer. The difference among the commentators rests therefore on the degree of translucency that they are ready to ascribe to sattva. Thus Bhoja does not feel the necessity of assuming any reflection from the purusha beyond the mere excitation of the sleeping intelligence of the sattva itself. Vācaspati thinks that such a reflection is necessary but the other reflection from the buddhi to the purusha unnecessary whereas Bhikshu required them both. The *Bhāshya* merely states the real analysis and is indifferent with regard to the metaphysical fictions over which the commentators quarrel.

The arguments on behalf of the existence of the purusha as summarised in the *Sāṃkhyakārikā* are, (1) because an assemblage of things is for the sake of another and thus there must be some other persons different from the three guṇas and their modifications for which they exist; (2) because there must be simple experiencers different from the complex assemblage of the guṇas; (3) because there must be a superintending power; (4) because of the existence of active exertion for the sake of salvation or emancipation.[1] The first is teleological, as has already been noticed.[2] The second is that the prakṛti being a composite of the three guṇas cannot itself be the seer. So the seer must be taken as an unchangeable actionless entity, pure intelligence. The third is that there must be a supreme background of pure intelligence, standing on which all our experiences may be co-ordinated and expressed. This background is the pure actionless intelligence, the purusha, by a reflection from which all our mental states are intelligised.[3] The fourth is that as the prakṛti is non-intelligent there must be one who enjoys the pains and pleasures and experiences the states.

[1] *Sāṃkhya-Kārikā*, 17.

[2] We have already noticed that Bhoja differs on this point, and says that it only excites cit in the sattva as movement in the iron by the magnet. Bhikshu however takes the simile of *cittamayaskānta-maṇikalpam sannidhimātropakāri* in the sense that as the magnet draws out an iron nail stuck in the hand and thus benefits the man, so the citta also brings the objects of experience to the purusha and brings about its experience.

[3] Davies commits a mistake in his translation of the *Sāṃkhya Kārikā* in interpreting the simile "*yathā rathādayaḥ yantrādibhiḥ*" to mean that the purusha must have some activity like the charioteer, for the comparison holds only as far that the chariot can take a particular course only when there is a particular purpose of the charioteer to perform.

The next important point is the multiplicity of the buddhis. The *Kārikā* says that "from the separate allotment of birth, death, and the organs of knowledge, action, etc., from the diversity of occupations at the same time and also from the different conditions of the three modes, it is proved that there is a plurality of souls. "Pātañjali, though he does not infer in this way the plurality of the purushas, yet holds this view, as we find in the sūtra "*kṛtārtham prati nashṭamapi anashṭam tadanyasādhāraṇatvāt.*"

If the different selves be the reflections upon different buddhis from one purusha, or ātman as in the Vedānta then the notions of self or personality would be false. For then the only true being would be the being of one purusha. So the knower being false the known also becomes false; the knower and the known having vanished, everything is reduced to that which we can in no way conceive, *viz.*, the Brahman. It may be argued that according to the Sāṃkhya philosophy also, the knower is false, for the pure purusha as such is not in any way connected with the prakṛti. But even then it must be observed that the Sāṃkhya-Yoga view does not hold that the knower is false, but analyses the nature of the ego, and says that it is the seeming unity of buddhi and the purusha, both of which are reals in the strictest sense of the terms. Purusha is a real knower there. Its seeing is the reflection of buddhi on it and simultaneously with it the modification of ego comes in the buddhi and this ego then appears as the person who identifies his experiences as his. Purusha thus always remains the real knower. The knower, the ego and the knowable, none of them are false in the Sāṃkhya-Yoga system in any one of the stages preceding emancipation, *kaivalya.* Śaṅkara's Vedānta has to admit the modifications of the māyā but has at the same time to hold it as unreal. The Vedānta says that the māyā is as beginningless as the prakṛti and as " sānta " (ending) as the buddhi of the Sāṅkhya with reference to the released person. But according to the Vedānta the notion of the self as the experiencer is only false knowledge—an illusion imposed upon the formless Brahman as many. The māyā according to Śaṅkara can neither be said to exist nor to non-exist. It is anirvācya, *i.e.*, can never be described or defined. Such an unknown and unknowable māyā by its reflection upon the Brahman causes the many of the world. But according to the Sāṃkhya doctrine, the prakṛti is as real as the purusha itself. They are the two irreducible metaphysical remainders, the purusha and the prakṛti. Their connection is beginningless. But the connection is not unreal in the Vedānta sense of the term. We see that according to the Vedānta system, all notions of ego, or personality, are false and are originated by the illusive action of the māyā, so that when they ultimately vanish, there are no other remainders except the Brahman. But this is not the case with Sāṃkhya, for as the purusha is the real seer, its cognitions cannot be dismissed as unreal, and so the purushas or the knowers as they appear to us must he held to be real so far as they are not identified with the contents of knowledge. As the prakṛti is not the māyā of the Vedantists the nature of whose influence over the spiritual principle cannot be determined, we cannot account for the plurality of the purushas by supposing that one purusha is being reflected into many buddhis and generating the many egoes. For in that case it will be difficult to explain the plurality of their appearances in the buddhis. For if there be one spiritual principle, how should we account for the supposed plurality of the buddhis? For to serve the supposed one purusha we should rather expect to find one buddhi and not many, and this will only mean that there will be only one ego, his experience and release. Supposing for argument's sake that there are many buddhis and one purusha, which being reflected into them is the cause of the plurality of selves, then also we cannot see how the prakṛti is moving, for the experience and release of one purusha, it

22

would rather appear to be moved for the sake of the experience and release of the reflected or unreal self. For the purusha is not finally released with the release of any number of particular individual selves. For it may be released with reference to one individual but will remain bound in connection with others. So the prakṛti would not really be moved in this suppositional case for the sake of the purusha, but only for the sake of the reflected self. If we suppose that it takes place in such a way as to avoid the said difficulties, then with the release of one purusha all purushas must be released. For on the supposed theory there would not really be many different purushas, but one purusha, which had appeared as many, so that with its release all the other so-called purushas must be released. On the experience, birth, emancipation, or death of one purusha we should expect the same for all purushas.

So we see that from the position in which Kapila and Patañjali were standing, this plurality of the purushas was the most consistent thing that they could think of. Any compromise with the Vedānta doctrine here would have greatly changed the philosophical aspect and value of the Śāṃkhya philosophy. The purushas are nothing but pure intelligences; though many they are regarded as all-pervading. But there is another objection that number is a conception of the phenomenal mind, how then can it be applied to the purushas which are said to be many? But that difficulty remains unabated even though we should regard the purusha as one. When we go into the domain of metaphysics, and try to represent the reality with the symbols of our phenomenal conceptions, we have really to commit almost a violence to it. But this must be allowed in all our attempts to philosophise or to express that pure inexpressible, free illumination which exists in and for itself beyond the range of any mediation by the concepts or images of our mind in terms of our conceptions.[1]

[1] Bhikshu however thinks that the determinations of number or content does not in any way make the thing *pariṇāmin* or changeable. *Yogavārtika*, II. 17.

CHAPTER VI

YOGA COSMOLOGY

We have seen that in order that a connection should be established between the prakṛti and the purusha the sattva type of Reals must completely dominate the other two constituents—the rajas and tamas. But the prakṛti is acknowledged to be the state in which these three guṇas are in such a state of equipoise that all their individual characteristics are in a state of absolute potentiality. The guṇas are of course in motion even then, but in this movement they are in a kind of inner oscillation against one another so that the movement is confined to the unified whole and only serves to maintain equilibrium and stability. This kind of movement which serves to maintain the state of equipoise is called *sadṛśa pariṇāma* as distinguished from that which breaks the equipoise and sets the three guṇas rolling on in the road of development, called the *visadṛśa pariṇāma.*

We must assume (*phalabalāt kalpyaḥ*) that the first step in the development is a state of sattva predominance, for otherwise it is difficult to explain the connection of the three guṇas with the purushas in the earliest stage. If the connection with the purusha is not admitted as the initial state, then such a transformation, being out of touch with the purusha, would be meaningless and the general teleological attitude that the developments of prakṛti are for the experience of the purushas has to be sacrificed.

But the question is how and why the prakṛti should of its own accord change its type of inner movement in a state of equipoise, so as to accept the other movement which produced the transformations. Prakṛti is non-intelligent and it cannot have any desire of its own to follow any particular course and change its own movement of itself. The difficulty is enhanced when we consider that the Sāṃkhya-Yoga in common with other Indian systems believed in the doctrine of dissolution—a state in which the world returns back into the original state in the prakṛti and again comes forth after a time as it existed before, through gradual transformations. The connection of buddhi with purusha cannot therefore be regarded as beginningless or *anādi* as it is taking place anew at each new creation after dissolution, and is broken up again at the time of every new dissolution (*pralaya*). Thus the question arises as to how or why the prakṛti should disturb its original equilibrium in order to form the first modification as represented by a state of predominance of the sattva? Why after it is once cut off from connection with any particular purusha should the buddhi again strive to find him and again become connected? If it be a matter of accident, then the buddhi might as well accidentally entrammel an emancipated purusha. Moreover the emancipation also would be no emancipation, for even after emancipation the buddhi might equally well again entrammel purusha.

This question brings us to the difference between the state of dissolution and the state of emancipation. The state of dissolution, pralaya (*apīti*), is like the state of deep sleep for the purushas, for just as when we go to sleep we lose all consciousness, feelings and experiences of the awakened state, but get them back again when the sleep is broken, so also in the pralaya, the purushas remain for a time in themselves, only to be again associated with old experiences at the time of the new creation. Pralaya is not a state of emancipation but almost a state of saṃsāra. Prakṛti has two movements, forward (*anuloma*) and backward (*pratiloma*). It is then the karmas of all purushas which come to such a state of harmony that they by their united force demand a state of temporary cessation from the bonds of prakṛti and the prakṛti takes its backward movement and retraces the stages through which it developed. The state of pralaya is also a state which has been as much earned as saṃsāra by the purushas owing to their karmas or deeds. We have remarked in the last chapter that the purusha is pure intelligence without any movement of any kind; knowledge, feelings, desires, actions all belong to the prakṛti; so all karmas also belong to the prakṛti and there cannot be any karma at all in the true sense for the purusha. But as we have said, the purusha experiences and takes the experiences as his own, on account of the reflection of the buddhi in the purusha, or merely owing to proximity. It is this false identification and false knowledge that constitutes the ignorance of the purusha. The prakṛti is impure and changing and it is when the purusha identifies this prakṛti with himself as pure and unchanging that the saṃsāra begins. It is this wrong or false knowledge, this taking that for the self what is not the self, that is called ignorance (*avidyā*), and emancipation only comes when avidyā is destroyed by the rise of a pure state of modification in the buddhi, which closely resembles the pure purusha (*sattvapurushayoḥ śuddhisāmye kaivalyam*). When such a state comes, the purusha experiences its true state through the states of buddhi which shows to it that all the modifications of the prakṛti, the objective physical states, as well as the mental states do not belong to it, and the result is that the buddhi returns back to the prakṛti once for all and cannot again serve to bind that purusha; and like a dancing girl, the prakṛti retires from the stage when its performance is over.[1]

There is however a technical difference between the Sāṃkhya and the Yoga avidyā, for while the Yoga holds that it is a positive knowledge opposed to the right knowledge, the Sāṃkhya takes it to be a mere non-distinction (*aviveka*) between the nature of the purusha and that of the prakṛti and calls this the avidyā, cause of the saṃsāra (*anyathākhyāti*). But without entering into details as to the significance of this difference we see that from the Yoga point of view it is the taking of the buddhi as the purusha, that is the cause of the bondage of the purusha. This avidyā however exists in the buddhi and manifests itself in diverse ways in the diverse modifications of the buddhi. At the time of dissolution when everything returns to the potential state, this also as a mere potential tendency returns back to the prakṛti. When the time of new creation comes, the transcendental influence of the purusha acts, and Īśvara removes the barrier of the prakṛti in accordance with the potency of the avidyās of the buddhis which had returned back into the prakṛti. The barriers being removed the prakṛti by the transcendental influence of the purushas acting like a magnet, moves on for the realisation of the experiences

[1] *khyakārikā*, 59-61.

of the purushas. These potential avidyā tendencies (*avidyā vīja*) serve to bring the peculiar modifications suited to the realisation of their potency into actuality and to show them again to their respective purushas, as their separate buddhis. These buddhis are but inherent parts of the stuff of consciousness called the mahat tattva, for at the time of the retirement of these avidyās into the prakṛti, their potencies had in them the peculiarities which were inherent in them by being in association from beginningless time with the particular purushas. Sāṅkhya finds a difficulty here, for the theory of non-distinction (*aviveka*) has no positive content in the avidyā of Yoga. For non-distinction can only take place so long as the buddhi and the purusha are present and it cannot be said to exist in the prakṛti when there is no buddhi; consequently, it is difficult to discover the agent which could modify the prakṛti as the buddhi of a particular purusha in the Sāṃkhya system. Bhikshu is therefore forced to admit that this aviveka is not a mere negative phenomenon of non-distinction, but has a positive stuff of existence or potency which resides in the buddhi and serve the same purpose as the Yoga avidyā. Moreover the Sāṃkhya does not think that the interposition of an Īśvara is necessary for removing the barriers of the prakṛti; though non-intelligent the prakṛti by its own inherent teleology under the magnet-like influence of the purushas, can bring about the order of development necessary and suitable for the experience of the respective purushas.

Considering the different kinds of evolutes that come out from the prakṛti, we find that these are classified as the aviśeshas and the viśeshas. The former (slightly modified evolutes) are those which being modifications or products themselves are capable of originating other products like themselves. The viśeshas (thoroughly modified evolutes) are themselves the products of some causes but cannot themselves be the cause of the origination of other existence like themselves. Thus the five tanmātras and asmitāmātra (*ahaṃkāra*) are called the six aviśeshas; the eleven senses and the atoms of the five mahābhūtas are called the viśesha. Mahat itself, called also sattāmātra, is properly speaking an aviśesha, for it has been produced from the prakṛti and is the mother of all other aviśeshas, but still as it has got its special name liṅga, it is not generally included under the aviśeshas. The production of these aviśeshas and the viśeshas are called *tattvāntarapariṇāma*, as distinguished from the changes that take place among the viśeshas themselves. Thus for example when the tanmātras are produced from ahaṃkāra, the state of being, involved in the tanmātras, is altogether different from the state of being of ahaṃkāra. It is not merely a mere change of quality but a change of existence or state of being. Thus though the tanmātras are derived from mahat through ahaṃkāra, the traces of ahaṃkāra cannot be easily found in them. This derivation is not such that the ahaṃkāra remains principally unchanged and there is only a change of quality of the ahaṃkāra, but it is a different existence altogether, and has properties which differ widely from that of ahaṃkāra. So it is *tattvāntarapariṇāma, i.e.*, evolution of the different categories of existence. The evolution of the senses and the five gross elements cannot be of this nature, for they are the viśeshas which have been too much specialised to allow the evolution of any other substance of a grade of existence different from themselves. With them there is an end of all emanations and the changes or modifications that they suffer are brought under the dharma, lakshaṇa and avasthā-pariṇāma. Thus mahat, ahaṃkāra and the five tanmātras are themselves emanations as well as the source of other emanations. The mahat has been called the liṅga (sign or ground of influence) as it is the basis from which the existence of the prakṛti and purusha can be inferred. Prakṛti from which no other primal state is inferrible is called the aliṅga, or that which is not a sign for the existence of any other primal and more unspecialised state. In one sense all the emanations can with justice be called the liṅgas or states of existence standing as the sign, by which the causes from which they have emanated can be directly inferred. Thus the five gross elements may be called liṅga of the tanmātras, and they again of the ego (*ahaṃkāra*) and that again of the mahat, for the unspecialised ones are inferred from their specialised modifications. But this technical name liṅga is reserved for the mahat from which the aliṅga prakṛti can be inferred Prakṛti is the eternal state which is not an emanation itself but the basis and source of all other emanations.

Thus the first stage in the onward course of the development of prakṛti is the mahat which comprises the knowable, the empirical universe, cosmic matter or stuff of consciousness, the intelligible essence of the cosmos evolved by differentiation and integration within the formless, characterless, inconceivable prakṛti. The relation of this stage to the individual buddhis is that they are only the parts of this universal, first great stage of being. There is however according to Sāṃkhya-Yoga no ultimate difference between a whole and its parts, but yet it is to be understood that if the creation had been from the individual buddhis then each person would have his own separate creation and there would be no stability of the objective world as the common field of experience for all persons. It is probable that such a view was held by the primary (*maulika*) Sāṃkhya school mentioned by Guṇaratna, who for the sake of consistency held that there were separate prakṛtis for each individual. The reduction of the many prakṛtis to one in the Uttara Sāṃkhya school naturally necessitated the joining together of the buddhis as one tattva which in its aspect as whole was the cause of the cosmic world, and as individual parts of the separate buddhis at the disposal of each purusha, the cause of his experiences.

This consciousness-stuff is described as "sattāmātra"—having no other determination than the pure being, and it is this pure being, which is at once the one and the same mind-stuff and the matter-stuff. It is a state of pure sattva where the rajas and the tamas elements are extremely subordinated. The confusion in understanding the system comes in when according to popular conception the buddhi is thought of as being of the nature of individual intelligence or idea, and as a result of that the world is thought of as having sprung from individual ideas, ego-hood or ego. It is therefore to be pointed out again that the buddhitattva is the universal consciousness-stuff of matter from which on one side the mental and on the other the physical take their origin.

The next stage of development from the buddhitattva is a non-individuated indeterminate stuff which bifurcates into two series, the subject experience and the object experience. It comprises on the one hand the indeterminate unity of apperception or the empirical ego, as the co-ordinating principle of the subject series (*asmitā*) and on the other hand the indeterminate material potencies, the subtile vehicles of potential energy (*sūkshmabhūta tanmātra*), the ultimate subtile constituents of the object-series of the external world. The genesis of the bhūtas from the tanmātras and the tanmātras from the ahaṃkāra (ego) and the ahaṃkāra (ego) from the buddhitattva has sometimes misled some scholars to suppose that according to the Sāṅkhya philosophy matter has been derived from thoughts and ideas. Thus Mr. J. C. Chatterjee says in the introduction of his *Hindu Realism*—" There has been much confusion in the West as to the exact nature of this standard. It derives the material from the mental and the psychical, that is to say from things which are of the nature of thoughts, ideas and feelings. But in spite of this fact Prof. Garbe has yet taken it to be a form of materialism ; so much so that he has seen no place for psychology in this standard and has substituted a physiology in its stead. This is indeed strange not only because it is absolutely against the universal tradition of the Hindus, but also because it is absurd to call a system of philosophy materialistic which derives matter from thoughts and ideas." From the description of the genesis as generally found in the Sāṅkhya treatises such an idealistic explanation may apparently appear to be justifiable at first sight. But if we look at it in connection with the most important passage on the subject in the *Vyāsa Bhāshya*—"*liṅgamātram aliṅgasya pratyāsannaṃ tatra tatsaṃsṛshṭaṃ vivicyate kramāṇativṛtteḥ*, etc.," the whole system assumes such a position that it can neither be called altogether materialistic nor idealistic in the ordinary sense of the terms. For here it is said that the separation, evolution or determination of mahat as such takes place in such a way that it remains itself integrated with the prakṛti all the while. Mahat is therefore not posited in opposition to the prakṛti as its differentiated evolute, but what we find here is rather differentiation in integration. Mahat is no doubt differentiated from prakṛti, but is at the same time integrated with it (*saṃsṛshṭā vivicyante*). The course of evolution here described points out that in each stage, it is the prakṛti itself which becomes more and more differentiated, determinate and coherent. The evolution of mahat means that the absolute homogeneity of the prakṛti being negated and broken, there is the predominance of the sattva which justifies its christening with the new name mahat, sattva, liṅga, or sattāmātra. This differentiation, however marked it may appear, cannot be thought of differently from the aspect of its integration with prakṛti. As Dr. Seal points out "increasing differentiation goes on hand in hand with increasing integration within the evolving whole, and by this double process, what was an incoherent, indeterminate homogeneous whole becomes coherent, heterogeneous and determinate." Mahat can never be regarded as a product of prakṛti outside of it but it is the prakṛti which has been differentiated within itself in order to be more integrated within itself; there is viveka, differentiation in saṃsṛshṭi or integration. Integrated with the mahat we find that the ahaṃkāra and the five tanmātras are differentiated, in a like manner. It is said no doubt that the five tanmātras are evolved from the ego or ahaṃkāra; but this evolution cannot be regarded as being of the same kind as the evolution of the bhūtas from the tanmātras. With the evolution of the stage of mahat, there is an oscillation consequent upon the liberation of rajas, which takes three different courses according to the predominance of sattva, rajas or tamas. The transformation which mahat undergoes by this liberation of rajas gives at one moment a shake to sattva and tamas and asserts its own predominance, and thus the differentiation which is the product of this liberation of rajas, though associated with integration, represents the root of the development of this stage in three distinct directions. Thus according to these three phases, the ego is called sāttvika, rājasika and tāmasika. These different phases represent the disturbance caused in the three constituent entities or guṇas of mahat which will lead the ego to develop in three distinct directions. The ego however in spite of its differentiation from mahat is however integrated with it all the while, for it is mahat itself which by an element of differentiation within itself has become more determinate and coherent in the form of ego and has thus become integrated with itself in a new form. But it is said that the five tanmātras together with the ego are evolved from the mahat—"*tathā shaḍaviśeshā liṅgamātre saṃsṛshṭā vivicyante pariṇāmakramaniyamāt.*"[1] To understand this passage clearly we must remember that the tanmātras are generated with successive accretions from the bhūtādi (*tāmasa ahaṃkāra*); thus from bhūtādi the rudiment matter by the action of rajas, the śabdatanmātra or sound potential being generated, there is an accretion of bhūtādi, and by the action of rajas, the touch potential is produced and so on; each new tanmātra is

[1] *Vyāsa-bhāshya*, II. 19.

generated at each successive accretion. We must also remember that though bhūtādi or the tamas side of ahaṃkāra is regarded as being one with the conception of the ego or ahaṃkāra, it being a preponderance of tamas is essentially different in nature from the sattva side of ahaṃkāra. Its inclusion in ahaṃkāra with the other two phases is due to the fact that all the three of them are associated and taken up in the very first moment of the oscillatory movement in the mahat. The successive accretions of tanmātras for the formation of the tanmātras are made from the mahat through the bhūtādi ; or rather the bhūtādi represents the tamas side of mahat which is in a state of activity by the inherent rajas for the formation of the tanmātras. Bhūtādi is the tamas or rudiment matter, mass, just when we conceive it to be unmoved by rajas for the formation of the tanmātras by successive collocations of gradual accretions and their definite combinations. It is the transitional state through which differentiations and determinations of tamas take place with the help of rajas in the very body of the mahat with which they are integrated. The being of these determinations and differentiations cannot be conceived in any way as being outside of mahat.[1]

[1] This interpretation is based on Dr. Seal's interpretation of the evolution of Sāṅkhya categories in his "*Positive Sciences of the Ancient Hindus.*"

In the production of the atoms however from the tanmātras the differentiation and integration take place in the tanmātras and not in the mahat. Those tattvas or categories, the genesis of which depends directly upon the differentiation and integration of the mahat are classed as aviśeshas. Though the tanmātras are derived from ahaṃkāra yet the very fact that the basis of their originating collocations lies directly in the mahat makes an idealistic explanation of the Pātañjala-Sāṅkhya doctrine an impossibility. The ahaṁkāra also, it should be remembered, is not a mere idea of "I" or mine "as is sometimes understood, for it is also a substance, an ego-stuff. Thus Bhikshu says, *ahaṃkāraśca abhimānavṛttikam antaḥkaraṇadravyam.*

The confusion that has arisen on this point is, I imagine, due to the confusion which was probably caused owing to the transition of the idealistic school of the Maulika Sāṅkhya to the Uttara Sāṅkhya. For the idealistic explanation of deriving the tanmātras purely from the ego could well have been defended if the ego of any individual person created his own matter, and if the matter and the prakṛti vanished altogether at his emancipation; but here in the Uttara Sāṃkhya, with the world as one common reality and ground of objective experience for all persons, such an explanation becomes wholly untenable. But the divergence is due, as I have just pointed out, to the difference of view which naturally arose at the time of the modification of the idealistic Sāṅkhya to the realistic Sāṅkhya. Here is the lacuna of an imperfect modification. But that the Yoga view, as I have explained, was also a genuine Sāṅkhya doctrine is suggested by the inconsistency pointed out by Śaṅkara in his refutation of the Sāṅkhya doctrine "*tathā kvacit mahatastanmātramupadiśanti kvacidahaṃkārāt.*" Vācaspati being a Vedāntist himself seems to be inclined to explain the genesis from an idealistic point of view, which could certainly be traced in it owing to the original idealistic form of the school from which the realistic one grew up. Thus Vācaspati says, "I am, mine are the objects, no one but I myself am entitied to do it; this is the abhimāna and its functioning is the ahaṃkāra; and feeding on this the buddhi decides or posits itself for the creation in the two series, and hence the twofold creation—the subject series and the object series."[1]

The bearing of this doctrine on Yoga ethics and psychology will be dealt with later on.

The three stages of bhūtādi, tanmātras and the atoms have thus been described by Dr. B. N. Seal. "The ultimate condition of matter is a question of the profoundest interest in the

[1] Vācaspati's commentary on *Sāṃkhya-kārikā*, 24.

Sāṃkhya-Pātañjala system. These stages clearly stand out in the genesis of matter : (1) the original infinite units of mass or inertia absolutely homogeneous and ubiquitous on which energy does work, when the original equilibrium comes to an end (*bhūtādi*, *tāmasāhaṃkāra*) ; (2) the infra-atomic unit potentials, charged with different kinds of energy, which results from the action of energy on the original units of mass (*tanmātra*) ; and (3) the five different classes of atoms, the minutest divisions of which gross matter is capable, but which are themselves complex tanmātric systems. The first stadium Bhūtādi is absolutely homogeneous and absolutely inert, being devoid of all physical and chemical characters (*rūpādibhiḥ asaṃyutam*) except quantum or mass (*paricchinnatva parimāṇa*) ; and this admits neither of addition nor of subtraction, can neither be created nor destroyed. The second stadium tanmātra represents subtile matter, vibrating, impingent, radiant, instinct with potential energy. These potentials arise from the unequal aggregation of the original mass units in different proportions and collocations with an unequal distribution of the original energy (rajas)—"*tanmātrarūpādeḥ kiṃ kāraṇam iti cet sa kāraṇadravyāṇāṃ nyūnādhikabhāvena anyonyam pratisaṃyogaviśesha eva svājatīyopashṭambhādinā vṛddhihrāsādikaṃ ca yuktam.*" The tanmātras possess something more than quantum of mass and energy. They possess physical characters, some of them penetrability (*avakāśadāna*), others powers of impact, others radiant heat, others again capability of viscous and cohesive attraction. In intimate relation to these physical characters they also possess the potentials of the energies represented by sound, touch, colour, taste and smell, but being subtile matter they are devoid of the peculiar forms (*viśesha*) which these potentials assume in particles of gross matter, like the atoms and their aggregates. In other words the potentials lodged in subtile matter must undergo peculiar transformations by new groupings and collocations to be classed among sensory stimuli, gross matter being supposed to be matter endowed with properties of the class of sensory stimuli, though in the minutest particles thereof, the sensory stimuli may be infra-sensible (*atīndriya* but not *anudbhūta* : "*tasmin tasmiṃstu tanmātrāḥ te ca aviśeshiṇaḥ te ca padārthāḥ śāntaghoramūḍhākhyaiḥ sthūlagataśabdādiviśeshaśūnyā ekarūpatvāt, tathā ca śāntādiviśeshaśūnyaśabdādimattvameva bhutānām śabdāditanmātratvam.*"[1]

"The tanmātras then are infra-atomic particles charged with specific potential energies; first, the potential of the sound stimulus is

[1] *The Positive Sciences of the Ancient Hindus*, p. 25.

lodged in one class of particles, tanmātras, which possess the physical energy of vibration (*parispanda*) and serve to perform the radicle of the ether atom (*ākāśa-paramāṇu*); then the potential of the tactile stimulus is lodged in another class of tanmātras, particles which possess the physical energy of impact or mechanical pressure, in addition to that of vibration, and serve to form the radicle of the gas atom (*vāyu paramāṇu*); next the potential of the colour stimulus is lodged in a third class of tanmātras, particles which are charged with the energy of radiant heat and light in addition to those of impact and vibration, and serve to form the nucleus of the light and heat corpuscles; then the potential of the taste stimulus is lodged in other tanmātras particles which possess the energy of viscous attraction in addition to those of heat, impact, and vibration, and which afterwards develop into the atom of water, and lastly the potential of the smell stimulus is lodged in a further class of tanmātras, particles which are charged with the energy of cohesive attraction in addition to those of viscous attraction, heat, impact and vibration and which serve to form the radicle of the earth-atom.

A very wide divergence of views is however found about the genesis of the tanmātras; thus according to *Vishṇupurāṇa* bhūtādi in conjunction with mahat, the sound potential, and this in conjunction with bhūtādi produced the ākāśa paramāṇu. This ākāśa paramāṇu in conjunction with bhūtādi produces the touch potential, and that in conjunction with bhūtādi produces the vāyu atom. Parāśara again says that the śabdatanmātra is produced from bhūtādi ; and from the śabdatanmātra is produced the sparśatanmātra and from it the rasatanmātra and so on. From śabdatanmātra as centre surrounded by bhūtādi the ākāśa paramāṇu is formed ; from śabdatanmātra as centre surrounded by sparśatanmātra and the ākāśa aṇu, the vāyu paramāṇu is generated and so on. According to *Yogavārttika* on *Vyāsabhāshya* however we find that it is the bhūtādi or the tāmasa ahaṃkāra, the rudiment mass which being acted on by the rajas (or rājasa ahaṃkāra) produces the sound potential or vibration potential. This subtle sound potential with a further accretion from bhūtādi generates the touch potential (impact potential) which is impingent and oscillating. This touch potential with a further accretion from bhūtādi generates the rūpatanmātra or the light-heat-potential From this again in a similar manner comes the taste-potential and from that again in a similar manner with a further accretion the smell-potential.

Coming to the production of atoms we find that the sound potential forms the ākāśa paramāṇu with an accretion from the bhūtādi. The touch potential combines with the sound potential to produce the Vāyu atom. The light-heat potentials combine with the two previous tanmātras of touch and sound and produce the tejas atom. Thus in the same way by the combination of the first three tanmātras, the ap atom and of the first four tanmātras with kshiti tanmātra, the earth atom is generated.

The ākāśa atom possesses penetrability, the vāyu atom impact, the tejas atom heat and light, the ap atom viscous attraction and the earth atom cohesive attraction.[1]

There is a characteristic difference between the tanmātras and their respective paramāṇus, such that though the former are sufficiently modified to be classed as kshiti, ap, tejas, marut, and vāyu, yet they are not in themselves sensible, but are rather the rudiments by the peculiar combination of which the atoms or the sensible elements are produced. Thus Bhikshu says :—

"*tanmātrāṇyaviśeshāṇi aviśesāstato hi te*
na śantā nāpi ghorāste na mūḍhāścāviśeshiṇaḥ

The atoms of the Sāṃkhya-Yoga system are not partless (*niravayava*) like that of the

[1] Many other views regarding the genesis of tanmātras and atoms have been elaborately discussed in Dr. Seal's most erudite introduction to Dr. P. C. Ray's Hindu Chemistry and need not therefore be repeated here unnecessarily.

Vaiśeshikas, but have parts (*sāvayava*) or what is called mahat parimāṇa. The guṇas alone are here taken to be partless or (*niravayava*) and can be compared in that sense with the atoms of the Vaiśeshikas. Thus Bhikshu says, "*vaiśeshikoktā paramāṇavaḥ api asmābhiḥ abhyupagamyante, te ca asmaddarśane guṇaśabdavācyā ityeva viśeshaḥ, Yoga-vārttika*, iii. 52." But even the guṇas themselves are not wholly of an infinitesimal nature, for then the all-pervasive nature of the prakṛti has to be abandoned. It is therefore to be admitted that those guṇas from which the partless antaḥkaraṇa and ākāśa are produced are to be regarded as pervasive; if they were wholly ubiquitous, then the contact necessary for the first movement of the prakṛti would be inexplainable. But these atomic guṇas have of course no differentiation as earth, water, etc., as in the case of the Vaiśeshika atoms. But these questions were not probably solved in the older Sāṃkhya-Yoga speculation, so the *Vyāsa-bhāshya* is also almost practically silent on these points. Bhikshu however in his *Yoga-vārttika* comes to these conclusions on the supposition that the opinions of other schools could be accepted so far as they did not run counter to their own conclusions.[1] In other places however Bhikshu himself has said that the guṇas stand

[1] *Yoga-varttika*, III, 52 and II, 18.

for all the eight substances of the Vaiśeshikas, and it is these which are the permanent causes of the creation as the modifications of mahat, etc., which vary in various creations after the final dissolution (*pralaya*).

Turning to the development of the eleven senses we find that these are produced from the sāttvika side of ahaṃkāra with the help of the rajas. The internal organs are therefore buddhi, ahaṃkāra, manas and the five cognitive and the conative senses. Of these the first three form together the three inner mental organs, and hold good for all experiences, past, present or future, whereas the other senses hold good only in taking the objects at the present time. Now to take a review. When at the outset of the last pralaya the guṇas had taken their backward movement, and all the aviśeshas had returned into the mahat, which with all the ignorance-stuff (*avidyā*) of the purushas inherent in it had returned back into the prakṛti, there came the pralaya. Prakṛti is now in a state of equilibrium consisting in a uniform diffusion of the reals. The tendencies to conscious manifestation as well as the powers of doing work are exactly counterbalanced by the resistance of the mass (*tamas*). The process of evolutionary creation is at rest. The transcendental (non-mechanical) influence of the purusha, whether it be contact (*saṃyoga*) or mere passive attraction of proximity, puts an end to the state of arrest and the equilibrium is disturbed. But how the actionless purushas can by their influence disturb the state of equilibrium of prakṛti is a point which Sāṃkhya cannot properly explain. The Yoga has tried to solve the difficulty by admitting that the disturbance is directly effected by the removal of obstacles by Īśvara. When once the disturance is set afoot, the affinity comes into play and leads to unequal aggregation, and therefore to the relative preponderance of one or more of the guṇas, and the process of formative combination (*ārambhakasaṃyoga*) commences. It has to be imagined that the first stadium of evolution is a state in which the sattva or intelligence-stuff, the principles of manifestation, should preponderate, for, otherwise the mutual reflection with the purusha becomes inexplicable. This stadium is the stage in which out of prakṛti a development has come which holds the first germs of all things as the stuff of consciousness. When we speak of such a development, it does not mean that the whole of prakṛti has been transformed into the mahat, but it only means that some portions of it has been transformed into it. Just as portions of the ocean are transformed into foam while still the great ocean lies within itself, or just as a tree grows up knot by knot, so this universal pure being as stuff of consciousness contains within itself as inherent in it many separate buddhis or individual conscious planes which form its part. These buddhis, though they have been treated as new, contain within themselves the particular and peculiar avidyās or ignorance-stuff with which the buddhis of a former creation had returned into the prakṛti at the pralaya. It is also in accordance with or for the realisation of the function of these buddhis that Īśvara had disturbed the prakṛti. When once the disturbance was set up, the old avidyāvījas or ignorance potencies prevailed and that stadium evolved, in which new buddhis with old avidyā potencies could find scope and bind their respective purushas by mutual reflection. If the potencies had been absolutely burnt by true knowledge of any purusha then that purusha could no longer be bound again, for the potency being lost no separate buddhi would evolve for him. This stadium is then on one hand the first stage through which prakṛti would evolve itself towards the creation of meterial objects, and on another the whole in which the individual buddhis were held up in one plane. Thus from these two aspects there is a twofold creation. For the first movement or undulation of this mahat creates a strife amongst the three different guṇas, and this state being a new differentiation as integrated in the mahat is called the three different ahaṃkāras. The sāttvika ahaṃkāra which expresses itself as "I," "mine," is the co-ordinating principle of the subject series which with the help of the rājasa ahaṃkāra produced the eleven senses. So this sāttvika ahaṃkāra is one product of the mahat whereas the other product is the tanmātras by the action of the tāmasa ahaṃkāra. The sāttvika ahaṃkāra is as much a new kind of consciousness-stuff as the tanmātras with this difference that the latter charged with the predominance of tamas is ultimately reduced into the matter-stuff by a further accretion of tamas. So all these actions up to the production of the tanmātras and the asmitā go on in the mahat and through it in the prakṛti herself. The tanmātras are therefore not a product of asmitā but of mahat directly, while they along with asmitā were still in a state of differentiation as integrated in the mahat. It should again be noted that when mahat transforms itself into its evolutes it is not wholly transformed, but as some forms of it are evolving onwards, it is being fed by the fresh formations of mahat-stuff from the prakṛti. Thus it is that we find that by a peculiar transformation, the guṇas (comparable to Vaiśeshika atoms) through the stage of a stadium as cosmic matter of experience of the predominance of sattva-stuff bifurcate into two lines, the subjective series through asmitā, and the world or gross matter through the tanmātras. Every transformation is nothing but a new state of existence generated by the groupings in of the guṇa particles in varying proportions with the predominance of a particular type of guṇas ; sattva, rajas or tamas are but names to denote the classes of guṇas giving their own peculiar types of manifestation, actualisation, or existence. The names sattva, rajas and tamas only serve to differentiate the characteristic differences of the guṇas as are seen in the state of their development.

CHAPTER VII

Yoga Physics

The existence of the external world as the common ground of experience for all men, in the past, present, and future, forms the most essential characteristic of the Sāṃkhya-Yoga realism as against the Buddhistic idealists. Of the two schools of Buddhists, one asserts that the external world exists, but its guarantee of existence or truth is (*arthakariyākāritva*) its capacity of producing effects ; the things must be coming into existence only at the moment that the ideas about them are produced, and destroyed the moment the ideas are destroyed.[1] The ideas have only momentary existence, and such must be the case with the external objects. Another class of Buddhists says that since the things and ideas are taken at the same point of time, both of them have the same identical reality (*cf. sahopalambhaniyamāt abhedo nīlataddhiyoḥ*) ; the awareness and that of which we are aware are one and the same and apart from the ideas the things have no separate

[1] *Kshaṇabhaṅgasiddhi* of Ratnakīrtti.

existence. Against the first class of Buddhists Yoga holds that if the thing rises into existence and dies away with the rise and destruction of the ideas in any person, then how can it at the very moment of its destruction be found to be existing, by virtue of the idea it has generated in another person who has directed his attention towards it. Moreover simply because I do not see a thing I cannot call it non-existent; I do not see the back of a thing and it cannot be argued that the back does not therefore exist.

Against the second class of Buddhists, Yoga holds that from the fact that wherever there is the idea there is the thing, it cannot be argued that the thing and the idea are one and the same, for there may be things without there being any one to represent them in his ideas; or in other words the maxim of sahopalambha is not corroborated by the negative test that every case of absence of knowledge is also a case of absence of reality (*sahopalambhaniyamaśca vedyatvaṃ ca hetusandigdhavyatirekitayā naikāntikī*). Moreover the external world appears before us by its presentative power, and its truth is guaranteed by the testimony of our ideas which possess extension and co-existence and are thus realised as being different from the external world. The things persist as the same, though they generate diverse emotions in diverse persons. So it is that we are to admit that external things exist apart from and independent of our ideas, and they are not momentary as the Buddhists would like to assert (*tasmāt svatantro'rthaḥ sarvapurushasādhāraṇah svatantrāṇi ca nityāni pratipurusham pravarttante*).

These are in short the contentions of the Yoga school in favour of an external world as the common ground of experience as against the idealists. With the exception of some schools of Buddhism and Vedantism almost all the other Indian systems are properly speaking realistic systems.

But the extent and nature of the admission of this external reality, as also the methods of its workings, were divergently conceived in different systems and it is here that the ideas of Indian physics differ. Thus to take a brief review of these, before we come to the Yoga physics, we find that the Cārvākas regarded life as the product of combinations of matter, just as we get red colour from the combination of white and yellow. Life according to them, was only a property of matter (*madaśaktivat caitanyam*) which manifested itself under conditions of particular combinations.

According to the Sarvāstivadin Buddhists the eternal dynamics of action conglomerated the different classes of atomic reals, and in particular cases of such combination, life shone forth as the product. There were two classes of such combinations, the mental conglomeration of the five groups consists of *rūpa* (perception), *vijñāna* (consciousness), *vedanā* (feeling), *saṃjñā* (name), and *saṃskāra* (association). The conglomeration (*saṃghāta*) of these clusters formed the psychical plane of man, whereas the atoms of the five bhūtas formed the basis of the physical bodies of men, animals, the vegetable and the inorganic world. The inference of the existence of the diverse atomic reals reminds us of the Herbartian argument for the doctrine of reals, as it consists in positing as many different reals as there are diversities of experience; for the same real cannot have contradictory qualities. These reals exist by themselves independently and there are no actual combinations to form wholes. But there are only conglomerations which are more or less of a mechanical nature of loose atoms rising up in existence and being destroyed the next moment. These conglomerations are brought about neither by a conscious principle as soul nor by an omnipotent God but by the dynamics of the eternal chains of causes and effects. Each particular being of the moment, vegetable, inorganic or organic, is determined by the particular nature of the conglomeration that is brought about. There is no other reality either in man or in nature save the force of actions which rolls on.

In each conglomeration each of the elements entering into it performs its own function of the conglomeration. The number of conglomerations forming the reality of the universe at any particular moment is destroyed at the next moment and further conglomerations spring up and so on. The order of the world is to be found in the regulative world-order of the forces of the actions. Thus is explained the manifold reality of the material world by the force of dying conglomerations by which new conglomerations are brought forth and so on. The universe is thus undergoing change at every moment; there is no stability anywhere but only change. No conglomerations can ever be the same at any two moments. They are breaking up at every moment and fresh conglomerations are being formed by the breaking up of the old ones and all this on the physical side is the result of the collocations of the atoms and the eternal potential energy associated with them which becomes kinetic at every stage of the progressive march—the *pratītya samutpāda*.

According to the Nyāya-Vaiśeshika view, generally, a molecule of any bhūta could not contain more than two atoms. But there was another view as we find from the accounts of Utpala in his commentary on *Bṛhat Saṃhitā* that two, three or four atoms are admitted to unite together by their natural vibratory motion to form molecules. So long as there is no action of heat, these molecules of the different bhūtas instead of displaying any diversities of qualities and characters show only their homogeneous characters. But by the action of heat these molecules of the different bhūtas are diversely rearranged and collocated, and it is on account of this diversity of collocations that the different genera and species are formed. Molecules or the atoms of the same bhūta, say for example kshiti, may rearrange themselves in diverse ways by the action of heat and form thousands of different substances. The factors which operate in the formation of these different substances are: (1) the density of the grouping, (2) the position of the atoms, (3) the different kinds of pāka or heat associated with them in the making of the different arrangements. Thus Uddyotakara says that "there is no differentiation of species in the atoms themselves." Śrīdhara also says, "there are no ultimate differences between the atoms of semen and ovum, as they are all but modifications of earth. The changes produced by heat upon a body suffering through the thermal influence are conditioned by the previous characters according to which heat generates further new changes of colour, etc. Nyāyabodhinī judging from the diversity of effects speaks of different kinds of heat. To take a concrete example of such atomic changes, we find that when a cow eats grass, the grass matter being broken up into atoms and by the touch of some kind of heat, the old colour, taste, touch and smell being destroyed, there comes in that kind of heat which generates those kinds of colour, etc., which are found in milk, and now the atoms being possessed of those kinds of taste, etc., generate a binary molecule, and by the aggregation of these, gross milk is formed. Thus it is that we find that all the objective world of matter is formed generally by the various kinds of groupings of the spherical atoms of the same bhūta, or by the groupings amongst the atoms of the modifications of the same bhūta entering into the compound for the formation of the same substance and sometimes really amongst the atoms of the different bhūtas when one of them acts as the radicle. The atoms were conceived to be spherical in shape, but it was something like a point without any dimension ; and it is by the grouping of these that the whole universe is formed

There can never be any change of substance or quality without the action of the components upon one another ; and no molecule can have any quality which is not possessed by any of its components. The character of any atom cannot manifest itself until it can link itself with other atoms of its own class. The whole world is explained on a basis of chemical synthesis, and all things are looked at from a detached point of view rather than from the point of view of the conservation of energy. Life itself is the product of diverse chemical syntheses. All action of matter on matter is reduced to motion with the exception of conscious activity. The combination of the atoms to form the diverse substances had a controller in the background in the shape of the unseen moral destiny, which in its turn was presided over by God. The atoms themselves were neither created nor were they the evolved products of simple elements. There is no separate entity or force apart from the modes of motion. The effect is in all cases the resultant of the combined motion of the various causes involved (*kāraka cakra*).

Taking the validity of the objective world as an established fact we have noticed in brief the two classes of atomists: the Buddhists and the Vaiśeshikas. The Sāṃkhya-Yoga view differs from both as it combines the dynamic aspect and the momentariness of the Buddhists with the static and detached character of the Vaiśeshikas into a system of evolution of the three types of reals. "This evolution in its formal aspect," as Dr. Seal says, may be defined "as differentiation in the integrated (*saṃsṛṣṭaviveka*). In other words the process of evolution consists in the development of the differentiated (*vaiṣamya*) within the undifferentiated (*sāmyāvasthā*) of the determinate (*viśesha*) within the indeterminate, of the coherent (*yutasiddha*) within the incoherent (*ayutasiddha*). The evolutionary series is subject to a definite law, which it cannot overstep (*pariṇāmakramaniyama*). The order of succession is not from whole to parts nor from parts to whole but ever from a relatively less differentiated, less determinate, less coherent whole to a relatively more differentiated, more determinate, more coherent whole. That the process of differentiation evolves out of homogeneity as separate or unrelated parts, which are then integrated into a whole, and that the whole again breaks up by fresh differentiation into isolated factors for a subsequent redintegration, is a fundamental misconception of the course of material evolution. That the antithesis stands over against the thesis and imposes unity *ab extra* on these independent and hostile moments is the same radical misconception as regards the dialectical form of the cosmical development. On the Sāṃkhya view increasing differentiation proceeds *pari passu* with increasing integration within the evolving whole. So that by this twofold process what was an incoherent, indeterminate, homogeneous whole evolves into a coherent, determinate and heterogeneous whole."

It should be remembered in this connection that though the individual combinations may be said to be subject to addition and subtraction, growth and decay, the guṇas themselves are infinite and eternal, and there cannot be any increase or decrease of them. Considering the cosmic changes as a whole, the guṇas remain for ever as their permanent substrata. The changes come and go, the combinations break and form but the reals remain ever the same, though they may seem to appear in diverse characters. The characters and qualities are the results of the diversity of their combination. Thus the totality of the mass and energy also remains constant if we take account of both the manifested and the unmanifested, the actual and the potential. Such is the bond of teleological relation between the guṇas and the purushas, that the course of evolution follows an unalterable definite law, not only as regards the order of succession but also about the appearance and mutual relations of the separate units of like and unlike energies. Had there not been such a definite order, the world would have been a chaos instead of cosmos, in spite of all the three guṇas. All things being composed ultimately of the three guṇas, there are no intrinsic differences amongst them (*sarvvam sarvvātmakam*). The only difference is the difference in the constitution of the collocation of the guṇas, or as expressed in the phenomenal world of matter as the collocations of the atoms. It is theoretically therefore possible to change anything in the world to any other thing provided the necessary collocations of the atoms could be arranged. The change or modifications only give expression to the latent varieties of the substance. As the atoms change their position by their innate rajas or energy, the substance changes its form and manifests diverse new qualities which could not be perceived before. But still such a change is not possible to an unlimited degree, for in the constitution of the relation of the guṇas there are limitations and obstacles which cannot be overstepped. These limitations may generally be counted in the phenomenal world of change, as being of the nature of time, space, form and disposing cause. Thus Kashmere being the country of saffron, it does not grow in the Pāñcāla country, even though the other causes of its growth may be present there. Similarly there are rains in the summer season, therefore the growth of rice is possible only in that season; so also the form of a man cannot take its rise from that of a deer.[1] Thus though all things are intrinsically the same yet the obstacles to change, of the constitution of the guṇas in the formation of different substances in certain directions, are such that these cannot be removed, and so those modifications though

[1] *Tattvavaiśāradī.*

theoretically possible will ever remain a practical impossibility.

This brings us to the relation of cause and effect and the part which is played by concomitant conditions in transforming the cause into the effect. We know that there is no other difference between cause and effect than this that the former is only the potential state of which the latter is the actual. The sum of material causes is only the vehicle of the power which is efficient in the production. The concomitant conditions are said to help the effectuation of this transformation from the potential to the actual state. Thus the work of the sculptor may be regarded as the concomitant condition which transforms a piece of marble into a statue. The oilman has helped the oil which was already in existence in the mustard to manifest itself as such. Thus, looked at from this point of view, all concomitant causes may be regarded as helping the passage of the effect from its potentiality as the cause, into the effect as an actuality.[1]

But apart from this surface view of the matter there is a deeper side of it which has been pointed out in the Vyāsa-Bhāshya which looks upon the concomitant conditions as only removing the obstacles in the way of the transformation

[1] *Pravacana-Bhāshya*, 1, 115.

of the cause into effect. This explains causation on the basis of conservation and transformation of energy, for the potential energy is here viewed as being stored up in a substance (or guṇa collocation), and as soon as the concomitant conditions remove the barrier, the energy flows out of itself and produces the necessary transformation. Thus the Bhāshya explains the situation of the theory of potentials thus: "As the husbandman desirous of carrying water from an already well-filled bed to another, does not draw the water with his own hands to places which are on the same or lower level but simply removes the obstacles or impediments, and thereupon the water flows down of itself to the other bed, so it pierces the obstacles or impediments in the way of the development, and thereby the creative causes naturally pass through the respective changes of themselves, or similarly the same husbandman does not possess the power of transforming the earth and watery juices to the roots of rice in the same bed. What then? He weeds the mudga, the gavendhuka, and the śyāmāka out of the common bed and when they have been weeded out, the juices themselves enter the roots of rice."

Thus we see that the energy conserved in one form naturally passes into another by manifesting consequent changes or transformations designated by the name of evolution. As natural flow is obstructed in various ways by the resistance offered by space, time, form, and causality, it has naturally to take the course in which there are no impediments and obstacles; at each stage new impediments may come in and interfere with the evolving process and compel the flow to change the direction of its course at every stage; so it is that we find that the evolutionary process has naturally to take a curvilinear line rather than the straight one It is this resistance against the evolutionary flow which compels it to reject thousands of courses open to it and select a particular one in which there is no resistance. It is this therefore that gives niyama or a regulation (*pariṇāmakrama-niyama*).

The pariṇāmakramaniyama, or the deśakālākāranimittāpabandha, takes the question of natural selection to a firmer basis and seeks to answer the question from the principle of the conservation of energy. It seems that by attributing the resistance of Nature to the particular atomic constitution of things and environments, it includes not only the modifications of the vegetable and the animal kingdoms but also those of the inorganic world. It suggests that the force which guides the evolutionary process is not a peculiar thing different from other kinds of forces of Nature, but reduces all forces of Nature to that one kind generated by the continual displacement of the vibratory atoms of substances and the natural obstruction involved in the adoption of any mode of displacement other than the one which belongs to the atoms owing to their particular constituent arrangements and environments. Only that kind of evolution can come out or remain unmolested which has not to face the opposition of time, space or the particular atomic arrangement of things. For unless retarded by these, the liberated energy will continue to form transformations which will again undergo a course of changes forced upon them by the varying retardation and oppositions either from environments or from the peculiar nature of their own constitution. What we call qualities of things are only modes of energy acting in these collocations (*yogyatāvacchinnā dharmiṇah śaktireva dharmaḥ*).

The question of cause and effect naturally brings with it the conception of time in the Sāṃkhya-Yoga system. For time is merely the scheme of the understanding for representing the course of evolution or recording the changes. Whenever we want to take note of any change these naturally fall into a series, and it is this series that is called the time series or order in time. If the finest constituent of matter is taken as the atom, then the finest unit of time would be that required by an atom to move its own dimension of space. But the atoms are constituted of the tanmātras and these are constituted of the guṇas, so if we are to rest anywhere we have to rest in the guṇas as the ultimate units of matter having no parts. So the ultimate unit of time must be the time required for these absolute units of matter to change. Time is here therefore wholly discrete as opposed to the Nyāya-Vaiśeshika view of an infinite continuum perceptible by direct experience. Bhikshu has argued in *Yoga-Vārttika* that though the time is defined as buddhi-nirmāṇa (a scheme of the understanding) yet it may be taken as real, for it is really identical with the unit of change of the guṇas in phenomena. But it is important to note that even this relative reality of time fails when we consider that in nirvicāra samādhi, the space-unit of the guṇa change is not of any use, as the sages then perceive only the guṇas without the space relations of ordinary consciousness. Discrete time therefore being only the scheme of the understanding in taking the phenomenal changes, and its ultimate unit being measured by the ultimate unit of change of space of the ultimate units of matter, it comes to this that there is no metaphysical existence of time. Time as an absolutely existing continuum is also illusory. It is only the present moment which exists and it is here that the whole world suffers a change ; the future and the past have no meaning apart from potential and sublatent phenomena. Only the present moment is the actual and the time of transformation is the change of the potential into the actual and from the actual into the sublatent.

Space as mere extension (*deśa*) is an existent external entity and it is not reduced to unity of position as in the moments with regard to time. We have seen that the grossness of things has been defined as the space they occupy. Dik however which means relative position results only from the different relations in which the all-pervasive ākāśa stands to the various finite objects. Space as extension is to be distinguished from this, for the former is an unalterable entity which stands as the measure of all finite things and these are themselves unanalysable into the infinitesimal extensive quantity inherent in the guṇas. The difference however between the reality of relative position and time lies in the former being absolutely illusory and having no real existence at all, whereas the latter is admitted to exist as mere moments. The difference here between the Buddhist and the Yoga position is this that here it is only the time which is regarded as momentary but things are regarded as permanent, whereas in Buddhism both the things and time are regarded as momentary; between the Naiyāyikas and the Yoga, the difference consists in this that the former holds that there is an eternal substance called time apart from the moments called kshaṇa. What we hear ordinarily as eternal time is but this eternity of flow or succession. We should however remember that the substance of both time and space is the ākāśa or vacuous ether so they are also not different in essence from guṇas. Vācaspati however contends that the moments being the scheme of the understanding are absolutely imaginary, illusory and false.

The close relation of ākāśa with time and space brings the ākāśa for our consideration. There are two kinds of ākāśa according to the Sāṃkhya-Yoga system, as has been noticed by Vijñāna Bhikshu in the *Yoga-Vārttika.* These are kāraṇākāśa and kāryākāśa. The kāraṇākāśa is the absolutely ubiquitous mass as bhūtādi which is devoid of all potentials and is merely the seat of the rajas. It is from this aspect called vibhu—all-pervasive. This should not be regarded as a mere negative vacuity, though it occupies the same space as all the gross forms of matter and is devoid of all impenetrability. From this comes the tanmātric ākāśa, when by the action of rajas it forms itself as a unit of vibration potential or ākāśa tanmātra. This ākāśa tanmātra with a further accretion of mass and fresh redistribution of energy forms into the ākāśa atom which is integrated and limited and is the sound medium. This ākāśa remaining itself in the kāraṇākāśa forms the medium of all gaseous bodies and also of light and heat corpuscles. This atomic ākāśa is called the kāryākāśa and we may conceive it for all purposes as being another kind of atom. Coming to the domain of evolutionary changes we find that the bhūtādi is pure ubiquitous mass and it is from this that the tanmātras are produced in a gradual order by the action of energy. These tanmātras have all the characteristics of differentiations as the bhūtas, but these are in such a state of potentiality that they cannot directly manifest themselves to our senses. These tanmātras combine themselves, as we have already seen, to form the atoms of the five bhūtas. The smallest part of any bhūta is called an aṇu or atom. These are not however partless (*niravayava*) like the atoms of the Vaiśeshikas but are composed of the tanmātras which are their parts. These are not also eternal like the Vaiśeshika aṇus. Sāṃkhya holds that these form into the dyaṇukas after the Vaiśeshika fashion, but Yoga holds that no such dyaṇukas are formed, but the mass of different bodies is formed by the conglomeration of atoms. These atoms are of five classes, kshiti, ap, tejas, vāyu and vyoman. These five bhūtas should not be taken to mean elements in the ordinary chemical sense of the term, for the classification is ultimate in the sense that there are only five types of qualities which can be grasped by the five senses. Whatever qualities may be grasped by any particular sense may be said to form a class and according to that the substance possessing them may be said to be a particular bhūta.

Formation of aggregates (*samūha*) may be said to be of two classes : (1) those of which the parts are in such intimate union as to form an individual whole (*ayutasiddhāvayava*), and (2) aggregates of a mechanical character where the parts are comparatively separate (*yutasiddhāvayava*). The combination of atoms which form substances may be said to be of two kinds: (1) the rearrangement of the atoms of the same bhūta which form different substances ; (2) the union of the atoms of different bhūtas which form substances. The contact of atoms in the former case is called sajātiya saṃyoga and in the latter vijātīya saṃyoga. Now the Vaiśeshikas laboured under the belief that there cannot generally be any union between the atoms of different bhūtas In cases where such combinations are possible only one should act as a radicle, round which the others may form a system of co-efficient causes.

The brief Sāṃkhya account as we have it from Utpala supposes that the atoms of five bhūtas could combine together to form the different bodies. *Vyāsa-Bhāshya* also in the line "*jalabhūmyoḥ pāriṇāmikam rasādivaiśvarūpyam*" suggests that different bi-bhūtic compounds of water and earth substances are formed in plants in different combinations. Vācaspati says in *Tattva-kaumudī* that with the water atom at the centre and the earth atoms grouped round it, new energies are produced which are manifested as the different kinds of fruit-juice and acids. In another place Vācaspati says that in the constitution of things, the atoms of different bhūtas are arranged side by side. Thus an object of perception is not constituted of the light or heat atoms merely, but these are also alternated by earth and water atoms ; so from it we can infer that Vācaspati held that compounds amongst the atoms of diverse bhūtas were allowable. But Vijñāna Bhikshu, probably under the Vaiśeshika influence, denies the possibility of such combinations except after the Vaiśeshika fashion, namely, with the atom of the principal bhūta as the material cause (*upādāna kāraṇa*) and the other atoms in a comparatively unattached condition as efficient causes (*nimitta kāraṇa*) called upashṭambha. So the human body is formed with the earth as the material cause and the other four bhūtas as upashṭambhaka.[1] About the union

[1] *Sāṃkhya-Sūtra*, I, 102.

of the tanmātras however no such objection was felt, and the *Bhāshya* also holds that the union of the five tanmātras form the liṅga deha. As all the substances according to the Sāṃkhya-Yoga view are but collocations of the guṇas there is no reason why Sāṃkhya-Yoga physics should object to the combination or collocations of the atoms of diverse bhūtas to form substances. All change here is but the transformation of energy due to the change of collocations of the atoms or guṇas.

Matter then can exist in three forms in the infra-atomic stage as tanmātras, as aṇus or the atoms of the bhūtas, and also in the actual combined stage as extensive earth, water, air, etc.

The physical characteristics of these five bhūtas have thus been described by Vācaspati:

The characteristics of earth are:—form, heaviness, roughness, obstruction, stability, manifestation, difference, support, turbidity, hardness, enjoyability by all.

The characteristics of ap are:—smoothness, subtlety, clearness, whiteness, softness, heaviness, coolness, preservation, purification, cementation.

The characteristics of tejas are:—going upward, burning, lightness, shining, destruction, power.

The qualities of vāyu are :—transverse motion, purification, throwing, pushing, strength, movability, throwing no shadow, roughness.

The characteristics of ākāśa are :—motion in all direction, non-agglomeration, and non-obstruction.

The atoms of the five bhūtas combined together to form the different material objects and the bodies of plants, animals and men. They all being only the collocation of the bhūta atoms there is consequently a circulation or passage from one state to another. Thus inorganic matter when assimilated as food in the plant or in animal systems, serves to form their bodies; the bodies of men and animals also when disintegrated are reduced into the atoms of the bhūtas as inorganic substances. All things are formed of mass (tamas) and energy (rajas); the action of rajas is going on always; and as Vijñānabhikshu says, the atomic constitution of things has to be admitted to make the action of the rajas possible, as we cannot but associate units of energy with units of mass. The difference between the diverse species of the same bhūtas as well as of the compounds of many bhūtas is due to the diversity of the arrangement of the atoms. All changes of all kinds, physical or chemical, are reduced to this one kind, namely, that of diverse redistribution of atoms and energy. Thus it is that the water atoms and the kshiti atoms combine together in the plant bodies and produce diverse kinds of juices in the roots, trunk, leaves, flowers and fruits by the diversity of their arrangement. The atomic arrangement of the plant bodies again changes and forms the bodies of animals and attain other characteristics. Bodies of animals also can be assimilated by plants and changed into such atomic arrangements as are suitable to plant-bodies. So there is a constant transformation from one state to another according to the diversity of the aggregation of the atoms and consequent appearance of new energies manifesting themselves as diverse qualities.

It may not be out of place here to notice that the practical nature of the Sāṃkhya-Yoga physics and the emphasis that it gave to the method of concentration by which a man could by his own endeavours attain truth readily attracted scientific workers to accept its general conclusions in the formulation of the principles of their special branches of enquiry. These were mainly the medical schools of Caraka and Suśruta, and other works in alchemy and medicine. Caraka devoted a whole chapter (*Śārira*) in explaining the Sāṃkhya-Yoga system of philosophy, and drew up its system on the basis laid down by it. We know that in Alberuni's "Book of Pātanjal" an alternative way of salvation through alchemy was proposed. In many alchemical works we find that processes of making the body immortal are suggested as the best kind of salvation and it is attainable through chemistry.[1] Thus Dr. P. C. Ray says in his lecture delivered in the University of Madras: "In our country though the pursuit of this science was made an auxiliary to the healing arts, it made rapid strides by entering into an alliance with the Yoga philosophy. In later times, the philosophy of the Yoga was pressed into the service of science and degenerated into Tāntrika rites especially in Bengal." These became so much associated with the Yoga philosophy that Yoga became the common name for medicine as well as alchemy.[2]

The fact that all objects in nature and all forces are reduced to the movement of atoms should not lead us to suppose that life itself is a product of the combination of the atoms like the *madaśakti* of the Cārvāka which we have described before; for we know that the Sāṃkhya has combated the Cārvākas on the ground that the difference of consciousness from intoxication lies in the fact that the intoxicating power is a force which is the resultant of the intoxicating tendencies of the different particles of

[1] *Kasārṇava.*

[2] Compare the names *Yogachandrikā*—a manual of materia medica, *Rājamārtaṇḍayogasārasaṃgraha*—a treatise on the preparation of medicinal arts, or *Yogaśatābhidhānam*—a work on the practice of medicine, etc., etc.—R. L. Mitra's Catalogue of Sanskrit MSS.

the fermented molasses; but consciousness is not motion and hence cannot be the resultant product of other motions or tendencies. Neither can the consciousness of the person be regarded as the product of any consciousness distributed over the particles of the body and it is a more legitimate hypothesis to admit one superintending intelligence than to accept the theory of an assemblage of consciousnesses latent in different bhūtas or material particles.[1] Life is only a reflex activity, a resultant of the various concurrent activities of the antaḥkaraṇas or the sensori motor, the emotional and the apperceptive reactions. It is thus the united action of the senses that is called life. Life is neither the five vāyus (bio-mechanical force) nor is it a sort of subtle rarefied ether principle (adhyātmavāyu) pervasive of the organism which is not gross vāyu, but is all the same subtilised matter like the manas itself of the Vedānta. It is the side of rajas or energy which first emanates in the emanation of the mahat from the prakṛti, and then shows itself in the formation of the senses, etc. Prāṇa presides over all the organs and pervades them and as such is but the active manifestation of the mahat. Thus Bhikshu says in Vijñānāmṛta-Bhāshya "*mahat tattvam hyekameva*

[1] See *Sāṃkhyapravacana-Bhāshya*, III, 22.

prākṛterutpādyamānam jñānakriyāśaktibhyām buddhiprāṇaśabdābhyām abhilapyate." Thus it is the different active manifestations of the mahat which holds together in union the different organs as its states that is called the prāṇa.[1] The five vāyus only represent the diverse types of the manifestation of life as the psychical co-ordinating and regulative activity of mahat. All movement thus, whether of matter or of mind, is derived from the stuff of consciousness, the mahat.

Thus we find that all the multifarious kinds of objects of the inorganic world are but the products of the displacement and rearrangements acting in accordance with a definite law. At certain stages of their development they become suitable to reflect life or soul. This soul though absolutely inactive in itself is the goal for which all the activities of life are produced which are in themselves but material products of the activities of the mahat or the supreme stuff of consciousness. Matter particles conglomerate together to form the different bodies for different souls according to their merit or demerit until we come to man wherein we find the soul wedded to the most perfect body of evolution. Man's body, so far as it is a physical object, is like any other object of

[1] *Vijñānāmṛtabhāshya* and *Pravacana-Bhāshya*, II, 13.

nature passing through the processes of evolution. In considering the objects of the material world we had so long altogether neglected its sattva side which had no other manifestation than that of making them cognisable in terms of thought and feeling of the purushas. But it is when the bodies gradually develop into the body of man that we find that the sattva of matter begins to manifest itself in developing the translucent character of the buddhi by removing the obstructing elements; and it is thus that we find that from the manifestations of simple feelings of joy and grief we come to the most developed consciousness of the philosopher.

If we look at the history of the investigation into the nature of matter we find that Locke found the concept obscure and of little use; Berkeley dismissed matter as an abstraction and a superfluity; Hume similarly banished spirit. Kant retained the conception in the sense of the permanent in all change. Modern phenomenalism regards it as denoting the unknown existent upon which physical properties depend. In the physical science matter is the "stuff" of which the universe is made. The happy guess of Democritus of matter as being composed of simple impenetrable hard atoms was revived by Dalton as a genuine scientific theory. But if the atoms had no elasticity many of the physical phenomena would not be explained. It is considerations like these that led Boscovich to speak of matter as being made of points which were the centres of attractive and repulsive forces. Lord Kelvin had proposed that a vortex-ring of ether in an ethereal plenum capable of transmitting vibrations should be the definition of an atom Kelvin's theory of matter differs from that of Boscovich in that it offers a plenum instead of isolating an empty space; this plenum provides for action and reaction wi t the need of any action at a distance. It differs again from Dalton's in dispensing with hard atoms, while furnishing atoms which are not only extended, but also, in virtue of their rotational movement elastic. Natural science however in spite of its high pretensions does no more than describe natural phenomena in so far as these are to be regarded as changes in the motion of masses. It abstracts from the qualitative properties and changes of matter, because these are not amenable to scientific method and replaces them by hypothetically representative movement of masses. Matter with its diversities of qualities of perceptual experience is not only one in kind for science but as the goal of abstraction is reached, physics passes into mathematics and matter becomes indistinguishable from space.

So far as the indivisibility of atoms and unchangeability of elements are concerned the views of the scientists were so long quite orthodox. But quite lately the old beliefs have been reversed. It is now believed that atoms are not simple but that portions of them can be split off and exist separately and that these detached fractions or corpuscles are identical from whatever kinds of atoms they may have been broken off and possess the same mass or inertia. Thus atoms are complex systems in spite of their differences as built up of parts or corpuscles which are identical. The corpuscles have been found to be a constant electrical charge (electron). Corpuscle and electron would seem to be identical because the whole mass of the corpuscles appear to be due to its electric charge and motion. The ultra-atomic character of matter and the non-fixed character of the elements have now been demonstrated by experiments. But the ultimate question as to what matter is in itself is still unsolved. It is moreover gratifying for an Indian to notice that in the bustle and crowd of the controversies of the scientific world it has been steadily approaching in a direction which, so far at least as the general scheme is concerned, is quite familiar to a student of the Yoga Philosophy. The highly specialised and experimental character of modern investigations may well be contrasted to the crude and speculative character of Sāṃkhya-Yoga physics. But we should remember that the Sāṃkhya-Yoga built up a whole system of philosophic thought and did not busy itself merely in giving a detached view of physics alone. We should also remember the remote period when it flourished, and we should also be alive to the shortcomings of the speculations of the scientific world of the past as well as of the present.

CHAPTER VIII

Sāmkhya Atheism and Yoga Theism

Atheism as a philosophic creed did not develop, it seems, in systematic forms in an early age in any country other than India. From Dr. Legge's edition of Mencius we know that a practical type of materialistic atheism developed in China about the third century B. C. A certain Yang Choo advises men "to care nothing for praise or blame, virtue or vice; to seek merely to make themselves as happy as they can while happiness is within their reach; to eat and drink for to-morrow they die." Looking to Greece we find that Plato asserts that while other erroneous views about the gods might be permanent, no one, after embracing in his youth the doctrine of atheism had ever continued in it up to old age. There were thinkers who denied the popular gods but did not deny God in its entirety. A sceptic like Protagoras declared himself unable to affirm of the gods either that they were or that they were not. Diagoras of Melos is said to have turned to atheism because the gods failed to visit with punishment a flagrant wrong which had been committed against him. The charges of atheism also against Euhemerus or Prodicus also may be said to be true only in the sense of their opposition to received religion. It is only of Theodorous of Cyrene, the follower of Aristippus, that we have definite information of an uncompromising atheism which was subversive of the foundations of customary morality. But these forms of atheism must be distinguished from the schools of atheism which developed in early India as a reasoned utterance of philosophy. Atheism as a system presupposes the existence of theism, the conception of a self-existing cause on whom all things and persons depend. The mere disbelief of the gods of the national pantheon of a race, does not constitute atheism. But here again distinction must be made between ordinary atheism as mere doubt and negation with regard to some essential elements of theism and the philosophic or scientific atheism which discards God as an unnecessary hypothesis as we had in India.[1]

Early in the Ṛgveda the national God Indra is derided in several passages [2]; and we read of people who absolutely denied his existence.[3] These traces of old atheism are not the result of any philosophical reflection, but simply

[1] See E.R.E., article on "Atheism."

[2] Ṛgveda IV. 24; 10, X. 119.

[3] Ṛgveda II. 12. 5; VIII. 100. 3.

the refusal to believe like the Lokāyatas, what cannot be visualised. This atheism must be distinguished from those types of atheism which developed as the result of serious philosophical speculations.

But atheism was being seriously worked amongst certain sections of the people to such an extent that by the time we come to the Śvetāśvatara, it had differentiated itself into diverse schools in more or less organised forms as can be inferred from the Śvetāśvatara texts :— *kālasvabhāvo niyatiryadṛcchā bhūtāni yoniḥ-purusha iti cintyaṃ saṃyoga eshāṃ na tvātma-bhāvādātmāpyanīśaḥ sukhaduḥkhahetoḥ.*

We find from the above text that the origin of the universe was ascribed by some to time, to nature, to moral works, to chance, to matter, to soul or to all of them combined as the soul was not itself the master of the causes of its pleasures and pains.[1]

The Sāṃkhya atheism seems to be a combination of all these forms excepting the chance atheism much advocated by the Cārvākas and amply criticised by the Naiyāyikas.[2]

In the Sāṃkhya system we find that there are many purushas but one prakṛti. Prakṛti is the composite of the three guṇas in a state of equilibrium. The guṇas are themselves non-

1 Śvetāśvatara Bhāshya of Śaṅkara, I. 2.

2 See *Kusumāñjali*, 1. 4, and *Prakāśa* of Varddhamāna on it.

intelligent but there is this instinctive tendency in them that all their diverse movements amongst themselves whether in the forward line as cosmos or in the backward line as the return into the prakṛti are for the sake of the infinite number of purushas. The formation of the state of equilibrium and its break are both the unbroken parts of the same chain of its movement as *sañcara* and *pratisañcara*.[1] The Sāṃkhya holds, that the question "who breaks the state of equilibrium" is meaningless, because the prakṛti is as much a state of becoming as any other state is. The state of equilibrium far from being a state of absolute motionlessness is one of the highest tension. The state of ultimate passivity is due to the arrest of motion on account of their mutual opposition. It is their nature that the guṇas disturb themselves for the sake of the purushas.[2] This state of arrest is only a moment in the process where the returning forces of the guṇas being set against one another had produced the equilibrium only to be negated by the disturbing series of modification called the *visadṛśapariṇāma*. Time, we have seen, is ultimately nothing but the movement of the guṇas, and all movement of the guṇas being in a state of arrest, it is time in its timelessness, it is the pure duration, if we may

[1] *Kapila-sūtra*, 6.—*sañcaraḥ pratisañcaraḥ*.

[2] *Calañca guṇavṛttaṃ guṇasvābhāvyantu pravṛttikāraṇamuktam*.

call it so. Time has vanished, because the data of its manifestation are not to be found. But the reality of time so far as it is indistinguishable from the guṇas, and so far as it is also a state in the process, still remains. The disturbance is as much a moment as the return, and if the whole process is thought of or conceived as existing in time one may say that the ultimate disturbances of the prakṛti happens as much in time as the disturbance of the mahat in the production of ahaṃkāra. It should always be remembered that from the Sāṃkhya point of view prakṛti herself is of a moving nature and no agent is necessary at any stage to disturb her. The influence of the purusha also does not move it, but such is its nature (*svabhāva*) or material disposition that all its movements are directed to the service of the purusha. The question how the prakṛti became originally connected with the purusha cannot be allowed, for it is eternal and there is no beginning of it.[1] The teleology of the prakṛti for the service of the purusha is not a conscious one, but a mere material disposition of the supreme

guṇānāmiti. (*Vyāsabhāshya*, iii, 13.)
cāñcalyaṃ hi guṇānāṃ svabhāvaḥ (*Yogavārttika*, iii. 13).

[1] *Bhāgavata purāṇa* gives a view in which it states that the union of Prakṛti and Purusha is due to mere chance coincidence on the part of Prakṛti and mere playfulness on the part of the Purusha. *Bhāgavata purāṇa*, III. 26.44.

mind-matter-stuff, the prakṛti, like the oozing of the milk from the udder of the cow for the calf. The introduction of a conscious intelligence, Iśvara cannot explain the position, as such an interposition cannot be justified otherwise than on egoistic or altruistic grounds. Īśvara must have some interest of his own to serve or He must have been moved with pity for others before he could wish to launch upon such an endeavour. But he cannot have any interest of his own to serve. Neither is there any scope for pity for no person had any affliction or sorrow before creation, and sorrow during the creation cannot certainly be the cause why he should move the prakṛti for the creation. Evidently this involves the vicious circle. Moreover if the sṛshṭi is for the good of the creatures, they all ought to have been made happy. If everything depended on karma what is the use of admitting an Īśvara to control it? The non-intelligent movement might as well serve the purpose, and karma might as well bring its own fruit itself. Moreover there is no way how the supposed Īśvara could act upon the prakṛti without running the risk of being sullied by its impurities. If it is admitted that it acts like a magnet through mere proximity, then the proximity of the purusha might as well be regarded as causing the disturbance in the prakṛti. Iśvara cannot be perceived; neither can His existence be inferred, as there is no way of determining any universal concomitance with Him. This atheism of Sāṃkhya, however, has no reference to the ordinary popular gods who are only more highly organised and happier beings than men ; like men they are within the saṃsāra cycle of life, and unless they gain the saving knowledge which enables them to withdraw from worldly existence, they are obliged to change their bodies again. Nor have they escaped the power of death or the fears of dismissal from office. Consequently they are lower than men who have reached the highest goal. These gods are called the *janyeśvaras* or *kāryeśvaras*, and they are evidently different from God as *nityeśvara* regarding whom the theists assume that he made the world by his will.

The denial of God is thus based firstly on the doctrine that there is inherent in unconscious matter (prakṛti and its evolutes such as bhūta, etc.) a force which operates with physical necessity, and develops it for the sake of the pure souls (purusha) and secondly, on the general Indian conception of the after-effects of the actions of living being (*karma* and *niyati*) which excite that natural force and guide its activity into definite channels.

If we take a bird's eye view of the Jaina, Buddhist or the Mīmāṃsā forms of atheism we find that the denial of Iśvara is mainly due to the fact that all that he could do is really determined by karma. For how could a Jaina assent to the existence of an omnipotent, omniscient God, when karma alone is regarded as responsible for the state of bondage as well as salvation ? In Buddhism also it is the force of karma which brings about all momentary existence. Moreover as the *Bodhicaryāvatāra* says, God has created neither souls nor elements which are eternal. He does not bring about the birth of knowledge in the mind since knowledge is produced by the object ; He does not allot pain and pleasure, which result from karma. Then, if God acts without desiring to act, He becomes subject to another's will; if he acts because He desires to act, He is subject to desire, and therefore dependent, if He were independent of others, He could have accomplished the creation, preservation, and destruction of the universe at one and the same moment. The Mīmāṃsā also does not think the existence of any God necessary firstly because the world as a whole cannot be thought to have any beginning in time, and secondly because all the individual pains and pleasures can be explained on the basis of dharma and adharma, which instead of being presided over by God really belong to the doers themselves.

But though these different systems agree with Sāṃkhya in point of atheism, yet to Sāṃkhya really belongs the credit of producing a systematic philosophy competent to do away with the hypothesis of an Īśvara as the ruler of the universe.

The atheism of Europe has not been able to go much beyond materialism. Thus Hobbes held that even sensations were nothing but the motion of corporeal particles. Holbach substitutes for God, matter and motion. Laplace, when he was asked by Napoleon why he had written nothing about God in his treatise the Mécanique Céleste had said, "Sire I had no need of that hypothesis." Carl Vogt argued that thought stood in the same relation to the brain as the bile to the liver or the urine to the kidneys and that all vital phenomena could be explained as a perpetual circulation of matter from the inorganic to the organic world and then back again from the organic to the inorganic. Moleschott says that without phosphorus there is no thought and thought is a movement of matter in the brain. Haeckel characterises the original substance as having a psychical as well as a physical side. The first substance passes by condensation first into imponderable ether and then into the elements of imponderable matter. The souls of animals and men have no origin separate from that of their bodies. The point in evolution at which consciousness first clearly presents itself, is however not known to him. Professor Clifford's theory of mind-stuff is also similar to that of Haeckel. With Holycake and Dubois-Raymond he regards the existence of a self-existent personal cause as highly improbable, owing to the want of evidence for the existence of a corresponding brain. Huxley tries to avoid the charge of materialism by saying that he is incapable of conceiving the existence of matter if there is no mind in which that existence would be pictured, but holds at the same time the doctrine of human automatism that while the states of consciousness depend upon the molecular movements of the cerebral substance, there is no proof that any state of consciousness is the cause of change in the motion of the matter of the organism. But comparing the Darwinian evolution with the teleological argument he holds that the teleological and the mechanical views of nature are not mutually exclusive. On the contrary the more purely a mechanist the speculator is, the more firmly does he assume a primordial molecular arrangement of which all the phenomena of the universe are the consequences. All these forms of modern atheism, are however but forms of materialism.[1] Sāṃkhya would abhor them all, as but the reappearance in diverse forms of the Bhūta-caitanya schools of Cārvākism which deny the existence of souls. The arguments of theists

[1] See E. R. E. article on Atheism.

against these forms of atheism consist in the contention, that movements of matter or the generation of new forces cannot explain consciousness, memory, ideas or personality and that the harmonious co-operation of matter particles or mind-stuff in the creation of this orderly universe would be inexplainable if it was not arranged under the direction of a conscious purpose or will.[1] Sāṃkhya will give the same answer to these atheists as it gave to the Cārvākas, with this modification that there was no need of admitting the purpose of a conscious Being, as the unconscious disposition of matter may be said to be working for the experiences of the souls. The primordial limitations in the guṇas, which may be compared with the primordial molecular arrangement of Huxley, is at once the basis of mechanism and teleology in Sāṃkhya. There is no conscious design, but an unconscious purpose or disposition in matter which develops it in unison with the moral merit or demerit of persons by its mechanistic teleology. Teleology is here the end and mechanism the means subserving to that.

The ordinary form of Nyāya theism supposes the world to be an effect, and thence argues

[1] Compare the Satkāryyavāda dictum with the main points of theistic objection to the generation of consciousness from matter that no effect can contain more than is contained in the ground and cause from which the effect has proceeded.

that it must have an all-intelligent creator who by his eternal and absolute will and knowledge acts upon the eternal atoms to bring about this orderly creation.[1] The principal points of the arguments may briefly be noticed as follows :—

(1) All the objects of the world are made up of collocations of parts like any of these common objects such as jug, etc., which are made by us (*sanniveśaviśishṭatvameva hetumabhidadhmahe—Nyāyamañjarī*, p. 194). The particular differences of collocation are immaterial, for it is the universal aspect of being made up of collocated parts which is to be made the ground of inference ; even those cases which are

[1] The form of theism as we find in the *Nyāya-sūtra* and Vātsyāyana's bhāshya is not as much of an intellectualistic character as the later form, as can be found from the time of Jayanta onwards. Thus Īśvara is acknowledged as the person who organises the world-order for the adjudging of rewards and punishments according to the actions of men. Īśvara has no interest of his own to realise; but he is like the father who works for his sons, though it must be observed that he cannot bestow any such blessing on men as are not guaranteed by their karmas *evaṃ ca svakṛtābhyāgamasyālopena nirmāṇaprākāmyamīśvarasya svakṛtakarmaphalaṃ veditavyam* ; *āptakalpaścāyaṃ yathā pitā apatyānāṃ tathā pitṛbhūta Īśvaro bhūtānām—Vātsyāyana-bhāshya* (4, 1. 21). He is an all-intelligent self (*ātmāntaramīśvaraḥ*) He can act as he wishes. He associates the individual with their respective dharma and adharma and moves the world order and living beings accordingly (*saṅkalpānuvidhāyī cāsya dharmaḥ pratyātmavṛttīn dharmādharmasañcayān pṛthivyādīni ca bhūtāni pravarttayati*—Vātsyāyana, *ibid*). Thus the formal side of the inference has hardly any importance so far as the Sūtra and the Bhāshya are concerned.

universally acknowledged to be made by men do not agree in the collocation of the parts.[1]

(2) The fact that young shoots of trees are directly found to be collocation of parts but are not seen to be made by any Being does not afford any room for doubt ; all that can be said of them is that the agent of their collocation is not visible. The inference could have been proved to be invalid if it could be definitely shown that they had no creator, though they were made up of collocations of parts. Unless that can be done, we are justified to infer, on the basis of the collocation of parts, that these have been done by an agent or creator ; for an inference cannot be nullified in spite of the presence of the hetu as collocation, merely on the strength of a meaningless doubt that there may not be a creator (*sadasatpāvakatayā parvate sandigdhe vipakashe varttamānasya dhūmasya hetutvaprasaṅgāt ; sarva eva ca sādhyāṃśa-saṃśayād vipakshā eva jātāḥ iti pakshavṛttayo hetavaḥ idānīṃ vipakshagāmino bhaveyuh ityanumanocchedaḥ.—Nyāyamañjarī*, p. 197).[2]

(3) It is not necessary for the conception of a creator that he should have a body, for it is enough that he should have knowledge, will

[1] *Nyāyamañjarī*, pp. 194-195.

[2] For the Jaina objection against the Nyāya argument, see *Syādvādamañjarī* and Guṇaratna on the Jaina philosophy in *Shaḍdarśanasamuccaya*. Compare also the logical form of the inference as given by Varddhamāna and Śiromaṇi.

and effort. Thus it is that by the mere will of our spirit or soul the body is directly moved.[1] The karma itself cannot create the world as it is non-intelligent. The souls of man also cannot be thought of as presiding over it in order to create the world, for the interests of men being different there cannot be any co-operation for a common end. So it is that one Iśvara has to be acknowledged as presiding over the karma, and by whose will creations and dissolutions take place. Yet he is not a despot for he only acts in accordance with the karmas of men. He is omniscient as he knows how to destroy and create the universe. His will and knowledge eternally exist His knowledge is not in succession but in eternal perception, so he has no need of memory or of mind. He is eternally happy.

It is easy to see that the Yoga could not have such a God, inasmuch as it denied all activity even to the human soul. Flint rightly says that in order to think of God as a cause, to apprehend the universe as an effect, we must have some direct experience of causation. And such experience we have only in the consciousness of volition. When the soul wills, it knows

[1] *Yathā hyacetanaḥ kāyaḥ ātmecchāmanuvarttate*
Tadicchāmanuvartsyante tathaiva paramāṇavaḥ
(*Nyāyamañjarī*, p. 202.)

There was however a school of Naiyāyikas who wanted to call the atoms the body of Īsvara. See *Muktāvalī*.

itself as an agent, as a cause. The Yoga attributed all movements and changes to the prakṛti, the primal matter. It was difficult therefore for it to assign any place to Īśvara consistently with its system of metaphysics. The "*sannivesa*" or the collocation of the atoms in an orderly manner, which with the Nyāya was the main ground of inferring an external intelligent cause, was with Yoga brought about by the natural movement of the prakrti herself. It is therefore that we find that in the Yoga sūtras Īśvara is but loosely introduced, more as a matter of traditional faith than as having a place in the system of philosophy. He is introduced as only one of the alternative objects of concentration; but concentration on God is more useful than concentration on other objects, for God is pleased by the direction of concentration on Him and may thereby be pleased to remove the obstacles and make the attainment of the goal of the Yogin much easier. He is himself but a purusha, with this difference that unlike them he had never the least semblance of any connection with the prakṛti. He had never any ignorance, karma, the fruits of karma or the residual instincts of karma as vāsanā. He has in him the seed of the highest omniscience. As he is not limited by time he is the preceptor of all past teachers even. I have elsewhere tried to show that Yoga as a system of mental discipline had originally existed independently of Sāṃkhya, and that it was subsequently incorporated into the Sāṃkhya school, as the latter could in all probability explain its phenomena quite satisfactorily. It is probable therefore that the belief in an Īśvara was associated from the earliest times with Yoga traditions as being revealed by the spiritual experiences of Yoga. Thus in Śvetāśvatara, immediately following the verse which contains references to diverse atheistical doctrines, we find the verse which says that " the sages devoted to meditation and concentration perceived the power belonging to God himself, hidden in its qualities (*guṇa*). He being one, superintends all causes, time, self and the rest.' It is true no doubt that the Upanishad period is a time when the Īśa and Brahman were hardly sufficiently distinguished and differentiated from the point of view of later philosophy. The word Īśvara or even Īśa was not a favourite word with the early Upanishads.[1] It was the Brahman who (from the point of view of the distinction raised in later philosophy) served both the purposes of Īśvara as well as that of its colourless character as Brahman. The comparatively free introduction of the name Īśvara in

[1] The word Īśa is used only once in the Īśa Upanishad though it occurs no less than six times in the Śvetāśvatara ; the word Īśvara is used twice in Bṛhadāraṇyaka (1. 4. 8 and 6. 4. 14) but not in the sense of God.

the later Upanishads might have probably been due to the fact that the name Īśvara was being separately chosen as the importance of the active side of Brahman was being gradually felt. In the early Upanishads the word Brahman seems to be loosely used to denote the supreme reality as infinite knowledge, as the self within, as the supreme cause of the world and also as the ruler and dispenser from the fear of whom all the forces of nature fulfilled their duties. The Upanishad culture, as we have noticed elsewhere, was the product of the consciousness of a ruler and upholder of all. The Brahman as pure knowledge, the Ātman as the only reality, the immutable and the eternal, forms no doubt an essential element in the Upanishads as Śaṅkara had so clearly shown in later times; but it has to be admitted that the word Brahman was also used to denote the all-intelligent creator, ruler and upholder of the world and this, as an important element of the Upanishad thought, had never lost its force. That the opposition between the Brahman as static and the Brahman as the upholder and ruler was not felt, was due to the fact that philosophy as a system of dialectic reasoning had not yet grown in the Upanishad period. It seems therefore that the later affiliation of the Yoga doctrines to the Sāṃkhya system of thought had not been able to shake off its old characteristic association with Īśvara the supreme Lord. Professor Garbe's remark that Patañjali, the founder of the Yoga system, introduced the idea of a personal god in the hope that he would thus make the Sāṃkhya philosophy acceptable to his countrymen is more an example of ingenious imagination than a fact justified by tradition and evidence. Had Patañjali introduced Īśvara from such prudential considerations as Garbe ascribes to him, he would surely have been a little more cautious and have given his Īśvara a place in the system of his philosophy, instead of keeping him in a floating condition. The belief in the existence of Īśvara and the profession of a philosophy which agreed so much with the atheistic Sāṃkhya philosophy gave such a peculiar position to the Yoga philosophy that in many ancient works one of the most familiar topics of controversy was the difference between the Sāṃkhya and the Yoga. Thus for example in the Mahābhārata Śāntiparva, Yudhiṣṭhira asks Bhīshma about the difference of Sāṃkhya and Yoga, and Bhīshma points out that the Yoga differs from the Sāṃkhya in this that it holds the existence of Īśvara necessary for salvation, whereas the Sāṃkhya holds that salvation comes by knowledge. Later discussions with Bhīshma show that though the difference of views with regard to the existence of Īśvara generally distinguish the one system from the other, their real difference lay in this that the Yoga laid all emphasis upon practice whereas the Sāṃkhya was essentially an advocate of science. As regards external ethical morality they were in complete accord. But the Sāṃkhya wanted to exhaust the field of knowledge in all possible ways and then ultimately to attain salvation by the knowledge of self. Truly it was this which was the original difference between the Sāṃkhya and the Yoga, but the difference which was apparent on the surface was the faith of the latter in Īśvara and the denial of the former.

To take account of the manner in which the problem was handled by the commentators we come first to *Vyāsa-bhāshya*. Vyāsa says that Īśvara has a pure body made of the purest sattva, and the evidence that we have of its existence is the creation of the śāstras, and if the body had not been so pure the śāstras could not have been so pure and infallible.[1] It is easy to see that Vyāsa had no other way of proving the existence of Īśvara, which had no place in the system, than by appealing to the śāstras, a device so rarely to be found in the general metaphysical discussions. It is on account of the pure body of Īśvara that he can have knowledge and action by which he could produce the śāstras for the benefit of the people and it is from the śāstras again that his pure nature could be inferred; such is their

[1] Compare the *Brahma-sūtra* "*śāstrayonitvāt.*"

mutual relation from eternity. His is the highest power ; there is none like him ; he is one, for if there had been many Īśvaras, then there would have been quarrels for supremacy, or the desire and will of one would have been baffled by that of another. He who has no equal and who has the ultimate perfection of all powers and omniscience is Īśvara.[1] He has nothing to realise for himself but he acts for the good of all beings and gives instruction in true knowledge and virtue for the emancipation of men. It is only natural for the pure souls to show mercy to others who are wretched : thus it is that Kapila with the help of a pure body first instructed Āsuri in the Sāṃkhya system. But Īśvara is the instructor of all previous teachers in all past ages. The praṇava or the oṃkāra has from eternity been the name to designate him. Thus we find that so far as the *Vyāsa-bhāshya* is concerned Īśvara is an unfettered soul, which is ever existing as the most exalted person with the purest body who brought forth the Vedas, and who is always engaged in doing good to the beings of the world. He is thus the omniscient, all-powerful, all-merciful, unfettered object of meditation, as he is of the same nature as the unfettered purusha, the object of Yoga meditation. Īśvara is a fit object of meditation, as he is of the

[1] Compare the Nyāya Īśvara as found in *Vātsyāyana-bhāshya*.

same nature as the purusha himself and as he being attracted (*āvarjita*) by bhakti fulfils his purpose by the merest wish.

Vācaspati however tries to find out a place for Īśvara by conceiving him elsewhere as removing the barriers of the prakṛti. This is indeed a very ingenious and happy device; for we know that prakṛti has the movement in herself. There is also the inherent teleology in the prakṛti by virtue of which all her movements become such that they are suited to the purpose of the purushas determined by their previous karmas, and it is this which gives the order and system of the universe, for these only signify that the universe is in harmony with the knowledge and expectations of men. Prakṛti again winds and unwinds of herself as pralaya and sarga. But the point which still remains to be questioned is that when at the pralaya all energy and matter are reduced to a state of pure potentiality, how can it (without any external movement) again reduce itself into its kinetic forms. Sāṃkhya says, as we have already seen, that prakṛti itself unwinds from the state of pralaya but the Yoga can maintain here with much reason that so far as the positive content of unwinding is concerned it is certainly due to prakṛti, but there is the negative affair without which the flow of the unwinding process would have remained in a state of pure potentiality, namely, that of removing the obstacles and the impediments in prakṛti herself which arrested its outgoing flow. The flow of energy is always on the way to actualise itself, but it cannot do so unless the inherent obstacles which kept it in a certain form be removed. This is true not only of the state of pralaya, but in all subsequent stages; for whenever prakṛti is in any of her forms of development, it means that the constituent elements have so stood in relation to one another as to effectuate the desired form; but this form can only change if any one of the guṇas gets greater ascendency than the others than was found in the existing form; but how can the guṇas change the relation of their relative strength? Thus it has to be admitted that the obstacles in the way of the flow of the guṇas in an appropriate direction must be removed before such a transformation can take place. In our ordinary phenomenal experience of conscious or volitional energy also we find that we have but to remove the obstacles in the way of the flow of the material energy consequent upon which the flow commences to actualise. It is for the removal of these obstacles that the Yoga Īśvara is of use as an important element in the metaphysical system of the Yoga. Īśvara removes the barriers of the prakṛti in accordance with the merits and demerits of men and as a result of that she can flow of herself to fulfil the purposes of the purushas; for merit and demerit being but modifications of the prakṛti cannot of themselves remove her barriers and all purushas are absolutely inactive. Vācaspati holds that at the time of the pralaya, Īśvara renounces his body with a desire that it should rise up again when the period of creation commences. As a result of that his pure sattvamaya body returns to the prakṛti and again rises up and connects itself with Īśvara, who then continues to help the order of the creation by his will by removing the suitable obstacles.

Vijñāna Bhikshu differs from Vācaspati in holding that the pure body of Īśvara never returns to prakṛti during the pralaya but that he is always in possession of his pure body, for Īśvara's pure body cannot be regarded as being either limited by time or as possessing potency or saṃskāra which is due to avidyā.

As regards the general Yoga position about Īśvara, Bhikshu says in the *Vijñānāmṛtabhāshya* that the Yoga in order to avoid the difficulties of meeting the imputations of a partial or a cruel Īśvara has accepted the independence of prakṛti in all its winding and unwinding processes. Īśvara is only one of many objects on which a Yogin can concentrate his mind. The only purpose of Īśvara is to do good to his devotees.[1]

1 *Vijñānāmṛtabhāshya*, p. 129.

Bhikshu himself had an ardent religious zeal and he could hardly think of his dear Sāṃkhya to be atheistic in spite of its clear and distinct professions on that side. Thus when he has to explain the atheistic declarations of the *Sāṃkhya-sūtra*, he remarks that these atheistical statements are only exaggerations (*prauḍhivāda*) to show that for acquiring dispassion towards worldly pleasures it is not necessary that one should know Īśvara; or in other words ethical and moral qualities of a man when combined with true knowledge are quite sufficient to bring about salvation for a man, even without a belief in Īśvara.[1] In another place in *Vijñānāmṛta-bhāshya* he says that Sāṃkhya cannot be regarded atheistic, as the Upanishads refer to the Sāṃkhyas as professing an Īśvara in such passages as "*tatkāraṇaṃ sāṃkhya-yogādhigamyam*" and the atheists were held in great disrepute in the Upanishad age.[2]

Vijñāna Bhikshu's comment on the *Vyāsa-bhāshya* shows that he believed that in the pralaya as well as during creation Īśvara was always connected with his pure body as the permanent basis of his eternal knowledge and will. With that pure body Īśvara has his joyous experiences though he has no bondage of abhimāna with them, as is the case with ordinary purushas. It

1 *Pravacana-bhāshya*, 5. 12.

2 *Vijñānāmṛta-bhāshya*, p. 129.

is because Īśvara does not identify himself with his happiness that he is generally spoken of as nirguṇa or without any attribute. Bhikshu thinks that both the prakṛti and the purushas have their truth and reality in his being, and it is by his will that the purushas are connected with the prakṛti. The disturbance of the prakṛti is also due to Īśvara's will (*prakṛtervaishamya-hetuḥ kshobhopi Īśvarecchāta eva—Yogavārttika,* 1. 24). The purushas are regarded as mere sparks of Īśvara. The reality therefore of prakṛti and the purusha cannot be distinguished from the reality of the Īśvara, though their separate existence as such is not denied. Purushas are the parts of which Īśvara is the whole. Bhikshu however controverts the Vedānta view of one Brahma-intelligence as appearing as Īśvara and the individual souls. His main objections are, (1) that in that case the limitations through which the individual could appear should be regarded as limiting Īśvara as well, inasmuch as the limitations which obstruct the pure consciousness (*caitanya*) are to be regarded as the sum-total of the limitations of the individual souls; (2) if again the limitations of individual souls be regarded as different from the limitation of Īśvara then also he cannot be regarded as dominating and controlling the individual souls; moreover if one limitation of an individual soul is broken then also the pure intelligence of that soul may again connect itself with other available limitations, just as the vacuum (*ākāśa*) of a broken jug may again be found as occupying the interior of another jug; (3) the reflection theory of the Vedantists is untenable, for reflection being absolutely unreal, jīva also becomes absolutely unreal, and so the question of its identification with Brahman also fails. Bhikshu says that in his view these difficulties have no place, since the souls are always like sparks of fires, parts of Īśvara at all times; the difference is only apparrent, on account of the semblance of a connection of the souls with their respective buddhis. Emancipation comes in when by true knowledge the soul finds that the prakṛti is distinct from itself, and as a result of that the soul is freed from the bondage of prakṛti and is then lost in its true nature as a part of the Brahman or Īśvara. Concentration as meditating on the meaning of praṇava is therefore of two kinds, namely that of thinking the self as a part of Īśvara the whole, or that of thinking the spiritual nature of the self as distinct from the prakṛti and her effects. In this procedure Īśvara is not affected by the connection of the individual souls with their prakṛti because in the pure sattva there is no room for ignorance and afflictions of the individual souls; but both the prakṛti and the purushas are held in the person of Īśvara, and cannot be thought of as being separate from Him though their independent realities cannot be denied, in the fashion of the monistic Vedānta. The position is designated as one of avibhāga as of milk and water. This view has been only referred to in brief in the *Yogavārttika* as the right conception of Īśvara, and it has been elaborated in great detail in the *Vijñānāmṛtabhāshya.* Thus Īśvara here in the theological aspect appears as the father of us all, and He is always engaged in doing good to us in accordance with our moral conduct. We are at once separate from him as being his sons and yet one with him as he is our father : so long as we are under the bonds of passions and afflictions we are separate from him though in reality we are still in Him; but as soon as these are removed we are free in our essence and again one with Him, though we do not still lose our identity as ourselves all the while. Thus the prakṛti in the Yoga system was generally regarded as being presided over by Īśvara, though there was a difference of views as to the exact nature of His influence. This idea of Bhikshu however is an old one which appears in the diverse Purāṇas and in the *Gītā* in slightly modified forms. We notice in the *Mahābhārata* also that the prakṛti is said to return back to the Paramātman on the release of the purusha. In the Vaishṇava schools of thought also the same line of thinking may be found.

But it is best that we should not discuss this subject at length, as it may leave the impression that the question of determining the relation of Īśvara to souls was one of the main problems of the Yoga philosophy; the sole aim of the later Vaishṇava systems was to bring out the relations between the individual and the Absolute Īśvara as can be determined in thought, emotion and action, and to realise them in devotion; but with Yoga the subject of Īśvara is of secondary interest, whereas the main interest is to remove the afflictions of the *citta* by the cultivation of dispassion and habits of concentration for the release of the purusha; Īśvara is described only as being one of the many objects of concentration; by fixing the attention on Him the Yoga goal may be achieved in a more convenient manner, as He may be pleased to remove the obstacles of the Yoga and thereby make the way smoother for the Yogin; there is also a general belief in Him that He is the father of us all and the dedication of the fruits of all actions to Him has been described as being one of the principal ways of purifying the mind.

CHAPTER IX

Yoga Psychology

The difficulty of putting the ideas of an antique age into modern forms is that they do not often suit them. Not only are the modes of expression different but the methods of enquiry, as well as the interest which guides them in each case, are also different. The interest of the present generation is of a positivistic nature; it generally likes to take the phenomena as they are, and to study their relations, and the end in view is to serve the usefulness of the present world. The modern sciences are tending towards utilitarian ends and psychology is gradually being studied more and more in the light of other exact sciences, and the action and reaction of the mental and the material worlds are daily becoming matters of laboratory investigation, instead of abstract conjectures under the domination of metaphysical theories. It is therefore hardly justifiable to devote a chapter to Yoga psychology in the modern sense of the subject, but it cannot be gainsaid that the problem of knowledge as well as that of the principle on which the arrest, movement and annulment of ideas and emotions depend, was of great importance for the Yoga philosophy. For unlike the other Indian systems of philosophy, emancipation is achieved here not by mere knowledge but by a process of psychological discipline by which it is said that the mind-stuff is absolutely disintegrated and merged in the Prakṛti.

It is therefore necessary before we enter upon a discourse on this Yoga method of mental discipline of an ultramoral type that we should discuss the essential characteristics of the Yoga theory of mind or citta. Translating the word citta as mind in absence of a better word, we may put the question in the form in which we get it in ordinary text-books of psychology, what is citta or mind? The common answer of modern psychology is that it is that which knows, feels and wills. The answer of Yoga is that it is the stuff of consciousness formed of the three guṇas sattva, rajas and tamas with an absolute preponderance of the first; its existence is involved in the mahattattva, and as such it is all-pervasive in its nature. It is infinite in number as each has to serve its respective purusha, and in this aspect it continues to exist till the time of pralaya. Mahattattva is but the collective aspect of this citta material, though the citta should be distinguished from the mahat in this that fresh citta materials are always being evolved in it from the prakṛti, which are always in a state of transformation into the tanmātras and the atoms. The mahat is thus the general name as upholding the mind-stuff and the matter-stuff. This citta in its all-pervasive character is called the kāraṇa citta. This kāraṇa citta holds within itself as its manifestation the kāryya citta transforming itself as the asmitā, the ten senses, the manas, and also the motor power prāṇa by which it transforms itself into the various life faculties. The citta is continually passing through its states, and as such resembles a flame; the movements of the senses and the ego are all absorbed in its movement as different moments, and its substance is composed of their substance. It has an appearance different from them in a continual state of transformation like the flame of a lamp (*vṛttiḥ pradīpaśikhāvat dravyarūpā*), though it remains all the same united with them. Thus the first is the buddhi stage, which has only the mere objective determination (*niścaya*); the second is the stage of asmitā or abhimāna, the ego, which feels all things as belonging to the self as "I am so and so," "mine is this or that;" then there are the five cognitive senses, five conative senses; and the faculties of desire and doubt; these however are all endowed with a dynamic of life called the prāṇa which again is associated with its five characteristic movements which preserve the life-functions called the prāṇavṛtti. The citta as thus associated with its modifications is called the kāryyacitta or citta as effect, and this citta pervades the whole body of the man or animal to whom it belongs and thus may be said to be contracting or expanding according to the extent of the body it occupies. The Sāṃkhya school however, as the *Yogavārttika* notices, does not admit the existence of one citta which contracts and expands according to the body it occupies and it is made up of the fine essence of sattva infinitesimals (the other two being extremely subordinated).

It is however with the kāryyacitta and its modifications that we are directly interested; for the kāraṇacitta is only a hypothetical all-pervasive ground for explaining some of the Yoga miracles. It is this ground, the kāraṇacitta, which in connection with different bodies manifests itself as the kāryyacitta. Its existence is the same as that of the kāraṇacitta under particular limitations.

Thus to repeat our question, what is citta? We find that it involves feeling, willing and knowing in the way that all the three are but the three aspects of the same state. The citta is continually transforming itself into its diverse states, and each state is as much a state of knowing as a state of feeling and willing. The citta and all its transformations are but the modifications of a subtle kind of matter, namely, the three guṇas with the preponderance of sattva. In reality these three guṇas, the substratum of the mentality, are but the three feeling-stuff entities which being plastic and translucent can reflect the objective world or transform themselves into its exact copies. These transformations can be looked at from three distinct aspects : (1) the mould or the form that it has taken of the objective world or any other representation, (2) its flow or movement, (3) its reality as feeling-stuff. These three aspects of any state of citta appears as knowledge, willing and feeling, when it comes in connection with purusha, the pure intelligence. The whole process of intellection consists in the intelligisation of these unconscious modifications of the states. The citta we know is regarded here as being spread all over the body just as the Jains thought of the soul. The contact of citta with the external world takes place through the medium of the active modifications of the senses. External objects are not represented in the citta as they really are but as they are modified by the senses through which they are transmitted. The sense data therefore vary with each individual according to the special characteristic qualities of his senses through which the objects are perceived. The spatial qualities of things as lying about in space are perceived by the senses directly, but the time-order is a scheme of the citta, mind or understanding. As regards the action of the senses in relation to manas Bhikshu says that the Sāṃkhya-Yoga supposes that the senses can directly perceive the determinate qualities of things without any intervention of manas, whereas Vācaspati ascribes to manas the power of arranging the sense-data in a definite order and of making the indeterminate sense-materials determinate. The first stage is the stage of indeterminate percepts (*vālamūkādi-vijñānasadṛśaṃ mugdhavastujaṃ*) when the world of objects is transmitted before the bar of buddhi. The next stage is the stage of assimilation, differentiation and association, by which the indeterminate data are ordered and classified by manas. It is this activity of manas called saṃkalpa which co-ordinates the indeterminate percepts into determinate, perceptual or conceptual forms as class notions with particular characteristics; the different senses may act in succession, as well as simultaneously; the action of the categories of the mind, namely, the actions of buddhi, ahaṃkāra, as well as the senses, also take place sometimes in different moments and sometimes immediately as in the case of fear, etc. Bhikshu who supposes that the determinate character of things is directly perceived by the senses has necessarily to assign a subordinate position to manas as being only the faculty of desire, doubt and imagination. It is important to remember in this connection that citta must be distinguished from buddhi, the faculty of niścaya, co-ordination or determination and ahaṃkāra, the ego, the faculty which actively relates all things with the self as its experiences or as identifying itself with them. According to Yoga these two are to be regarded as the separate vṛttis of the citta in the process of cognition which first discerns a thing as such, and then identifies the thing or its experiences with the experiencer shining forth as the ego; looked at from another point of view these may all be regarded as the working of the same vṛtti, excited either by the senses of presentation or by the representative elements of memory, etc.

The Buddhists characterise the nirvikalpa concept as the mere characterless specific individuality (*svalakshaṇa*); the Bhaṭṭa school holds that it is not mere specific individuality but the appearance of a thing of which the parts and the relations are not distinct (*sammugdhākāraṃ vastu*). It later on develops into the savikalpa stage when it is associated with class notions, attributes, action, name, etc. The Nyāya distinguishes the two stages, the nirvikalpa as the specific individuality, as the basis of the notions of genus, etc., and the savikalpa as the thing characterised or determined by the notions of genus and species (*jātyādisvarūpāvagāhi na tu jātyādīnāṃ mitho viśeshaṇaviśeshyabhāvāvagāhi* —*Tātparyyaṭīkā*, p. 82).

Thus Vācaspati's view with regard to Sāṃkhya and Yoga perception agrees in the main with the Bhaṭṭa view in admitting that in the indeterminate stage neither the genus nor the differentia is presented in consciousness ; all that is present there being only the individual wherein those two subsist. Bhikshu's view runs counter to the other views and reduces the importance of manas in the perceptual process to a minimum, for it holds the nirvikalpa and savikalpa as stages produced by the prolongation of the work of the visual sense.

In discussing the nature of sense perception we find that owing to a defective knowledge of optics, the Hindus were much puzzled and could not explain how the visual sense came in contact with the external objects. Some of the schools of philosophy thought that the visual sense actually protruded itself and reached the objects whereas Yoga held that the visual sense could connect itself with the external objects (even without going over to them) by its processes called vṛtti.

About the auditory perception of words it is said that the sound is produced as vibrations of the air which touch the ear drum and produce the sensation of the sounds of alphabets. The object of the perception of the auditory organs is the śabda tanmātra and not the entities signified by those words.

In connection with the subject of auditory perception, the doctrine of sphoṭa attracts our notice. This doctrine has indeed little or no philosophical importance. But it is so peculiarly associated with the Yoga doctrine that I believe it may be expected of me to enter into a little digression to describe briefly the special features of the theory of sphoṭa. Vācaspati on describing sphoṭa says that each of the letters has the potentiality of manifesting endless meanings but none of them can do it individually; it is only when the alphabet sounds are produced in succession by one effort of speech that these individual alphabets by their own particular contiguity or distance from one another can manifest a complete word called sphoṭa. Thus owing to the variation of contiguity or distance, and by the intervention of another alphabet sound, they may manifest any meaning or word; for the particular order and the association of alphabet sounds depend upon the particular output of energy required in making their utterance. The sphoṭa is therefore a particular modification of the buddhi of that word, whereas the alphabet sounds have their temporary origin in the organ of speech, lasting there only so long as they are uttered, and lasting in the sense of hearing only so long as each one of them is heard. It is well to point out in this connection that the theory that the alphabet sounds themselves are of endless potentiality and can manifest any word sphoṭas according to their particular combinations and recombinations is quite in keeping with the main metaphysical doctrines of the Pātañjala philosophy, though the Sāṃkhya stands against it and denies the existence of any such sphoṭa.[1]

As regards the question of verbal cognition the Yoga holds that it proceeds only from a confusion of (1) the alphabet sounds which are perceived in the sense of hearing, (2) the whole word or śabda manifested in the buddhi, and (3) the corresponding objects existing in the external world denoted by the śabda. The three though altogether distinct from one another yet appear to be unified on account of the saṅketa or sign, so that the alphabet sounds, the sphoṭa word, and the thing can never be distinguished from one another. Of course knowledge can arise even in those cases where there is no actual external object, simply by virtue of the manifesting power of alphabet sounds

[1] In later times however there had been a tendency on the side of Sāṃkhya authors to accept the doctrine of sphoṭa. Thus Sīmānanda says :—*tāni padānyevārthasya karaṇatvāt sphoṭa iti ucyate; taddhi padam vāgindriyoccāryyapratyekavarṇebhyaḥ atiriktam, varṇānām āśutaravināśitayā melanabhāvāt naikam padamiti vyavahāragocaratvāsambhavāt arthasmārakatvāsambhavācca.*—*Sāṃkhyatattvavivecana*, pp. 27, 21.

(*śabdajñānānupātī vastuśūnyaḥ vikalpaḥ*). This saṅketa or convention is defined as the manifestation of memory of the nature of mutual confused identification of words and their meanings. This object is the same as this word and this word is the same as this object. Thus there is no actual unity of words and their objects ; it is only imagined to be so by beginningless tradition. This view may thus be well contrasted with the Nyāya view which says that the convention of words by which they signify objects are due to the will of God (*asmāt śabdāt ayam artho boddhavya iti Īśvarecchārūpaḥ*).

To understand the sphoṭa more clearly we find that first the vocal sound is produced in the mouth of the speaker ; the sound then moves in aerial waves until it reaches the ear-drum of the hearer ; by coming in contact with which it produces the audible sound called dhvani. This sound in the stage of pure varnas is called nāda. The third stage of śabda is that in which the varṇa *g*, *au*, and *ha*, as in the case of the word gauḥ are taken together and the complete word form 'gauḥ' comes before our view The comprehension of this complete word form is an attribute of the mind and not of the sense of hearing ; for the sense of hearing only receives the varṇa sounds as they are produced one by one. But each varṇa vanishes as it is generated, as the sense of hearing has no power to hold them together and comprehend the varṇas in a collective form in a definite order. The ideation of the complete word is called sphoṭa. It differs from the varṇa sounds which die the next moment that they are generated. All significance belongs to this sphoṭa form and it is believed that the varṇa sounds pronounced or heard in a particular order serve to give rise to such ideational word-images which possess denotation and connotation and are thus called sphoṭa. These are essentially different in nature from the varṇa sounds generated in the sense of hearing, which are momentary and evanescent, and can never be brought together to form one whole as the complete word form.

It may not be out of place here to notice that with the exception of Patañjali the grammarian and his followers there are in general no other adherents of the sphoṭa theory in the Yoga fashion in any of the prominent systems of Indian philosophy. Both Kumārila and Prabhākara deny the sphoṭa for they say that when the saṃskāras have to be admitted, even on the sphoṭa view it is better to admit that, with the help of the saṃskāra, the varṇa sounds are sufficient to explain the śabda directly instead of manifesting the śabda sphoṭa as the Yoga holds. The Nyāyavaiśeshika view also discards the sphoṭa on the ground that the varṇas pronounced and heard in a definite order are jointly called a name when they denote a particular meaning or object. The fact that the Yoga should differ on such a technical matter from Kapila Sāṃkhya with which it is philosophically so much united, and hold a view which is held only by Patañjali of the *Mahābhāshya* is therefore the most important argument in favour of identifying the Patañjali of the Yoga with the Patañjali of the *Mahābhāshya*.

We may now conclude the discourse on perception by briefly describing the principal moments involved in the production of the perceptual knowledge. Thus taking for example the visual perception we find first that the connection between the visual sense and the object takes place in absence of the natural obstruction to perception—such as too much remoteness (*atidūrāt*), too much proximity (*sāmīpyāt*), defect of the visual organ (*indriya-ghātāt*), too much want of attention (*mano'nava-sthānāt*), too much fineness (*saukshmāt*), as in the case of atoms, the existence of an obstructing barrier between the organ and the object as by walls, etc. (*vyavadhānāt*), the brightness of objects being overcome by other brighter things as in the case of the stars during day-time (*abhibhavāt*), the non-distinction which a thing suffers when it is lost in its own medium as in the case of drops of water in water. The connection once established between the sense organ and the external object, the citta being modified by the sense organ through which its connection with the external object is made, assumes the form of the object. So it is that the sense of colour, etc., are due in part to the visual organ too. It should be remembered that the citta may also suffer transformations quite simultaneously with the visual modification. The problem of acquired perception is solved here through saṃskāra as in the case of Nyāya. Thus as soon as the citta suffers any transformation through the senses and the saṃskāras acting through the tamas, the tamas or obstruction being removed, the pure citta is tinged and coloured according to the object with which it has been connected. Thus it is that the buddhi has the same form as the external object. In dream experience, though there is no presentation of an external object, the citta through saṃskāra assumes a shape which is akin to the mental object. This transformation of the citta is called a state or vṛtti of the citta; this state is in itself non-intelligent and a species of mind-stuff; but it is raised to the status of valid cognition by being connected with the purusha immediately it is produced. It is the purusha who intelligises these states by receiving the reflection from the buddhi states; the reflection again in the purusha of the buddhi appears as the notion of the ego, or the perceiver of the states.[1] For internal thought also the process of citta transformation is just the same.

The states or vṛttis of citta are described as of five kinds (1) right cognition, (2) illusory knowledge, (3) imagination, (4) sleep, and (5) memory. Right knowledge is said to be of three kinds namely, perception, inference, and scriptural testimony. Of these perception has already been described. Inference is of three kinds : (1) pūrvavat or that from cause to effect, (2) śeshavat, from effect to cause, (3) sāmānyatodṛshṭa, where the inference proceeds from general similarity alone. Anumāna is the process of ascertaining not by perception or by direct observation but through the instrumentality or by the medium of a mark, that a thing possesses a certain character. Inference is therefore based on the establishment of an invariable concomitance between the mark and the character inferred. It is not merely formal nor merely material, but it combines formal validity with material truth, inductive generalisation with deductive particularisation.

Whether we infer the effect such as the rain from the cause, the clouds as in pūrvavat, or infer the cause such as the rain from the flood in

[1] See for the *jñānotpattiprakriyā* of Sāṃkhyayoga, pp. 74-79, of *Vijñānāmṛtabhāshya* of Bhikshu.

the street as in śeshavat, a single condition called a cause is not invariably succeeded by the effect, nor does the phenomenon in general point to any particular cause as antecedent, for there may be a plurality of causes leading to a general effect. The skilful observer will therefore select the full complement of causal conditions, which is invariably succeeded by the effect, and also the specific effect which points to a specific causal antecedent. A specific assemblage of causes therefore has only one assemblage of effects and *vice versa* ; of course the observer is to find out the essential features (as distinguished from irrelevant ones) which being included will enable him to specify the particular cause of the particular effect, and this is done by what is called the knowledge of svabhāvapratibandha or vyāpti.

As regards viparyyaya or the psychology of illusion, Yoga does not hold like Sāṃkhya that the illusion of silver in śukti is due to the fact that the memory of the silver cannot be distinguished from the percept of the object under presentation ;[1] nor does it agree with Vaiśeshika in holding that the memory of silver appears in the form of the percept of śukti which is thus perceived to be thereby of the form

[1] This is virtually the admission of the Akhyāti theory of illusion. Thus Sīmānanda says :—*arthataḥ akhyātivādāṅgīkāraḥ. ata eva dam rajatamiti jñānam na bhramaḥ kintu svarūpataḥ arthataśca aviviktam jñānadvayam, yasya yādṛśamidaṃ rajatamiti rajatajñānavishayībhūtam tādṛśameva jagaditi nirṇayaḥ.—Sāṃkhyatattvavivecana*, p. 32.

of silver. But it holds that it is the śukti which appears in the mind in the form of the silver, for when such direct transformation is possible, there is no necessity of admitting memory of external silver existing at a distant time or place appearing as a present percept.[1] That such a transformation is only mental ideation and not a case of memory appearing as the object under perception, as being perceived, is proved by the fact that with regard to dream consciousness we say that we experienced it in dream but it is no longer present. Such an experience that it is not now but yet it was experienced, shows that the dream experience is a case of mental adaptation of a kind which is not in real existence; for if all illusion is analysed as the appearance of the memory of distant objects in form of things which are perceived at the present moment, then the dream existence could not be regarded as possessing any present existence, and then negated again in the waking time as an existence in the past during sleep. This theory of Yoga illusion is called anyathākhyāti. This illusion is a product of avidyā (ignorance), which we know is

[1] *Svarūpataḥ arthataśca aviviktam jñānadvayam, yasya yādṛśamidam rajatamiti rajatajñānavishāyībhūtam tasya tādṛśameva jagat iti nirṇayaḥ*—Ibid.

defined as a positive knowledge of a thing as that which it is not and not a mere negative non distinction between the right and the wrong thing.

Vikalpa is the existence of abstract imagination on the basis of language symbols, as when we say "the intelligence of the purusha" though we know that the purusha has no other essence than pure intelligence. Without such a characteristic mode of citta transformation abstract thinking would be impossible.

Dreamless sleep is also regarded here as a state of mind in which the tamas predominates over the sattva, on the ground that on awaking a man remembers it as a state of mind. This, as it is easy to see, runs directly counter to the Vedantic teaching that sushupti cannot be regarded as a state of mind for the ātman remains then in a state of its own pure bliss. Bhikshu however tries to make a compromise with the Upanishad texts which are in favour of the Vedantic view by supposing that there are two grades of sushupti, the *ardhasushupti* (half-dreamless sleep) and the *samagra-sushupti* (complete dreamless sleep) and that it is only to the latter case that the Upanishads refer.

When we perceive things, the act or the states of mind as perceiving as well as the perçeptual image of the thing generate in the citta corresponding saṃskāras, potencies or impressions. In the presence of things which have associative bonds with them these are revived, and as a result of that, comes the memory of the thing as well as the state of mind associated with its former perception. The dream state of mind is a result of memory, though the representations are all unreal, and as such the dream states are examples of viparyyaya or illusion. All these different kinds of cognition are the different classes into which the modifications of buddhi can be divided or rather the different images of the buddhi substance.

These modifications of citta as pratyayas or states of mind must however be distinguished from other aspects of citta which cannot be directly experienced, as they represent the character of the citta in its own nature. Thus first of all it has to be admitted that it is possible for the citta to remain in itself without transforming itself into its states, though this its existence in its own nature can never be cognised. This state is called the nirodha state. Ordinarily we find that the citta is incessantly transforming itself into its states in ordinary perception, in representative thought as smṛti and vikalpa, in dream as viparyyaya or as sleep. There is not a moment when the citta is divested of its states in our experience, but still it is the fundamental postulate of Yoga that such a state is possible when the citta remains in itself without transforming itself into the states, for the aim of all Yoga is to reduce the citta to this form. There is also the moral colouring of the citta as virtue and vice, merit and demerit. Then there are the saṃskāras or the impressions in the citta as the ground of memory. There is further the plasticity of the citta, the pariṇāma by virtue of which it is always transforming itself, and there is no t a moment when it is at rest. Then there is also the life functions which are, so to say, almost like bye-products of the citta transformations—the movement which is characterised as the movement of the five vāyus. Further there is the volitional activity or willing (ceshṭā) by which the conative and the cognitive senses are brought in relation to their objects. Then there is also the reserve potent power, śakti of citta, by which the citta can retain itself or change its course and directions. These characteristics are involved in the very essence of citta and form the ground work of the Yoga method of practice, which consists in steadying a particular state of mind and then giving it up and steadying a finer state and so on until the citta is reduced to its pure essence.

On the side of the feelings we know that the guṇas themselves are but feeling materials; so it is that every mental state has not only a tinge of feeling in it, but pleasure, pain and a *feeling* of *ignorance* are all present in the same state of mind, at one and the same time. But the Yoga holds that though all the three feelings are present simultaneously yet it is pain which is the most prominent among them. Even when a feeling of pleasure is felt, there is the pain also in it for howsoever a man may like to be the possessor of any pleasure, he has also the antipathy against its removal, and this antipathy is fraught with sorrow. This antipathy again leaves behind it its potency, and this potency will have a tendency towards repeating the pain feeling. From the feeling of pleasure also there will be new potencies, and these will again try to repeat themselves in new experiences, and these will associate with new turns of antipathy and pains. As our sensitiveness grows, we find that all our experiences are but experiences of sorrow, for not only are the best pleasures mixed with sorrow but they also directly lead to sorrow of themselves; the Yogin alone can feel these subtle shades of pain.

It is not out of place to note here that this pessimism of the Yoga does not necessarily follow from the metaphysics, for pleasure is as much an element of the composite of feelings of each state, as pain, and if owing to the presence of pain all states are to be styled as painful, they may as well be called pleasurable If pleasures lead to pains, pains also lead to pleasures. Sāṃkhya pessimism is not so deep, for there the ambition is to weed out all the roots of pain so that they may not come at all but here all the experiences are felt to be painful. It is well therefore that this pessimism should be distinguished as a special characteristic of the Yoga school.

With regard to the law which regulates the rise and disappearance of emotions, the most important thing is that the growth of the potencies of the contrary feelings always checks the other feelings. The surest mode therefore of driving away a particular type of feelings is to try to habituate oneself to their opposite emotions. Emotions which are of a similar nature always try to help their mutual appearance, and it is only with the rise of the opposite emotions either through self-initiation or through objective influence that the other emotions and their potencies can be destroyed. The law of the appearance or disappearance of any emotion or idea depends on the strength or weakness of their potency. The strength of the potency again depends upon the frequency of occurrence of the emotion or idea and *vice versa*. They may be said to be mutually the cause and effect of each other.

Thus the chief results of psychology with which the Yoga as a system of moral-intellectual practice is interested may be summed up as follows :—

(1) The buddhi is always transforming itself into its states either by the presentative or by the representative process and these states are in the main of the nature of pain.

(2) By concentration it is possible to bring forward any state of mind and by repeating it, its potency may be so far strengthened that that state gradually becomes steady, and all the movements of the mind are arrested.

(3) By the growth of practice and steadiness there might come such an ultimate steadiness, when the buddhi shrinks back to its own essence and there are no states at all.

To conclude the chapter with a brief review of the main problems of psychological interest, we find first that the problem of the interaction of mind and matter has been solved by the supposition that the mind is composed of the same three essences of which the external world is composed; so that the mind or citta being only a translucent counterpart of the same stuff of which the objective world is made up, it can easily tinge or transform itself automatically after the mould or pattern of the objects. In Buddhism we find that there is an apparatus capable of reacting to an impact not itself an impinging form (rūpa) producing an impact of one specific kind, an impact between these two, and the resultant modification of the mental continuum as the intellectual and the feeling result involving the two moments of mutual impact as causing the modification and as constituting the object of attention in the modified consciousness. The action and re-action of sense and sense-object are compared in realistic metaphor to the clash of two cymbals and the butting of two goats, and thus it is that we find it said in the *Aṭṭhasālini* that the "strikes on the eye are receptive of the object consciousness." From the discussions in *Śāstradīpikā*, *Nyāya-mañjarī*, and *Nyāyabindu* also, we collect that the raising of these indeterminate sense-data to the determinate stage is done from within, and so the objective world as it appears in our perception as having name and form and as appearing under class notions and as wholes containing parts and diverse characteristics, is more a creation of the inner imagination than a conglomeration of diverse reals (*puñja*). The Yoga as explained by Bhikshu differs from such a view of the origination of a precept in this that, according to it the indeterminate stage as the contact of the citta with the object, and the determinate stage as the modifications of the citta, both take place in association with the sense through which the unity took place.

Time and association as relative space (*dik*) are generally the only two elements imposed by the buddhi faculty of the citta; in auditory perception however the formation of the whole words on the basis of the dying alphabet sounds is also ascribed to the buddhi. The association of names with objects is also regarded as an illusory confusion between the auditory perception of the name with the objects of perception of the other senses. As regards the relation of the sense-material with the sensations also we find that in spite of the same sense-material there are different sensations for different persons according to the nature and character of the senses through which these are presented to the citta. But apart from limitations of this kind no distinction is made in the perceptual process between the sensory stage and the intelligible stage, and the latter is regarded as the continuity of the former, for the impinging here only brings the citta into contact with the object of presentation; once the contact is established the citta transforms itself into the form of the object. But this citta transformation should be distinguished from the Vedānta transformation of antaḥkaraṇa in that here corresponding with each moment of contact there is a separate modification of the citta, which is constantly changing its states, whether it be in the form of similar or dissimilar ones. In Vedānta however until the presentation changes, the form of the citta remains the same, and there is no such continual change of the citta as is described here.[1]

At this point again though with the Buddhists there is no permanent citta substance, yet there is a great similarity between the Buddhists and the Yoga idea; for with the Buddhists the rise of citta is a mere expression to fix the occasion for the induction of the whole concrete psychosis and also in a variety of other senses such as mental object or presentation (*ārammaṇam*), the process of connecting the last things arising in consciousness with that which preceded them (*sandhānam*), the property of imitative action (*pure cārikam*), etc. The citta is constantly dying and arising, according as it appears with all the sensory objects as its field and its special province of dhammas. Citta may thus be occupied with its past experience, memory, or ratiocination, etc., called sometimes manoviññānam as the dhammas of mano, as well as the cognition of the visual forms, etc., of objects. But in whatsoever mould it may be, its stages are rising and dying. In Yoga also we find that citta is used in all this diversity of senses and even more, and just as can be found here, each stage

[1] *vṛtteḥ svavirodhivṛttyutpattiparyantam sthāyitvābhyupagamāt* (*Vedāntaparibhāshā*, p. 27, Bombay, 1911.)

of citta is continually rising and passing away. But there is this difference that there is a citta substance here, and the states which arise whether in the form of external objects or in the form of inner reflection, etc., are all merely the transitory expressions of the citta substance, which in its essential form is below the threshold of the plane of consciousness. External sensations serve to bring out this potential citta into its actual states as coloured by them. When these presentations are absent, it transforms into the states naturally by the dynamic of its past impressions, and it is this continual burning of the sub-conscious stuff into the conscious states that is called the "flame of consciousness." Until and unless the sub-conscious is brought out in the form of the states it cannot be cognised; in spite of its pure essence it cannot catch the reflection of the soul. This lower region is a store-house of experiences of the most varied kinds in a latent state. The door of that treasure house which is also a work-house, is locked, so far as the conscious experiences of the purusha are concerned. The senses are like the chinks and crevices through which there is a constant coming and going, and the manufactured products of the lower world are continually returning to the upper plane of consciousness and once more entering into the train and sequence of what we call active life; both the invisible processes of this life as well as their root cause are as active as the visibles but from which these are derived. There is a continual movement from below upwards. A never-ending train of images, memories, and ideas keeps emerging into the light.[1] Thus according to the Yoga, citta has two classes of characteristics, visible and the invisible, and it is the latter that controls the former and *vice versa*; for the visible as it passes away into the invisible gradually grows stronger and stronger in the form of potencies according to its frequency and stronger these potencies grow, the more their chance of actualising themselves in the form of visible states.

But not only the plasticity, the change, the movement and life-functions are attributed to this citta, but there is also the reserve power in it called the śakti, by virtue of which it can reflect and react back upon itself and change the passivity of its transformations into active states associated with will and effort. Thus man's thoughts and actions are pure psychological determinations, but in the citta there is the reserve force by which it can act upon itself and determine itself. This force gets its full play in the strong effort required in meditation by which a particular state is

[1] *Cf.* James's description of the sub-conscious.

sought to be kept in a steady condition as a check against the natural flowing tendency.

Aonther point already noticed, which may also be regarded as the important feature of the Yoga psychology, is the distinction of kāraṇa buddhi and kāryya buddhi. The kāraṇa buddhis are pervasive and lie inherent in the stage of mahat. The kāraṇa buddhi expresses itself under the limitations of the body through which it is destined to play its rôle as destined by its karma ; it is the greater psychical store of which only a part is revealed in each individual experience as a fragment. If with certain reservations we may be given the liberty of reflecting upon it in the language of modern psychologists, we may remember here the lines of McDougall, that "each human mind is conceived as but a fragmentary and temporary expression of some larger psychical whole ; and it is sought to explain the supernormal phenomena by assuming that they are rendered possible by some temporary relaxation or breaking down of the conditions by which the isolation of the individual mind is commonly maintained, so that for the time being it may share in the larger life of the whole of which it is in reality a part and may draw psychical or spiritual energy from the common store more freely than is possible in normal condition." It will be easy to see that if this assumption of Yoga proved in future to be verifiable, it will explain many of the unexplained facts of abnormal psychology as also of telepathy, hypnotism and other kindred psychic phenomena.

CHAPTER X

Yoga Ethics

Probably the earliest instance in the history of ethical thought of the schism between the ideal as pleasurable and the good which has in recent times been so much emphasised by Kant is to be traced in the episode of Naciketas and Yama in the Kaṭha Upanishad. Naciketas is filled with a longing to know what becomes of man after death ? Yama asks him to cease from this enquiry, and offers in return all the sensual joys and pleasures of the world ; but Naciketas spurns them all. He would not be satisfied with these transitory pleasures, as he was stirred up by the longing of the infinite within him. And Yama commending this noble conduct says "the good is one thing, the pleasant another ; these two having different objects, chain a man. It is well with him who clings to the good; but he who chooses the pleasant misses his end. The good and the pleasant approach a man : the wise goes round about them and distinguish them. Yea, the wise prefer the good to the pleasant, but the fool chooses the pleasant through greed and avarice. Thou Naciketas after pondering on all pleasures that seem to be delightful, hast dismissed them all. Thou hast not gone into the road that leadeth to wealth, in which many men perish. Wide apart and leading to different points are these two, ignorance and what is known as wisdom. I believe thee Naciketas to be one who desires knowledge, for even many pleasures could not tear thee away." Later on Yama continues, that the self is not to be found by arguments but Naciketas has got it by true resolve, and by renouncing all that could be desired through motives of pleasure. It is this which is the ideal sought for in the Vedas and the goal of brahmacaryya and tapas. The path of truth or knowledge (*vidyā*) is that which leads man towards realising his own true essence as the self, whereas that which leads him to identify himself or his ideal with pleasures or their attainment is avidyā or the path of ignorance and untruth. We know that from the dawn of the Upanishad era of thought, the enquiry after the truth and reality had taken its firm hold upon the enlightened and the elevated, while the ordinary people were still under the sway of the popular gods, engaged in satisfying them with libations and sacrifices to ensure a prosperous and healthy lease of life with their help. This enquiry after true knowledge brought forth a new channel of work through tapas and self-culture, and must be regarded as the dawn of a new ideal which sought the good for its own sake as against the Vedic ideal which worked through the hopes of pleasure and enjoyment. It is no doubt true that we do not find here the ordinary ethical modes of expression with which we are familiar in modern times, but in its essence it has the same ethical character, though it has not yet emerged clear from the theological and metaphysical elements associated with it. We view things from two different points of view, as to how they naturally are or as to how they should be with reference to a certain standard, and call the one "natural" and the other "normative." Ethics thus is a normative science with its subject-matter as human conduct and character, not as natural facts with a history and causal connection with other facts but as possessing value in view of a standard or ideal. The claim of these ideals or ends to be universal and absolute for human life necessarily raises the metaphysical question of the place of human life itself in the whole scheme of things. The metaphysical character of the Upanishad quest consists in this that it had laid its hold upon the ātman as the supreme and permanent reality. But the ethical aspect is also quite as strong, for the knowledge of self is not a mere subject of metaphysical discussion, but it shows itself as an imperative upon all persons as the supreme ideal "Thou shouldst know the self." No one would be remoter from truth than he who should think that the result of the Upanishad teaching is a mere pantheistic creed, that it is the self which is the only reality and all else is māyā ; for even if this extreme Vedantic monism be taken to be the only teaching of the Vedānta, we find here a subjective ethical ideal which grows up with the evolution of thought, and the supreme creative and presiding power of the universe becomes identified with the psychical principle in man ; salvation lies in the personal recognition of this identity, and the ethical value of actions was reckoned not so much according to an objective scale of utility as according to a subjective calculus of their significance and result to the doer. Thus it is that we find that though the ultimate salvation was achieved by knowledge, and though there had grown up a general school of thought or tendency which exaggerated its supreme importance as the only end in view, a definite system of self-renunciation, self-culture and the practice of many cardinal virtues had come to be regarded as absolutely indispensable for qualifying oneself for furthering his great ambition of achieving this supreme subjective ideal. Thus not only do we find the commandments relating to the ordinary civic duties, such as that of truthfulness, right conduct, righteousness, obedience to parents and teachers, making gifts, etc. (as in the Taittīrīya Upanishad) but the much more advanced code, namely, that of controlling the senses and of keeping the mind in a state of steady meditation. The ideal of self-attainment presupposed the highest perfection of the ordinary ethical duties as being indispensably essential for the purpose. "He who has not first turned away from his wickedness, who is not tranquil and subdued, or whose mind is not at rest, can never obtain the self by knowledge" (Kaṭha., ii, 23). The Upanishads assert a hierarchy of joys, and the highest of all joys and blessings is the realisation of the good, the Brahman, the self. But yet it is not hedonism; the supreme realisation of man's own psychical principle as the ultimate cosmical reality is the ethical form to which all ethical actions are to be subordinated; the performance of objective moral duties are essential only so long as by their performance such a perfection of the mind is not brought about as may stand as a sure guarantee against any misdeed, and it is in such a perfect state of the mind that there may dawn forth the true knowledge. So we see also that as the true identification of the self with pleasure or with any earthly object is avidyā, it is the source of all that is ethically bad. The root of all good and evil is thus psychological as they are the direct results of right knowledge and ignorance respectively.

Yoga ethics also has to take this avidyā as the root of all evil, in the sense that all that is bad is due to it. We have spoken of avidyā in some of the previous chapters, but there we had only looked at it from the point of view of metaphysics ; but in Yoga it has a great importance from the point of view of ethical conduct as we shall try to show presently.

Ethics presupposes a conflict between the ideal and the actual which the will has to overcome, and this necessarily brings the question of the principle of evil. Prakṛti in herself cannot be regarded as evil in any way, as she is a reality existing side by side with the souls. But when they come to regard the worldly objects (all evolutes of prakṛti) as being endowed with attributes that they do not really possess, the psychological confusion leads to a series of blunders and misfortunes. The appearance, the ignorance, is the real cause of the evil. The evil does not therefore really exist it is the mere shadow that appears as the ghost and creates all the fear and unrest. It is an eternal psychological confusion, which having taken root from beginningless time is necessarily and naturally repeated again and again.

Thus it is through this ignorance that this changeful order of the universe is regarded by us as having been in existence permanently and eternally ; or that this body though impure from every consideration is regarded as pure, as is seen in the fascination, charm and passion that women generate in us, and we think "The girl is attractive like the moon. Her limbs are as it were made of honey and nectar. She looks as if she has emerged from the moon. Her eyes are large like the leaves of a blue lotus ; with playful flashes of her eyes she imparts life to the world of men ;" or again when a person thinks that merit (*puṇya*) is attained by the animal sacrifice for worldly happiness, or when a person takes to such works as most of our worldly duties are, which are in reality of no other use than of increasing sorrows and troubles ; or again in spite of the fact that all that appear as pleasurable are in reality fraught with pains, we think them as essentially pleasurable ; or again when we think of the mind, body, friends, or relatives as being ourselves and suffer in their sufferings thinking them to be our own. This is what is called avidyā, the ignorance which confuses a thing with such characteristics as it really does not possess. From such an ignorance comes egoism (*asmitā*) which is but the immediately succeeding moment of the confusion. Thus for example when once the confusion has arisen that the mind is the self, the self naturally proceeds to identify itself with the affections of the mind. We first identify ourselves with wife, son, relatives, and then think of their sorrows and pleasures as being ours. This egoism however is only a moment in the development of avidyā as it unfolds itself in its concreteness, and must, from the point of ethical value, be distinguished from its theoretical aspect as a cosmic principle of creation in metaphysics. From the psychological confusion and ignorance comes this tendency by which man begins to think of all things as his own, and from this comes his desire and attachment for pleasures and antipathy to pains called rāga and dveṣha, and the instinctive desire (*abhiniveśa*) to live, which man shares in common with all animals.

It is thus that ignorance which readily expresses itself as egoism works in the threefold way, namely the desire for pleasures, antipathy to pains, and desire for life. All other vices are but separate forms of manifestation of any one of these. The egoism acting through ignorance is the root of all evil.

But the question comes in that under such a supposition all experiences become evil, and there is no scope for good, nor is there any chance that some external agent should cut asunder the knots of ignorance. The ethical ideal or standard of actions also therefore fails, for, how should one strive after the true knowledge of the self, so long as the ignorance continues, for all strife and moral endeavours of the will are the productions of this ignorance, and can in no way therefore tend to its dissolution and the rise of self-knowledge. It is a fact that we are always prompted to action for the achievement of pleasures and for love of life, it does not matter if it is due to mere ignorance, for this ignorance is our very nature and existence, and all the world is moving under its guidance. Where is the saving virtue to be found? Where again are we to find the distinctions of moral and immoral, good and bad? And if ultimately there is no distinction why not follow Aristippus or Cārvāka?

The Yoga however thinks that it is possible for us to remove this ignorance, and it is on this possibility of the ideal being actualised by will that morality can find its scope. We have already discussed in detail how this ignorance came into being, and we have also noticed that there is also in prakṛti an innate tendency towards destroying this ignorance and releasing the soul. If prakṛti herself were not dominated by such a purpose, not only moral actions would be impossible, but even the existence of moral ideas and purposes would be inexplainable; and motives of pleasure and love of life would be the only motives, and morality would be reduced to mere prudence. Thus it is that there is not only an inclination in us towards pleasure, but also a tendency to turn away from pleasure and seek to discover our own true nature. Both these tendencies are therefore equally innate in our minds. This is not however a characteristic which is peculiar to mind, for it has only inherited it from prakṛti, the supreme mother. Thus it is therefore that the order of material events and things cannot throw any obstruction to the actualisation of the moral will. Mind and matter are both permeated by such a unity of purpose that it is as much possible for us to be good as to be bad.

The states of mind are good or bad according as they are calculated to loosen the bonds of ignorance or fasten them all the more. Such is the innate tendency of prakṛti that though she acts and relates herself to the purushas through ignorance and its manifold manifestations, she also takes a reverse process and is ready to continue it until the bonds of ignorance are finally removed and the purusha is let alone. It remains for us therefore to avail ourselves of this tendency of the mind towards the good—liberation and self-realisation—and to form a habit of associating ourselves with it and it alone, so that the other tendency which leads us after the wandering fires of pleasure may gradually lose all its strength for us. It is according to this difference of moral tendency that all states of mind may be divided as good and bad or unafflicted (*aklishṭa*) and afflicted (*klishṭa*). With the ordinary persons mental states are in a state of constant change and flow and the good and moral ones are peeping in and immediately passing away but in the case of moral men the good states preponderate, and bad ones visit them only occasionally like unwelcome guests. He alone can be good who has been straining himself to attain the habit of always cultivating moral emotions and ideas and eschew immoral ones. For such is the mechanical condition of mind that the more the good ones are repeated the more their potencies are formed, and the more do they mechanically reappear before the conscious plane; and the same is true of bad and immoral emotions and thoughts. To be moral therefore means to form a moral habit, to avail oneself of the moral emotion, will, and thoughts, and to habituate the mind to them.

The reason why it is so difficult to be moral or spiritual is to be found in the fact that we are more in the habit of placing ourselves under the power of the immoral emotions such as those of pleasure and of self-love. This has made their potencies so strong, that even quite against our will they are again and again revived, and we drift along with them. But the potencies of the higher demands of spiritual life and emotions, thoughts, etc., suited to that end are not altogether lost, and they also manifest themselves from time to time in the conscious plane and prompt us to follow their lead, and the more the suitable environments of good company, moral instructions, etc., are found the more is the chance of these moral potencies gaining in strength and overcoming the immoral potencies.

It is indeed a foolish hope to cherish that, as prakṛti has naturally a tendency towards destroying the avidyā bonds she will do it of herself naturally, and it is unnecessary for us to energise. For the moral purpose of the prakṛti towards self-realisation is shown in no other way than by that of interposing moral emotions and thoughts against immoral propensities; it remains therefore for us to energise, and by strenuous efforts of will to drive away the immoral propensities by the positive formation of moral habits. Thus if a man associates himself continually with evil thoughts, his moral emotions are gradually more and more stifled, and he may gradually be further off from the path of the good. But it may so happen that in some future time he may come into the midst of such good environment that moral potencies may be generated in him, and he may by his will so cultivate them that he may attain salvation. All men therefore have with them the power of being good and of attaining salvation, and though the fear of being immoral may forever be removed in the case of an emancipated person, the hope of redemption is never lost to man however degraded his present condition may be.

The ideal of conduct for a Yogin is the removal of ignorance and the realisation of the true nature of the self and thus ultimately to dissociate the soul from the bondage of matter. This end can only be attained when even the last germ of the avidyā potency has been removed. For such a complete removal it is first necessary that the Yogin should safeguard himself against the inrush of any new emotions of pleasure or self-love by dissociating himself completely from all attachments to all pleasures which are attainable in the ordinary course, by religious worship and sacrifices. He must weaken the strength of the immoral instincts by the formation of opposite moral habits of thought and the acquirements of positive mental virtues, such as that of purity, contentment, etc., which will help him in gaining equanimity and balance of mind. Last of all when the mind has once been prepared in that way to follow by the most strenuous effort of the will the process of Yoga meditation, the mind will be brought to a state of ultimate perfection, and the self will shine forth in its own clear and unsullied life. So far as this last Yoga process is concerned it is easy to see that it transcends the highest limits of our ordinary ethics. We shall therefore first describe the first stages which are generally called the Yogāṅgas or accessories to the Yoga, and then describe the Yoga process.

Like Jainism, Yoga counts ahiṃsā as the one moral ideal; for all external conduct, and all the other virtues are subordinate to it in the sense that ahiṃsā includes them all. These virtues are: (1) veracity (*satya*) which consists in word and thought being in accord with facts, (2) abstinence from theft, which consists not only in not taking the things of others unlawfully, but in removing even the desire thereof (*asteya*), (3) continence, (4) absence of avariciousness, the non-appropriation of things not one's own, consequent upon seeing the defects of attachment and of the miseries caused by accumulation, preservation, etc. (*aparigraha*). A Yogin must observe these duties universally and unconditionally. The maxims of moral conduct then are, "Thou shalt not injure any being, thou shalt not speak an untruth, thou shalt not steal, thou shalt not be avaricious." But the last three maxims can be brought under the one grand maxim, "Thou shalt not injure any being on any condition whatsoever." Thus it is that in case of a conflict of duties, say for example, between truthfulness and non-injury, it is the latter which is to be followed and not the former.[1] The fulfilment of these laws is technically called in Yoga, *yama*. According to the variety of circumstances, persons and conditions, the vices such as hiṃsā, etc., may be of infinite kinds, but in every case it brings to us sorrow and takes us down the path of ignorance, and hence away from self-realisation.

The other observances called *niyama*, which are said to help the Yogin, are cleanliness, contentment, tapas, study and making Īśvara the motive of all actions (*Īśvara-praṇidhāna*); of these cleanliness may be regarded as being of two kinds: (1) external, which consists of eating pure things, washing, etc., (2) internal, which consists in removing the impurities of the mind. Contentment is the absence of desire to secure more than the bare necessaries of life. Tapas or asceticism consists in the endurance of opposites such as that of the desire for food and drink, cold and heat, and, in the absence of speech and facial indications. Study refers to that of philosophy which shows the way to liberation. Īśvarapraṇidhāna means the performance of all

[1] It is important to remember in this connection that the Jains had also exactly the same code of morality and Hemachandra in his *Yogaśāstra* relates how Kauśikī having told the truth in pointing out the way of the bandits to the villagers had violated the law of ahiṃsā and gone to hell.

actions and the dedicating in mind of all the fruits to be reaped therefrom to Īśvara without the slightest personal desire.

So far we have seen that in external conduct the Yogin has to follow the universal law of not committing any harm to any being and to strengthen himself by limiting the course of all other actions in accordance with the observances, the niyamas. For merely by non-injury the Yogin only avoids the vices, but he is to see that his other works may also be suitable for his purpose, for such an end restraining himself from injury, he has to follow the niyamas or the observances.

But in his attempts to follow this procedure obstacles may come in, and the remedy lies in meditation on the evil effects of those bad desires (*pratipakshabhāvanā*). Thus in spite of his self-restraint when the desire of doing injury to others comes to his mind, he is to think of the troubles and griefs and rebirths which this injury causes, and he should make his resolve that when once he had forsaken it with difficulty he should not take it upon him again, as it is the source of all mischief. We have already noticed that the chief moral obstacles are the attachments to pleasure, self-love, and the will to be ; it is necessary therefore in order to weaken the strength of these manifestations of ignorance by trying to take them at their real value and by meditating upon their defects. Thus for example when pleasure attracts us, we may think that it is but a bubble which is not only fraught with pain itself but will gradually draw us into more and more pain, and there is pain everywhere in all the manifestations of avidyā. Sorrow, sorrow, sorrow, everywhere, excepting the right knowledge which releases the soul and takes it beyond the bonds of pain and pleasure.

This thinking of the contrary nature or the opposite character of things which appear attractive through ignorance or tempt us in the path of evil, reacts upon the will by tending to generate right estimates of things. The right observances serve to make the mind pure, remove desires, and tend to strengthen the will and prepare it for the great Yoga meditation. But still it may be said that until the mind is at peace with the world, the great duty of the yama of ahiṃsā cannot be performed merely by thinking of the evil effects of the corresponding vices (*vipakshabhāvanā*), particularly because in ordinary minds the desire for salvation is not strong enough to resist the temptation. It is therefore necessary that the mind should be at perfect peace with the world by a willing culture of the emotion of friendliness (*maitrī*) towards all those who are leading a life of pleasure, of compassion towards those who are virtuous, and indifference towards the vicious. Whoever shows friendliness towards the happy is purged of the dirt of envy, whoever wishes to remove the miseries of others through compassion (*karuṇā*) is purged of the propensity of doing mischief to others. Complacency (*muditā*) removes jealousy, and indifference towards sinners, removes impatience and anger. Thus by the culture of these positive emotions the mind becomes inclined to the side of mental restraint. When the mind is thus purged of its dross the Yogin takes his Yoga practice for the ultimate realisation of his purpose.

When the general tendency of Upanishad teaching referred to avidyā sometimes as the non-knowledge of the identity of the individual soul with the supreme reality the Brahman, and sometimes as the tendency which attracts men towards worldliness, we had a plastic and indefinite conception which could be interpreted by the later Vedantists as a mysterious metaphysical principle which in some mysterious way helped the Brahman in the production of this world-appearance (*cf.* the Śaṅkara view of māyā of Vācaspati). The other side of it as a mere want of right knowledge of things and one's true interests, was also however present in the same conception. Thus it is that when we enquire into the meaning of avidyā, which is placed at the beginning of the causal nexus in

Buddhism, we find that it is within the range of earthly tangible reality, as it means the ignorance of the four sacred truths. Sārīputta says, "Not to know suffering, friend, not to know the origin of suffering, not to know the extinction of suffering, not to know the path to the extinction of suffering is called ignorance." In Buddhism being is suffering, but ignorance totally deceives us as to this suffering, it causes us to see suffering as a phantom of pleasure and happiness, the impermanent as the permanent, the non-soul as the soul. Precisely the same is the definition of avidyā in Patañjali (*anityāśuciduḥkhānātmasu nityaśuçiduḥkhātmakhyātir avidyā*). But the content is different, for in the case of Yoga we have two entities—purusha and prakṛti which stands as the vehicle of all that is impermanent, sorrow, non-soul and impure, and thus though the psychological and moral positions are almost the same there is a difference in the conception of avidyā.

Again, when we look to the other derivatives which are said to be the root of all ethical troubles, we find that avidyā, rāga and dvesha are the same as moha, lobha and dvesha of the Buddhists. Thus Rhys Davids writes: 'The three bad roots are greed, hate and want of intelligence; the first three are so radical and inclusive as sources of all human suffering that, the extinction of them, is one of the few positive definitions given of Nibbāṇa."

The ethical function of ahaṃkāra or asmitā is also the same, and we read in the *Sutta Nipāta* :—

> "He who doth never think ''Tis mine,'
> Nor 'others have gotten something' thinketh this,
> There is nothing for me ! No 'mineness' (*mamatvam*) being found
> In him he hath no cause to suffer grief."

There is also the same analysis of saṃsāra as the source of all sorrows. In Yoga as well as in Buddhism, "the state as it surrounds us in this world, with its restless oscillation between origination and decease, is our misfortunes. The ground of our existence is our will. This is our besetting sin, that we will to be (*cf. abhiniveśa*), that we will to be ourselves, that we fondly will our being to blend with other beings and extend. The negative of the will to be cuts off being, for us at least."[1]

Not only in the origin of ethical troubles do we find Yoga and Buddhism the same, but we find also in the attainment of the ethical ideal that the method followed is the same. The

[1] Compare also the same Sāṃkhya teaching on this point in the *Kārikā*

> *Evam tattvābhyāsānnāsmi na me nāhamityapariśesham*
> *Aviparyyayādviśuddham kevalamutpadyate jñānam.*

same *maitrī*, *karuṇā*, etc., and *ahiṃsā*, the same (*śauca*, *santosha* and *tapas*). Thus it is that with the exception of *Iśvarapraṇidhāna* and the general metaphysics, Buddhism has almost the same ethical scheme as the Yoga, and when we consider the details, we find that the Yoga ethics remarkably agrees with that of the Buddhists.

But still so far as we understand Buddhism, it seems that there is little difference between the Buddhist and the Yoga ideal. For the Buddhist finds nothing but pain all round him, and the good for him is thus only good with respect to karma that is to pleasurable effect or eudaemonia. "With respect to the supremely good—arhatship or nirvāṇa," says Rhys Davids, "he might, it is true, have admitted a difference, namely that this state was absolutely good, and not good because of its results. It was the supreme result or fruit, and there was 'no beyond.' But then he did not rank Nirvāṇa exactly in the category of good, and precisely for this reason that in it moral causation culminated and ceased." It was rather a freedom than a good. Good at which we aim in all our lower quests is sukham, in the one high quest, vimutti or Nirvāṇa. But even the Nirvāna is spoken of in terms of pleasurable feeling and Gotama attaining his enlightenment is said to have experienced emancipation, bliss or vimuttisukham; Nāgasena also emphatically declares Nirvāna to King Milinda to be absolute happiness or ekāntasukham.

The *Sāṃkhya Kārikā* also describes the object of human endeavour as being the final removal of all pains ; Yoga also analyses all feelings and emotions as being nothing more than pain. It is through ignorance that we are deluded into thinking that the pains are pleasures. But it is also an ignorance that we are driven to hanker after pleasures and avoid pains. The avoidance of pain is not therefore the object of our endeavours but dissociation from saṃsāra. But why should we tend to dissociate ourselves from saṃsāra, because the tendency of our mind towards salvation (*kaivalyārtham pravṛtteśca*) is as innate as the tendency towards the attaining of pleasure and binding us with the saṃsāra. But why should we take the former course and avoid the latter, if both the tendencies are our own ? The latter is an unreal connection due to ignorance, and there is no particular reason for us to follow this tendency alone ; for if it be pleasure that attracts us to this course, a careful analysis shows to us that there are in reality pains and not pleasures. The final achievement also, mukti, is dissociation from prakṛti, and the testimony of the self in its own nature. It is not a state of pleasure but kaivalya—oneness. Thus it is that though the dissociation from the prakṛti involves the ultimate dissociation from all pleasure and pain, such a course is followed not with the purpose of the attainment of an ultimate state of happiness, but for removing that instinct inherent in our nature which seeks to be free. Prakṛti cannot realise herself only in drawing us through the bonds of ignorance but she wants to realise herself by setting us free. We are conscious of these tendencies of prakṛti through the mind, its product ; we find there that both are imperative with us, when we give ourselves up to desires of enjoyment (*bhogapravṛtti*) we have saṃsāra, and when we give ourselves up to the tendency of liberation (*kaivalyapravṛtti*) we have liberation. The schism of śreyas and preyas is therefore innate in our nature, and that course of conduct which binds us in the meshes of the preyas, the pleasurable, and bhoga, the enjoyment, is immoral, whereas the conduct which leads us onward to the śreyas or liberation is moral. The moral dignity of the Yogin will appear in this that with him the attractions of earthly pleasure and the great pleasure of heaven are worth nothing compared with the supreme happiness that comes from the destruction of lust When the gods tempt an advancing Yogin with the transitory sensual pleasures of their heaven, "Sir will you sit here, will you rest here, here is an attractive pleasure, here is an attractive girl, this elixir wards off old age and death," the Yogin turns his back to all these temptations and says "Baked on the pitiless coals of the round of rebirths, wandering about in the blinding gloom of birth and death,—hardly have I found the lamp that dispels the darkness of the moral defilements, the lamp of Yoga,—when, these lust-born gusts of the things of sense threaten to put it out; how then could it be that having seen its light tricked by the mirage of the things of sense, I should throw myself like fuel into that same fire of the round of rebirths as it flared up again? Fare ye well, like unto dreams are ye! they are to be pitied that crave these things of sense!" Howsoever great and supreme any happiness might be it must lead to pain, so happiness cannot be the goal towards which a Yogin should move. His goal is freedom from the bondage of the prakṛti and this ambition of his is ultimate and irreducible, for it is innate with prakṛti to tend towards liberating the purushas from their own shackles. It is through the tendency of prakṛti that men desire pleasures and thereby suffer pains, and it is through prakṛti again that men desire mukti and are freed from all pleasure and pain.

The stoics also wanted to turn away from nature; they also found the world to be full of pain, and thus sought to return to the philosopher's quietness of reason. But this life of reason was a life of happiness. It is only by a later modification of stoicism that cheerfulness or peace of mind, is taken as the real ultimate end, to which the exercise of virtue is merely a means. In Zeno's system it is good volition, and not the feeling that attends it, which constitutes the essence of good life. But even then pleasant feeling of some kind must always have been a prominent element in the popular conception of "well-being," and it is probable that the serene joys of virtue and the grieflessness which the sage was conceived to maintain amid the worst tortures, formed the main attraction of stoicism for most minds. It is this that gives stoicism its hedonistic tinge. The Yoga however did not aim at any such philosopher's serene happiness, but the extinction of the source of happiness and pain. In the emancipated stage there was not only no pain but no pleasure also, for it was prakṛti which was the feeling principle, and this was no part of a man's essential nature as pure reason. The stoics thought that pain came only because we could not reconcile our essentially rational nature to the happiness of the world, which in essence are all rational in the highest degree. The Yoga however found that pain formed an essential constituent of the three types of feelings —the prakṛti—and could only be avoided by a complete dissociation of the purusha from the feeling stuff, the prakṛti ; and consequently from the cessation of all the psychological experiences which are but composites of the ultimate feeling materials, the sattva, rajas and tamas. Such a psychological dissociation was but the other name for the dissociation from mind (*citta*). It is thus that the dissociation from mind and all experiences associated with it, is called mukti. When in the first stages we find that the Yogin analyses the world-experiences as painful and thus grows averse to them, we are led to trace a tinge of hedonism in it, but when we find that the practice of virtues, the cessation of worldly actions, the serene happiness and knowledge of meditation are all but means to the dissolution of Avidyā and the freedom of the pure intelligence to purusha, we are forced to say that it is not hedonism. Even the Vedantic ideal [1] had to offer a state of bliss in the supreme merging of the self in the Brahman though it be of a transcendental nature, but the Yoga has no such temptation to offer, for if the state of mukti is a state of painlessness, it is because it is the pure purusha absolutely dissociated from

[1] There are however Vedantists who deny that in Brahmanhood there can be any positive ānanda.

the feeling principle of prakṛti. To the question why we should move ourselves to attain such a state the Yoga answer is that it is as natural a tendency of the human mind as that which takes the world as its own and holds the experiences of pleasure, pain, etc., as belonging to the purusha, the pure intelligence. The highest end of the Yogin is not to avoid pain or even the world experiences that lead to it, for then he could have been satisfied when he passed into the nirvicāra or ānanda stage of samādhi; but no, he is not satisfied there, for the ultimate goal before him is the removal of avidyā and the dissolution of the prakṛti. It is easy to see that such a goal is not a goal of feeling but a goal of an innate tendency towards the destruction of avidyā and the absolute freedom of the spirit. If to the worldly person it is held as a state of absolute painlessness, it is because the state of freedom is also the highest good, even from the worldly point of view which seeks to avoid pain; any other attempt which aims at pleasure of any kind must fail, for it will necessarily bring pain; so the true aim of all persons ought to be the avoidance of pain, and the ultimate stage of such an aim is the dissolution of prakṛti. So the mukti is not only the natural ideal of man but also the highest good, as it involves the ultimate uprooting of the source of all feelings, the prakṛti.

The notion of mukti is indeed the pivot on which all systems of Indian philosophy revolve. The word *mukti* is derived from the root *muc* to be free from. Mukti therefore means the true transcendent nature of the self free from any touch or association with prakṛti. But apart from any such negative conception, there is also the positive content that in this state uncontaminated by any impurity, the self remains in itself ; of course the self cannot in any state be sullied by any impurity, but yet in the saṃsāra stage, since the prakṛti is continually transforming herself differently with reference to different souls, these transformations of prakṛti as thoughts and ideas carry with them the conviction that they belong to a person, and thus there is a seeming association of the self with prakṛti, by virtue of which the pure self appears as the person who enjoys and suffers, wills and thinks. Strictly speaking the self can have neither bondage nor freedom. The state of bondage is thus a state of prakṛiti in which the prakṛti can undergo such transformations (in the shape of thought, feeling and willing) with reference to any purusha as are interpreted with reference to it or as belonging to it. The self has no consciousness in our ordinary sense of the term, but it is the postulate of all phenomenal consciousness. The nature of the self is said to be pure cit (intelligence). This cit is not ordinary intelligence but a transcendent entity. It is devoid of any action or feeling. This cit is never demonstrated in its absolute purity in any of our ordinary conscious states, but is revealed at the stage just preceding mukti or final emancipation. The self is neither consciousness nor unconsciousness but the transcendent intelligence of absolute homogeneity. The Upanishads had spoken of such an ātman as pure transcendent intelligence and the Sāṃkhya-Yoga had accepted it as a legacy from them, and postulated it as being indispensable for the interpretation of conscious states. According to Sāṃkhya-Yoga, our mental states become conscious only because they happen with reference to a purusha from whom they catch reflection. The phenomena of mental states differ from the phenomena of happenings in the objective world in that they happen immediately and directly with reference to a purusha, and are made of such stuff that they can catch reflection from it (purusha). What the exact nature of this purusha as pure intelligence is, we cannot say, for it is a transcendent entity.

Sāṃkhya differs from Buddhism in holding that the mental states by their mutual correlation, movement collocation or conglomeration cannot generate consciousness. The element of consciousness in the mental states is derived from an extraneous principle. The ultimate purpose or realisation of citta is accomplished when it succeeds at the final stage in producing in consciousness an image of this transcendent entity, the purusha ; and when this is once done the purpose or teleology of citta being fulfilled, it cannot hold itself any longer, but is disintegrated and dissolved and the purusha, the absolute, shines forth alone by itself in the eternal state of kaivalya.

But how far is man responsible for his actions, how is the problem of the relation of free will and karma to be solved ? This question did not occur in this form in any prominent manner in Sanskrit works, for the supposition always was that man was free to work, and he was responsible for his karma or actions. The fact that man has to suffer for his actions to such an extent that he cannot avoid it even by death, as he will have to be born again for reaping their fruits, makes it not only necessary that there should be a harmony between the external order of necessity and change and the moral order dependent upon the realisation of an ideal by the will, but also that man should be free to act. All the systems of Indian Philosophy except the Cārvāka agreed upon the law of karma as determining the differences in the fortunes and experiences of pleasure and pain between man and man in social life, and the question of the opposition of freedom and karma did not rise at all as an important point of discussion. When we however approach it with our minds steeped in western philosophy to meet the discussion of free will and determinism we find it difficult to reconcile them. If the individual should depend upon his karma of a previous birth for his mental endowments and physical environments and sufferings and enjoyments, where is the scope of his free will to act? His previous karmas brought about his present state and through that determined his present karma, and this again determines a future state and karma. There is thus throughout a process of dependent origination and decease (*paṭiccasamuppāda*). The apparent soul is only a tool in the hands of this eternally moving causal nexus and it is thus that Buddhism which laid stress upon this process of karma had dismissed the soul altogether.

Looking at the problem from another point of view we find that it is determinism, psychological and external, which gives the scope for the moral struggle. If we had not to struggle against the forces leading us the other way there would be no moral conflict, no development of moral will, and the spheres of the normative and the natural would coincide. This modifies our position with regard to the problem of free will, and we ask ourselves how far we are free, and how far we are determined. Since all karma stands in Indian Philosophy as the principle of determinism, the question returns again, What is the nature of karma? How does it limit our freedom?

To enquire into this problem we find that as in Buddhism so in Yoga, karma means all that we do in thought, word and deed. The first one is called the mānasa karma, and the other two the vāhya karma. These are again divided as (1) kṛṣṇa, (2) śukla, (3) śuklakṛṣṇa and (4) aśuklakṛṣṇa. The kṛṣṇa (black) karmas are those committed by the wicked and as such are wicked actions which pass also by the name, adharma. These again are of two kinds: (1) external, of the nature of speaking ill of others, stealing others' property, and (2) mental as in having such states as are opposed to śraddhā, vīrya, etc. The śukla karmas are the virtuous or meritorious ones which can happen only in the form of good mental states such as, śraddhā, vīrya, smṛti, samādhi and prajñā, which are infinitely superior to any good actions that may be achieved in the external world. The śukla karma can thus only accrue to those who resort to study and meditation. The śuklakṛṣṇa karmas are the actions achieved in the external world and they are called white and black because actions achieved in the external world cannot be devoid of some wickedness as they must necessarily be associated with some harm at least to the living beings—*yadyāvat vahissādhanasādhyam tatra sarvatrāsti kasyacit pīḍā; nāpi vrīhyādisādhane karmaṇi parapīḍā nāsti avaghātādisamaye api pipīlikādibadhasambhavāt.* We in ordinary circumstances are thus always in all our external actions earning dharma and adharma, and may thus be said to be lying on the bed of karmas (*karmāśaya*). Dharma and adharma are thus called the karmāśaya and they proceeding from śukla and aśukla karma produce pleasures and pains. The aśuklakṛshṇa karma belongs to those who have renounced all the fruits of their good actions to Īśvara, and whose present body is the last one. They do not perform any black actions, nor reap the fruits of good ones, having dedicated them all to Īśvara.

The root of all karmas and hence of karmāśayas is the fivefold group of avidyā, asmitā, rāga, dvesha and abhiniveśa, so long as they are not removed; all karmāśaya, dharma or adharma must ripen and give their fruit, but once the roots are removed, all karmas and karmāśayas are also necessarily destroyed and cannot give their fruits. The afflictions or kleśas are like the streams of water which nourish the karmāśayas, and thus when once the afflictions are destroyed, the innumerable vehicles of actions accumulating from beginningless time having no scope for their fruition (as the very seed of their existence, the avidyā has been burnt) are destroyed.

Karmāśaya is again classified from the point of view of the time of its fruition as *dṛṣṭajanma-vedanīya* (ripening in the same life) and *adṛṣṭa-janmavedanīya* (ripening in another unknown life). The puṇyakarmāśaya which is generated by intense purificatory action, trance and repetition of mantras and the pāpakarmāśaya which is generated by repeated evil done to men who are suffering the extreme misery of fear, disease, and helplessness or to those who place confidence or to those who are highminded and perform tapas, ripen into fruit in that very life, and may thus be called *dṛṣṭajanmavedanīya.* Other kinds of actions take fruition in other future lives. The living beings in hell must be taken as an exception to dṛṣṭajanmavedanīya, for as their bodies and lives are intended for sufferance alone, no karmāśaya can accumulate for them. So also, those saintly characters who have destroyed their afflictions must be taken as exceptions to adṛṣṭajanmavedanīya karmāśaya.

The karmāśayas of both kinds described above ripen themselves into the life-state, life-time, and life-experience, called the three vipākas of karmāśaya. They produce pleasure or pain according as they are the fruits of puṇyakarmāśaya or pāpakarmāśaya. It is assumed that many karmas have combined together to produce one life-state, for if each karma for its fruition would require a life, there being endless karmas, there would not be sufficient lives available for fruition. It is therefore held that many karmas unite to produce one life-state (*jāti*), and determine particular life-time (*āyuṣkāla*) and pleasurable or painful experiences. The virtuous or sinful karmāśayas accumulated in one life (in order to produce their effects) cause the death of the individual, and manifest themselves in producing the birth of the individual, his life-time and particular pleasurable or painful experience. The order of undergoing the experiences is the order in which the karmas manifest themselves as effects, the principal ones being manifested earlier in life. Principal karmas here refer to those which are too ready to generate their effects. We see that there is a continuity of existence all through, as the karmas of this life, when they ripen, jointly tend to fructify by causing another birth, as a means whereto death is caused and along with it life is manifested in another body formed by the refilling from prakṛti (*prakṛtyāpūra*) and the same karmāśaya regulates the life period and the experiences of that life, the karmāśaya of which life again take a similar course, and manifest itself in the production of another life and so on.

But this karmāśaya regarded as ekabhavika or unigenital on account of its accumulating in one life, must be distinguished from the vāsanās regarded as anekabhavika as they remain accumulated from thousands of previous lives from beginningless time and the mind is pervaded all over with them like knots of a fishing net. The vāsanās result from a memory of the experiences of a life generated by the fructification of the karmāśaya and kept in the citta in the form of potency or impressions (*saṃskāra*). Now we have seen before that the citta remains constant in all births and rebirths that an individual has undergone from eternity. It therefore keeps the memory of these experiences of thousands of lives in the form of saṃskāra or potency. These vāsanās are the causes of the instinctive tendencies, habits of deriving pleasures and pains peculiar to different animal lives. Thus the habits of a dog-life and its peculiar mode of taking its experiences and of deriving pleasure and pain are very different in nature from those of a man-life, and must therefore be explained on the basis of an incipient memory in the form of potency impressions or saṃskāras of the experiences that an individual must have undergone in a previous dog-life of its own.

Now when by this fructification of the karmāśaya a dog-life is settled on a person, at once his corresponding vāsanās of a previous dog-life are revived and he begins to take interest in his dog-life in the manner of a dog.

If there were not this law of vāsanās, then any vāsanā might be revived in any life, and there would be no difference of human instincts and those of other animals. The vāsanās being of the nature of saṃskāras, potencies or impressions, can be revived again in time, though the time of their revival may come in even after many hundreds of years. For once the saṃskāra is formed in the citta, it cannot go out of it or be lost in the natural course, and whensoever the conditions recur they will be revived. So when the karmāśaya is on its way to fructification by the production of any birth-and life-time, it helps to revive the vāsanās as instinctive tendencies or memories. So the instinctive fear of death also comes from the innate memory of the experiences of the sufferings of past lives.

Returning again to the divisions of karmāśaya we find that dṛṣṭajanmavedanīya karmas of unappointed fruition (*aniyatavipāka*) have three different courses. Thus, firstly, in the case of a Yogin they may not find any scope of fructification, and may thus be lost for good, or secondly, as effects of minor actions they may show themselves gradually, along with the effects of major actions in instalments in many lives; or thirdly, they may remain overcome for a very long time by other (*adṛṣṭajanmavedanīya*) karmas of appointed fruition (*niyatavipāka*). A man for example may do some good actions and some extremely vicious ones, so that at the time of death the karmāśaya of these vicious actions becoming ripe and fit for appointed fruition may generate an animal life, but his good actions, the benefits of which are such as may be reaped only in a man-life will remain overcome until he by the fruition of his other deeds can earn a man's life and be born again as man.

Thus when we try to classify, we find that karmas are of two kinds: (1) those which are to be fruitful in this life (*niyatavipāka*) and (2) those which are to be fruitful in other lives (*aniyatavipāka*). Those which are to be fruitful in this life are also called ekabhavika by Vācaspati.[1] These may be those actions of the preceding life or lives which being on the point of fruition produced this body, or they may also be those intensive good or bad actions which produce their fruits immediately and are therefore called dṛṣṭajanmavedanīya as distinguished from the fruits of the karmas of other lives enjoyed in this life and called dṛṣṭajanmavedanīya (*niyatavipāka*). As regards the karmas accumulated in this life, some of them will be of appointed fruition and produce the life-state of another birth, but those which could not come to the stage of appointed fruition may either be

[1] Bhikshu and his follower Nāgeśa differ from Vācaspati in holding that ekabhavika is only that action which is fructified in the life immediately succeeding the life in which it is accumulated. So according to him dṛṣṭajanmavedanīya cannot be called ekabhavika.

lost through the man's attaining right knowledge or may be awaiting till the coming of such a suitable birth in which they can show themselves, or they may gradually fructify in connection with the fructification of major karmas.

When we attempt to get at the root of this artificial and detailed karma theory which bears a strong Jaina colouring, we see that by the karmas, some new kinds of matter stuff are produced which may be called virtue or vice. We have no reason to be shocked at such a theory in a system of thought, where ideas, emotions and all that we call mental, are but some subtle kinds of matter-stuff. This virtue-stuff or vice-stuff forms, so to say, a kind of sheath which is associated with the purpose of purusha. When these have accumulated and undergone certain transformations, they require some new conditions of body, etc., for manifesting themselves into their effects. Īśvara removed the barriers of the prakṛti in the suitable direction, so that through mahat new fillings-in might take place, and out of this new influx of matter-stuff from prakṛti a suitable body might through the processes of evolution be made, wherein the purusha had to manifest itself and suffer the pains and pleasures destined for it by the fructifying influence of dharma or adharma stuff. This dispensation of the experiences of pleasure and pain takes place through the particular modifications of the buddhi. So it is that dharma or adharma matter is also a particular modification of buddhi as much as other characteristics of change or life-sponteneity are. These dharma and adharma stuff remaining in buddhi subjectively, determine the pleasures and pains of the man, for it is a matter of common experience according to the Sāṃkhya-Yoga theory that the same object (*e.g.* a young wife) produces pleasure in the mind of the husband and pain in the mind of another co-wife looking at her with jealous eyes. All objects are composed of three primary feelings, and they excite different feelings in different persons according to the fructifying dharma or adharma with which their buddhis may be associated.

The karmas however do not penetrate into the purusha after the Jaina fashion and cannot therefore obscure his vision or weaken his will. There is no leśya here which can colour the soul. The soul in spite of all its bad works ever remains in its original purity.

It will moreover be seen that according to the karma theory of Yoga the limitations imposed by karma lie mainly in producing the suffering of pain and the particular environment in which we are born as men, in particular social positions with peculiar advantages or disadvantages.[1]

[1] We may contrast this view with the extreme view of Gosāla according to whom there is no such thing as exertion, labour, power,

But the scope of self-improvement is not stopped. Man holds within his mind in the form of saṃskāras all the good and bad lives that he has lived and he is free to determine himself as he likes; he has also the innate instinct in his mind to tend towards final emancipation or the ultimate good; he has around him the obstacles also as the past bad lives that he has lived, and he has to exert his will and achieve his moral ideal. The objection that purusha itself is without any will or movement cannot apply, for the answer is the same as that we have for all other mental states and experiences, namely that the buddhi and the purusha together serve for all phenomenal purposes to stand as a knowing, feeling, and willing self, and the transcendental aspect need not interfere at any state of our phenomenal experences.

energy or human strength; all things are unalterably fixed. The *Dīgha Nikāya* gives the doctrine of Gosāla's system thus: "There is no cause, either proximate or remote, for the depravity of beings; they become depraved without reason; they become pure without cause or reason. Nothing depends either on one's efforts or on the efforts of others; in short nothing depends on any human efforts, for there is no such thing as power, energy, human exertion or human strength. Everything that thinks, everything that has senses, everything that is procreated, everything that lives is destitute of force, power or energy. Their varying conditions at any time are due to fate, to their environment and their own nature."

(Dīgha Nikāya. Dial., Vol. 1, 71.)

CHAPTER XI.

The Yoga Practice.

When by observing the universal Mahāvratas and filling the mind with the sweet emotions of friendliness and compassion, and by adherence to such attainments as contentment, etc., the mind is softened, the Yogin looks to the Yoga practice for gaining a complete mastery over his mind. Yoga means the arrest of the flow of the states, and is thus a characteristic quality of the mind, for in all minds in the continual passage of the states there is always taking place a relative arrest of a certain state and the rise of another. But not until this arrest of states has become an object of the conscious efforts of will, and has helped the Yoga to loosen the knots of affliction by inclining the mind to a state of deep and steady inhibition, can it be of any use to the Yoga ideal. The river of mind, says the sage Vyāsa, flows in two directions: it flows towards the evil and it flows towards right knowledge, the good. So long as man does not find that his instinctive hankering after pleasure, sensual gratification, and worldly objects is incessantly drawing him into the meshes of pains, so long as he does not understand that the happiness of paradise of the popular forms of worship is not only transitory but is in reality dire pain with a mere varnish of pleasure, he will not try to turn his mind towards the right and the good. So disinclination towards worldly pleasures and their attainment, vairāgya, is the first desideratum. The stronger the vairāgya, the greater will be his inclination towards turning away his mind and controlling it from dissipating and corroding vices. The next desideratum is habit (*abhyāsa*). The habit is the habit of steadying the mind. In order to strengthen it, one must most assiduously continue to practise it for a very long time, put the utmost energy of his will into the attempt, and have a staunch faith and confidence in the method he is adopting. He must habituate his mind and body to bear with indifference all sorts of privations and acquire absolute continence, brahmacaryya, and be possessed of knowledge. It is when all these accessory conditions are thoroughly fulfilled that it becomes possible for a man to acquire a steady habit. The greater the chance of distraction either from ignorance, faithlessness or any other cause, the less will be the possibility of keeping the mind steady. The accessory virtues which gradually advance Yoga development are śraddhā, vīrya, samādhi and prajñā. Śraddhā means not only faith but includes a sweet hope which looks cheerfully on the practice and brings a firm belief in the success of the attempt. Such a cheerful hope saves the Yogin from all depressions and fears, and keeps him steady in his path of toil. Vīrya is the firmness of will and effort which comes naturally from the firmness of faith and hope as is exemplified in Buddha when he said, "Let my body dry up in this seat, let my bones, skin and flesh moulder away, but without attaining right knowledge which can hardly be secured even by the attempts of thousands of years, my body shall not move from this seat." From such an unflinching determination comes smṛti or samādhi—the steady meditation in which the thinker loses himself in the thought. From the development of such samādhi comes prajñā or right knowledge about the true nature of prakṛti and purusha; and then one should continually meditate upon this right knowledge, till at last this also loses all attraction for him and he is liberated according to the superior, inferior or middling attainment of these conditions of practice such as śraddhā, etc. The Yogins can be divided into three classes, and again each of these classes may be divided further into three classes according to the degree of superior, inferior or middling energy that the Yogin is able to devote to his task, and the time within which success can be attained is determined accordingly.

Turning to the actual Yoga practice we come first to the posture of the Yogin called the āsana. He must attain such a perfect posture that all efforts to that end should cease, and there should not be any movement of the body. One should think how this great earth is set at rest and thus secure strength for the mind to keep itself steady in its own posture.

After having secured stability in the posture a person should try the prāṇāyāmas. The pauses that come after a deep inhalation and after deep exhalation are each called prāṇāyāma: the first is called external and the second internal There is however a third mode, when the lungs are neither too much dilated nor too much contracted and there is another total restraint, where cessation of both these motions takes place by a single effort, just as water thrown on a heated stone shrivels up from all sides.

These can be regulated by keeping the eye upon space, span and numbers. Thus as the breathing becomes slower the space that it occupies also becomes smaller and smaller. Space is again of two kinds, internal and external. At the time of inhalation the breath occupies internal space which can be felt even in the soles of hands and feet, just like the slight touch of an ant. To try to feel this touch along with deep inhalation serves to lengthen the period of cessation of breathing. External space is the distance from the tip of the nose to the most remote point up to which breath can be felt by the palm of the hand or by the movement of any light substance like cotton placed there and just as the breathing becomes slower and slower the distance traversed by it also becomes smaller and smaller. Regulations by time are seen when attention is kept over the time taken up in breathing the shortest time being a moment which is the fourth part of the twinkling of the eye. So regulation by time means the fact of our attending to the moments or kṣaṇas spent in the acts of inspiration, pause and expiration. These prāṇāyāmas can also be measured by the number of normal durations of breaths. The time taken by the inspiration and expiration of a healthy man is the same as that which is measured by snapping the fingers after turning the hand thrice over the knee and is the measure of duration of normal breath ; the first mild attempt is called udghāta and mātrās or measures are measured by 36 such ughātas ; when it is double it is the second udghāta, middling, when it is trebled it is the third udghāta called intense. Gradually the Yogin acquires the practice of prāṇāyāma of long duration being daily practised and being increased in succession to a day, fortnight, a month and so on. He proceeds first by mastering the first udghāta, then the second and so on until the duration increases up to a day, fortnight, a month as stated before. There is also a fourth kind of prāṇāyāma transcending all those stages of unsteady practice when the Yogin is steady in his cessation of breath. It must be remembered, however, that while the prāṇayāmas are practised, the mind must be fixed by dhyāna and dhāraṇā to some object, external or internal, without which these will be of no avail. By the practice of prāṇāyāma mind becomes fit for concentration, and steadiness is acquired, and this steadiness is the same as concentration, as we find also in the sutra "*dhāraṇāsu ca yogyatā manasaḥ.*"

When by the prāṇāyāma the senses are restrained from their external objects, we have what is called pratyāhāra, by which the mind remains as if in its own nature, being altogether identified with the object of inner concentration or contemplation, and thus when this citta is again suppressed the senses which had already ceased from coming into contact with other objects and become submerged in the citta itself also cease along with it. Dhāraṇā is the concentration of citta on a particular place, which is so very necessary at the time of prāṇāyāmas mentioned before. The mind may thus be held steadfast in such places as the sphere of the navel, the lotus of the heart, the light in the brain, the forepart of the nose, the forepart of the tongue, or any other parts of the body.

Dhyāna is the continuance, the changing flow of the mental effort, in the object of dhāraṇā unmediated by any other break of conscious states.

Samādhi or trance contemplation results when by deep concentration mind becomes transformed in the form of the object of contemplation. By pratyāhāra or power of abstraction the mind desists from all other objects except the one to which it is intended to be centred; the Yogin as he thus abstracts his mind also tries to give to it some internal or external object, and this fixing on an object is called dhāraṇā. It should be borne in mind that in order to inhibit the obstructions arising from the shakiness and unsteadiness of the body it is necessary to practise steadfast posture and to cultivate the prāṇāyāma, as also for the purpose of inhibiting the distractions arising from breathing. Gradually as an effect of steadying the mind on one object by meditation called dhyāna, the mind flows steadily in that state without any interruption, and the mind even ceases to think that it is thinking the object ; it is then transformed into the form of the object under concentration and becomes steady therein. We see therefore that samādhi is the consummation of that process which begins in dhāraṇā or concentration. These three, dhāraṇā, dhyāṇa and samādhi represent the three stages of the same process, of which the last one is the perfection, and these three are together technically called saṁyama which directly leads to and is immediately followed by the samprajñāta state. Yogāṅgas or the attainment of moral virtues only help it indirectly. For asamprajñāta state however these three are not so intimately related, for a person who is very highly advanced, one who is the special object of God's grace may at once by an intense vairāgya and abhyāsa pass into the nirodha state or the state of absolute suppression.

As gradually the knowledge of samādi dawns through the possession of saṁyama, the saṁyama is strengthened. With the rise of samādhi-knowledge or prajñāloka the saṁyama also rises higher and higher. In the beginning, the mind can hold saṁyama or concentrate, and become one with a gross object together with its name, etc., which is called the savitarka state; the next plane or stage of saṁyama is that when the mind becomes one with the object of its meditation without any consciousness of its name, etc., called nirvitarka. Next come the other two states when the mind is fixed to subtle substances called savicāra and nirvicāra.

The savitarka stage is that in which the mind becomes one with the thing together with its name and concept and is regarded as the lowest stage; for here the gross object does not appear to the mind in its true reality but only in a false illusory way, in which it appears in ordinary life associated with the concept and the name. This state is not different from ordinary conceptual states in which the particular thing is not only associated with the concept and its name, but also with other concepts and their various relations ; thus a cow will not only appear before the mind with its concept and name only,but also along with other relations and thoughts associated with the cow, *e. g.*, this is a cow, it belongs to so and so, it has many hairs on its body, and so forth. This state is therefore the rudimentary stage, as the mind here does not become one with the heart of reality but is only attempting to become steady and is not yet beyond the range of ordinary consciousness.

From this comes the nirvitarka stage, when the mind by its steadiness can become one with the object divested of all other association of name, concept, etc. The thing in this state does not appear as an object of consciousness but the consciousness being divested of all "I," or "mine" becomes one with the object itself, so that there is no such notion here as "I know this," but the mind becomes one with the thing, the notions of subject and object drop off, and the result is the one steady transformation of the mind as the object of its contemplation. This state brings to us the real knowledge of the thing divested of other false and illusory associations, which instead of explaining the real nature of the objects serve only to hide them all the more. This samādhi knowledge or prajñā is called nirvitarka. The objects of this state are the grosser material objects and the senses.

When the Yogin has mastered this state, he then directs his attention to finer and subtler objects, those from which the atoms have been derived. Things now appear before the mind of the Yogin not as the conglomeration of atoms, but of the diverse tanmātras of rūpa, rasa, etc., under the limitations of time, space, and causality, and this is called the savicāra stage. It differs from the savitarka stage in that here the objects of concentration are the tanmātrā and not the gross bhūta. But this stage is also negated for the formation of the indeterminate tanmātric meditation called the nirvicāra. The mind here does not feel in the savicāra stage as perceiving the tanmātras as being associated with pleasures, pains, or any other characteristic qualities, but it becomes one with it, merged as it were, as in the nirvitarka stage with reference to gross objects.

These four stages are however often counted as two, vitarkānugata including as savitarka and nirvitarka and vicārānugata including savicāra and nirvicāra. The other two elevated stages that come after these are ānandānugata and āsmitānugata. In the ānandānugata stage the mind is filled with supreme bliss or happiness ; and in the āsmitānugata the mind is in the state of pure being when the self is one with the buddhi. It will be seen therefore that the first two kinds called the vitarkānugata, and vícārānugata are those where it is the grosser and subtler forms of objects that are made the objects of meditation. The objects may no doubt vary from the bhūtas up to the prakṛti herself, but still these forms of meditation have this characteristic, that unity with them is effected with themselves as objects, grāhyavishaya. In the ānandānugata however the self has elevated itself from this objective meditation and is one with the pure sattva or blissful aspect of the senses, the apperceivers of sensitivity, and this type of samādhi is therefore called grahaṇavishaya.[1] The āsmitānugata is the one where the buddhi turns back to itself, and the self being one with the buddhi there is only the steady light of pure being (sattva).[2] Samādhi thus comes to be of four kinds : vitarka, vicāra, ānanda, and asmitā, and if we take each of the other varieties of vitarka and vicāra, it becomes of six kinds and when

[1] Bhikshu however does not take the pleasure or bliss belonging to the senses but ānanda as a special object of meditation.

[2] Here also Bhikshu does not take it as any self-turning of buddhi but the shining of the proper nature of the purusha.

with it the nirānanda and nirasmitā varieties are added, it becomes of eight kinds.[1] All these types however have an object on which the meditation is based, and as such are known as the samprajñāta samādhi. The next stage is called the stage of nirodha when there is no actual mental stage of any kind. The mind in this state is in pure vacuity so to say; there are only some of the germs of thought in the form of potencies. The "I" of the mind remains long in this nirodha in a state of absolute objectlessness; all the potencies are destroyed, and at last the citta is annihilated in the sense that it returns back to prakṛti, never again to bind the purusha.

It appears that all the four forms of samādhi that we have just now described were in existence even long before Buddha. This fact with many other points of resemblance which we have noticed before would offer strong ground for inferring that Buddha might have derived a large part of the groundwork of his philosophy, theoretic as well as practical, from the Yoga doctrines which were then only in a floating condition. It has often been maintained that Buddha was much indebted to Sāṃkhya philosophy, but if that is true to any extent, nowhere does this indebtedness come out in so

[1] Bhikshu diffiers from Vācaspati and says that samādhi can only be of six kinds.

remarkable a manner as in Yoga ethics and practice, fields of enquiry which Yoga can particularly claim as its own as apart from Sāṃkhya.

Thus to give a brief account of Buddhist dhyāna after Anesaki and Takakusu, we find that dhyāna is divided into four degrees. Even the first and the lowest of the four dhyānas corresponds in its quality to a state higher than the sixth of the eight constituents of Yogāṅga. To reach the first dhyāna several preliminary practices are needed. These correspond to the first five constituents of Yoga. First of all one has to keep the precepts and rules (śīla) laid down by the Buddha (yama of the Yogāṅgas); secondly to keep one's body and mind pure and serene, living in solitary retirement away from the people in a forest or a cave and sitting cross-legged always thinking on an object. A novice should as a preparatory measure practise the meditation on love and compassion (mettākaruṇābhāvanā) in which he is to regard all sentient beings as his brothers, desiring their happiness and welfare as all the good that he would seek for himself. A novice who needs concentration of attention should practise at first the method of counting the number of his inspirations and expirations. A novice whose impure desire is too hard to be suppressed, should meditate on the impurity and impermanence of the human body.

Childers thus explains the four states with reference to the process of meditation:— He concentrates his mind upon a single thought. Gradually his soul becomes filled with a supernatural serenity, while his mind still reasons upon and investigates the subject chosen for contemplation: this is the first jhāna called vitakka. Still fixing his thoughts upon the same subject, he then frees his mind from reasoning and investigation, while the ecstasy and serenity remain, and this is the second jhāna vicāra; next his thoughts still fixed as before, he divests himself of ecstasy and attains the third jhāna sukham, which is a state of tranquil serenity. Lastly he passes to the fourth jhāna, in which the mind exalted and purified is indifferent to all emotions alike of pleasure and pain called upekkhā. The ideal of early Buddhism thus being the equilibrium of morals (śīla), meditation, dhyāna, and knowledge, prajñā, is quite in harmony with the Yoga teaching.

Returning back again to the Yoga meditation we find that as samādhi advances, knowledge advances too; for the reason why our knowledge is imperfect is that the states of our knowledge are continually flowing and passing and there is no opportunity for us to go into the heart of things. As the concentration becomes deeper and more steady the real and perfect knowledge of things begins to flash before the mind's eye. Thus it is that as the plane of samādhi rises higher and higher, knowledge also becomes clearer and clearer, so that by the time the Yogin reaches the nirvicāra stage the steady light of perfect knowledge burns, and this is the highest and the truest knowledge known as ṛtambharā prajñā. Thus the prajñā proceeding from samādhi differs from the knowledge that we derive from the scriptures and inference, as those are based upon concepts which only take notice of the general characteristics of things, and thus are only symbols which can never take us to the heart of reality. Perception also can take note only of gross things and is absolutely helpless with regard to the subtler essences of things. As the right knowledge of samādhi is gradually more and more sustained, the potencies of imperfect knowledge and ignorance of ordinary consciousness are superseded. These potencies being superseded, those states of consciousness cannot manifest themselves, and thus samādhi becomes strengthened and by the strengthening of samādhi, comes further prajñā ; new potencies of prajñā come to be accumulated, and these bring in the prajñā states, and thus further strengthen their potencies. Thus the potencies of ordinary consciousness being gradually rooted out, the Yogin remains in a new world of right knowledge or prajñā consciousness. But it is the peculiarity of this prajñā consciousness that neither it nor its potencies serve to bind the purusha except by loosening the knots of avidyā which gradually tend to disintegrate the citta and dissociate it from the purusha (*na te prajñā-kṛtāḥ saṃskārāḥ kleśakṣayahetutvāt cittam adhi-kāraviśishṭam kurvanti; cittam hi svakāryyād avasādayanti khyātiparyyavasanam hi cittaceshṭi-tam—Vyāsabhashya*).

When the mind is on its way to pass into the samādhi state, it is in a state of oscillation as it were between its passage into ordinary consciousness and the samādhi consciousness, until the samādhi power is sufficiently strong to prevent the invasion of ordinary consciousness. In the passage of the samādhi consciousness into higher and higher stages there is also the same oscillation, and then finally in the passage of the mind into the nirodha or asamprajñāta state of absolute contentless arrest, there is the oscillation of the mind between the asamprajñāta nirodha, and the śamprajñāta state of the asmitā type, till at last the nirodha potency having destroyed the samprajñāta potencies (saṁskāra), the citta having illuminated by its extreme translucent character, the true nature of the self finally returns to prakṛti. Here it is th: the returning process which had once begun in the samādhi state being continued and brought to the buddhi is led back to its ultimate equilibrium as prakṛti by the gradual process of the disintegrating power, and thus the returning tendency of prakṛti is finally realised. The forward movement of the prakṛti had begun from beginningless time, and was satisfying itself by binding the purusha, and now the backward movement brings it back to itself, never to come out again for the bondage of the purusha. The final prajñās which help the movement of this returning process are said to be of seven kinds. The first four are as states of consciousness associated with the four stages of samādhi. The first one dawns in the form: "I have known the world, the object of suffering and misery, I have nothing more to know of it." The second is of the form: "The grounds and roots of the saṃskāra have been thoroughly uprooted, nothing more of it remains to be uprooted." The third is of the form: "Removal has become a fact of direct cognition by means of inhibitive trance." The fourth is of the form: "The means of knowledge in the shape of discriminative knowledge has been understood." This is the four-fold freedom of conscious discrimination from external phenomena. The three prajñās that rise after this are not psychological states of mind but metaphysical and real states of the disintegrating process of the return of the citta to prakṛti. These moments are as follows :—(1) The double purposes of buddhi, bhoga (ordinary experience) and apavarga (salvation) have been realised : (2) The strong gravitating tendency of the disintegrated guṇas drive them into the prakṛti like heavy stones dropped from high hill tops ; and they finally collapse into the prakṛti substance where they remain merged for ever : (3) the purusha having passed beyond the bondage of the three, shines forth in its own pure and ultimate freedom.

It is interesting to note that though the Sāṃkbya metaphysics adopted by the Yoga was combated in many quarters, neither the Yoga practice nor the superior character of Yoga prajñā was ever opposed by any of the other philosophic systems of India. Throughout all the epochs of Indian culture we find the highest reverence paid to the Yogins who were believed not only to possess a superior sense, by which they could know the highest truth beyond the ken of ordinary vision, but also to wield the most wonderful miraculous powers which Patañjali has described as the vibhūtis of Yoga, by which the Yogin showed his powers not only over his mind and the minds of others, but also over inert external objects. It was not only superior knowledge that they possessed, but superior power as well, by which even the necessity of the normal pariṇāmakramaniyama could be effected according to their will. We in this positivistic age of science and scepticism have but little belief in these trances. But it may not be out of place to note here that the idea that man could pass into states of trance by which he could be in communion with the highest kind of reality was quite common in most countries.

Ecstasy was for Plotinus the culmination of religious experience, whereby the union with God and perfect knowledge of divine truth, and the ultimate goal of the moral will, are realised in direct though ineffable experience. Plotinus enjoyed this supreme initiation four times during the period when Porphyry was with him; Porphyry himself had it only once, when he was in his 68th year. It was a vision of the Absolute, "the one," which being above thought, can only be apprehended passively by a sort of divine lapse into the expectant soul. It is not properly a vision, for the seer no longer distinguishes himself from what he sees; indeed it is impossible to speak of them as two, for the spirit during the ecstasy has become completely one with the "One." This "flight of the alone to the alone" is a rare and transient privilege even for the greatest saint, and it is said that he who enjoys it "can only say that he has all his desire, and that he would not exchange his bliss for all the heaven of heavens." From neo-Platonism this philosophic rapture passed into Christianity though we seldom find it again in such a pure and elevated form. We trace the succession of metaphysical mystics from pseudo-Dionysius to Erigena, Echkart, Boehme, and Swedenborg. In extreme cases ecstasy produces complete insensibility. "Schwester Katrej who is spoken of as a pupil of Ekhart is said to have been carried out for burial when in a cataleptic trance. Anaesthesia of the skin is very common; the ecstatic feels nothing when pins are driven into his flesh. Aquinas says: "The higher our mind is raised to the contemplation of spiritual things the more it is abstracted from sensible things. But the final stage at which contemplation can possibly arrive is the divine substance. Therefore the mind that sees the divine substance must be wholly divorced from the bodily senses either by death or by some rapture." Professor William James also describes many kinds of trance experiences in his "Varieties of Religious Experience."

Even in such modern poets as Wordsworth we find an experience similar to that of Plotinus. Thus Wordsworth on revisiting the banks of Wye describes :—

These beauteous forms,
Through a long absence, have not been to me
As is a landscape to a blind man's eye:
But oft, in lonely rooms, and 'mid the din

Of towns and cities, I have owed to them
In hours of weariness, sensations sweet,
Felt in the blood, and felt along the heart;
And passing even into my purer mind,
With tranquil restoration ;—feelings too
Of unremembered pleasure : such, perhaps,
As have no slight or trivial influence
On that best portions of a good man's life,
His little, nameless, unremembered, acts
Of kindness and of love. Nor less, I trust,
To them I may have owed another gift,
Of aspect more sublime ; that blessed mood
In which the burthen of the mystery,
In which the heavy and the weary weight
Of all this unintelligible world,
Is lightened :—that serene and blessed mood,
In which the affections gently lead us on,—
Until, the breath of this corporeal frame
And even the motion of our human blood
Almost suspended, we are laid asleep
In body, and become a living soul :
While with an eye made quiet by the power
Of harmony and the deep power of joy,
We see into the life of things." [1]

Tennyson again records a similar experience. "A kind of waking trance I have frequently had, quite up from boyhood when I have been all alone. This has generally come upon me through repeating my own name two or three times to myself silently, till all at once as it were,

[1] "*Lines composed a few miles above Tintern Abbey*" on revisiting the banks of the Wye during a tour by Wordsworth.

out of the intensity of consciousness of individuality, the individuality itself seemed to dissolve and wave away into boundless being, and this is not a confused state but the clearest of the clearest, the surest of the surest, the weirdest of the weirdest, utterly beyond words, where death was almost a laughable impossibility, the loss of personality (if so it were) seeming no extinction but the only true life." [1] This experience is utilised by the poet in his "*Ancient Sage.*"

> " For knowledge is the swallow on the lake
> That sees and stirs the surface shadow there
> But never yet hath dipt into the abyss
> The Abysm of Abysms, beneath, within,
> The blue of sky and sea, the green of earth,
> And the million-millionth of a grain
> Which cleft and cleft for ever more
> And ever vanishing, never vanishes
> To me my son more mystic than myself."

William James also writes: " It is that our normal waking consciousness, rational consciousness as we call it, is but one special type of consciousness, whilst all about it, parted from it by the filmiest of screens, there lie potential forms of consciousness entirely different. We may go through life without suspecting their existence, but apply the requisite stimulus, and

[1] Tennyson—*A Memoir* by H. Tennyson.

at a touch they are there in all their completeness, definite types of mentality, which probably somewhere have their field of application and adaptation. No account of the universe in its totality can be found which leaves these other forms of consciousness quite disregarded ; looking back at my own experiences they all converge towards a kind of insight to which I cannot help ascribing some metaphysical significance."

But howsoever these experiences might be, they differ from the Yoga knowledge which is held forth as the ideal by Patañjali. The Yoga system speaks of five kinds of minds, namely, kshipta (wandering), mūḍha (somnambulic), vikshipta (occasionally steady or distracted), ekāgra (one-pointed), and nirodha (restrained). So far as Yoga is used simply to mean an intense stage of concentration where the ordinary mental states are arrested, it is the common characteristic of mind of all these kinds. Thus the kshipta and mūḍha stages are those in which even a deep self-forgetting experience may take place even through the extreme intensity of ordinary emotions or instinctive passions when the ordinary outflow of states is arrested. Thus Bhaṭṭa Kallaṭa writes in *Spanda-kārikā*, "The true nature of self is there where a man is in a state of intense anger, joy, or extreme indecision, or running after something through extreme emotion" and Vijñāna Bhairava also writes to that effect.[1]

But such stages of arrest have nothing to do with the Yoga arrest which Patañjali recommends. The states of hypnosis which belong to the vikshipta stage resemble these states more than the samādhi of Yoga. Thus Bhaṭṭa Kallaṭa and Utpala both describe the hypnotic method as an alternative means of producing the same kind of arrest as that which is achieved through the intensity of emotions thus described.[2] Thus

[1] *Atikruddhaḥ prahṛṣṭo vā kiṃ karomiti vā mṛśan, dhāvan vā yat padam gacchet tatra spandaḥ pratiṣṭhitaḥ.*

(*Spandapradīpikā.*)

krodhādyante bhaye śoke gahvare vāraṇe raṇe
kutuhale kshudādyante brāhmasattā samīpagā.

[2] There seems little doubt that the modern form of hypnotism through exterior suggestion and self-passivity was quite well-known in India. Thus Bhaṭṭa Kallaṭa writes :—

yāmavaśthām samālambya yadāyam mama vakshyati
tadavaśyam karishye'ham iti saṅkalpya tishṭhati.
tāmāśrityordhvamārgeṇa somasūryyāvubhāvapi
sāuśumṇedhvanyastamito hitvā brahmāṇḍagocaram
tadā tasmin mahāvyomni pralīnaśasibhāskare
saushuptapadavanmuḍhaḥ prabuddhaḥ syādanāvṛtaḥ.

and Utpala annotates ; *ayamesha Devadatto jñātā adbhūtasadvastvabhidhāyyanulaṅghyājño yat kiñcit mama vadishyati tadavaśyamaham karishye anushṭhāsyāmīti saṅkalpya yāmavasthāmaunmukhyarūpām vṛttim samālamvya gṛhītvā yastishṭhati tasya puṃsaḥ tāmavasthām āśritya ūrddhvamārgeṇa vishuvatpravāheṇa somasūryyāvubhavapi dvāvapyapānaprāṇau ...... svayamastamito astam gacchataḥ ... tadā tasmin kale tasminmahāvyomni ca paracidākāśe pratyastamitaśaśibhāskare praśāntajñānakriye jaḍaḥ anabhivyaktasvasvabhāvaḥ* according to Bhaṭṭa Kallaṭa and Utpala we find that the difference between the trance states produced through strong emotions or through instinctive passions of a somnambulistic nature, and those cases of hypnotism which are produced by the surrendering will of the subject in conjunction with the suggestion of the hypnotiser, is that the latter is a case of trance initiated by conscious will and surrender, and thus may be taken as the samādhi of the vikshipta stage. The difference between the mind of the vikshipta stage and that of the kshipta and mūḍha stages is that the former may under certain conditions be induced to go into the trance stage, whereas the latter is almost an unconscious and somnambulistic passage without any control of the subject.

svapnādinā amūhyamānaḥ prabuddhaḥ aniruddhaḥ syāt saushupta-padavat yathā sushuptapade tathā prabuddhastu anāvṛta eva bhavet. An instance of hypnotism is also found in the *Mahābhārata*, XIII, 40, where "Vipula," the disciple, being asked by his teacher Devaśarman to protect the latter's wife Ruci from attempts at adultery on her by Indra, sat down by her, and gazed steadily with his eyes into her eyes, so that her gaze might meet his, and filled her mind with longing for what was right. Vipula thus entered her body as the wind enters space and remained there motionless, and invisible. Then making rigid the body of his teacher's wife, he stayed there devoted to guarding her and she was not aware of him. When Indra came to tempt her, Ruci could not move a muscle under the influence of Vipula, and though she wanted to assent to Indra's proposal she could not utter a word, and only said, "Sir what business hast thou to come here ?" against her wishes. Indra being much disappointed went away with fright lest Vipula should curse him.

Almost all the different kinds of trance experiences which we find in Europe seem to belong to this vikshipta stage. These trances of the vikshipta stage must necessarily be transitory, and do not show any real spiritual development.

We should distinguish the Yoga ideal of trance which can only take place in the ekāgra and the final nirodha stages of the mind from the trances of the other stages in that the former presupposes a very high degree of moral perfection, which is not a necessary desideratum of the other stages. It is when the Yogin has by a high degree of moral perfection become passionless towards objective pleasures that he begins gradually to establish himself in the trance state. The Yogin is not satisfied only to transcend the objective world, but he wants to transcend the limits of his mind as well. The miraculous powers attained by the practising of the Yogin are useful to a person bent upon the Yoga ways in securing and strengthening his faith. Once he has become apathetic to all the attractions of pleasure and begun to travel in the road of Yoga, the states of trance through which he has to travel, will discover the true path for him ; Yoga is itself the teacher for those that take to Yoga.[1]

[1] *yogen yogo jñātavyo yogo yogāt pravarttate*
yo'pramattas tu yogena sa yoge ramate ciram.

The objects on which such a Yogin should at the beginning of his practice concentrate his attention have ordinarily no limits, and we find that the Yogin could meditate upon the passionless souls of many saints, upon dream consciousness, sleep or anything that he liked, for his only object was to stop the flow of his conscious states and to weaken for final destruction all the potencies of the states of consciousness. There was thus no limitation of the object of the samādhi, as the whole thing proceeds not in any miraculous way but quite naturally and consistently in accordance with the general principles of Yoga psychology. But yet the real road generally adopted by the Yogins was the meditation of Īśvara. It is most likely that from the earliest period of the growth of the Yoga method, the Brahman was the object with whom the individual soul wanted to connect itself and we read in the Śvetāśvatara: "And when by means of the real nature of his self he sees as by a lamp, the real nature of Brahman, then having known the unborn eternal God, who is beyond all nature, he is freed from all fetters."[1] When the Yogin thus meditated upon God, God was pleased to make the

[1] *Yadātmatattvena tu brahmatattvam*
Dīpopameneha yuktaḥ prapaśyet
Ajam dhruvam sarvatatvairviśuddham
Jñatvā devaṃ mucyate sarvapāśaiḥ.

advance of his trance realisation easier for him by removing all obstacles which could stand in the way. It was by his will that all the movements of the prakṛti were intelligently guided, and it was in him that the world was held, and it was unto him that the Yogin returned like a drop of water in the ocean. The knowledge that is brought about by the Yoga salvation is infinite ; all the hindrances and barriers which 'limit' our knowledge and serve to express them in concepts are removed, and there is little to know, till at last when salvation is earned, the supreme intelligence shines forth in eternal sunshine never again to be sullied, darkened or eclipsed—the oilless lamp that forever shines.

The state of Sāṃkhya emancipation is also the same, but more stress is laid there upon knowledge as the means of its attainment. So far as the need of the performance of outward morality is concerned Sāṃkhya and Yoga are one. The stage of liberation is one that transcends the sphere of moral works, and is only for those who have attained perfection in the latter. Yet it is not sufficient for a man to purge his mind of all immoral desires only, but in order to obtain salvation it is necessary that he should by continual thinking come to the thorough conviction that " he is not all that he had been supposing himself to be, nor is the world nor even the mind his in any way, he does not exist at all (*nāsmi, nāham, na me*). In Buddhism also we find a similar echo, when we find that their object also consisted in the extinction of the will to be, which is the cause of all suffering ; it is the Nirvāṇa, the extinction of what we call self and of all that we attribute to it, that is the summum bonum of the Buddhist. But the distinction remains that the destruction of the ego in Sāṃkhya is only the annihilation of the phenomenal qualities of the self, which caused the notion of ego and its relation to the environing mental states and the world of matter and the consequent restoration of the self to its individuality—the self which, though noumenally always free, had been in the sphere of suffering owing to ignorance or a mere non-distinction of its own nature with that of prakṛti. In Buddhism there is no such permanent entity as the self and the Nirvāṇa is an inconceivable existence which though a state of annihilation is regarded in many texts as being a happy one. The Sāṃkhya and Yoga liberation has nothing of happiness in it, it is the restoration of the individual to its own true and pure state.

The reason why Sāṃkhya does not think the Yoga method indispensable, as we can understand from a discourse of Bhīṣma and Yudhiṣṭhira in the *Mahābhārata* is that here self-knowledge is regarded as the culmination of all culture. The Sāṃkhya sage will on the one hand try to attain the highest moral perfection attainable, and on the other proceed on a scientific enquiry through all the departments of human knowledge. He must try to attain the highest and most wide-spread culture, until he can know the distinction of his self from the buddhi and all the products of the prakṛti. The true knowledge of self is thus regarded not as a shrinking away from all science and culture but as their highest culmination.

Yoga however holds that this self-knowledge is attainable by the methodical processes of trance; and fixed faith in the surety of this process as the means of salvation is the most essential desideratum of success. Proceed on the way, the Yoga says, you will have miraculous powers and miraculous experiences, which will convince you of the truth of this method. Yoga salvation is thus attained through the perfected discipline of the will as the Sāṃkhya goal is achieved through knowledge. As to the nature of the last existence in the emancipated states there is a view which is not only advocated by Vijñāna Bhikṣu but anticipated in the purāṇas as well, which holds that the emancipated souls return into the self of the Īśvara. It is through the highest moral elevation that this transcendent state comes when the soul attains its freedom, and then lives in eternal peace with itself. The saint is not merged in him in the Vedānta fashion but holds his individuality all the same as a pure intelligence.

INDEX

B

D

E

J

K

L

M

Q

R

S

V

Y